Death of the Beast

An In-depth Study of Revelation

Eli Borden, PhD

Third Edition

Except where otherwise indicated,
all "Scripture taken from the Holy Bible, New International Version®, NIV®
  Copyright© 1973, 1978, 1984 by Biblica, Inc.™
  Used by permission of Zondervan. All rights reserved worldwide.
  WWW.ZONDERVAN.COM"
"The "NIV" and "New International Version" are trademarks registered in the United States Patent and Trademark Offices by Biblica, Inc.™"

Death of the Beast

Previously titled: "The Death of the Beast"

Copyright © 2011 Eli Borden
ISBN-13: 978-1456525767 (CreateSpace-Assigned)
ISBN-10: 145652576X
LCCN: 2011900398

Printed by CreateSpace
https://www.createspace.com/3535123

All rights reserved. No part of this publication may be reproduced, stored in a retrieval system, or transmitted, in any form or by any means, electronic, mechanical, photocopying, recording, or otherwise, without the prior written permission of the copyright owner.

The Death of the Beast
Copyright © 1996 Eli Borden
ISBN 1-56794-118-4
Published by Star Bible, Ft Worth, Texas

The Death of the Beast
Copyright © 1987 Kendal/Hunt Publishing Company
ISBN 0-8403-4249-78
Printed in the United States of America

Dedication
Acknowledgements

Dedication: To Wilsie, my life's companion and best friend and to our children, grandchildren and great-grandchildren.

Acknowledgments: Thanks to my sister Fran Borden for hours of proofreading and for her consultation by phone. Thanks to Wilsie for designing the cover along with other family members who offered suggestions during the process. Thanks also to Wilsie for hours of working with formatting of the book. Thanks to all of you who have listened to my presentations and have encouraged me through brainstorming with your thoughts and questions.

DEATH OF THE BEAST

CONTENTS

Preface IX

SECTION I –

1 Thesis of *Revelation* 1

- Meaning of the word <u>revelation</u>
- Primary application relates to the fall of Rome
- *Revelation* is a letter to Roman citizens
- Blessings are promised to those who obey
- John states that the coming events were near
- The wicked kingdom was the fourth from Daniel's time
- The 6th King of the empire was ruling when John wrote
- The number <u>666</u> points to Rome
- The seven hills describe Rome
- Secondary application applies to every generation

SECTION II - Tools for Understanding

2 Daniel Prophesied the Fall of Babylon 31

- Nebuchadnezzar's dream about the golden kingdom
- Daniel's vision about the lion
- The handwriting on the wall
- The fulfillment of the prophecies.

3 Prophecies about Medo-Persia 39

- Nebuchadnezzar's dream about the silver kingdom
- Daniel's vision about the bear
- Daniel's vision about the two-horned ram
- The fulfillment of the prophecies.

CONTENTS

4 Prophecies about Greece 49

- Nebuchadnezzar's dream of the bronze kingdom
- Daniel's vision of the leopard
- Daniel's vision of the he-goat
- The extended vision of the Grecian empire
- The fulfillment of the prophecies.

5 Prophecies about the Roman Empire 85

- Nebuchadnezzar dreams about the iron and clay kingdom
- Daniel's vision about the ten horned beast
- The King of kings and Lord of lords arrives on earth

6 Daniel Wrote about the Kingdom of God 91

- The time of the King's arrival
- The purpose of the heavenly kingdom on earth
- The eternal nature of the kingdom of God

7 John Used the Imagery of Ezekiel 103

- Three writers in exile
- Sixteen parallel visions seen by Ezekiel and John.

8 Number Symbols in *Revelation* 123

- The importance of numbers in *Revelation*
- The basic meaning of each number.

CONTENTS

SECTION III - Analysis of *Revelation*

9 The Beginning of the Letter 137

- John penned the letter
- The authorship is divine
- The primary audience is the seven churches of Asia
- The message is to prepare for tribulation
- Seven letters to seven churches of Asia

10 The Seven Seals 165

- God is the center of the universe
- God and the Lamb are praised
- Jesus opens the seven seals.

11 The Seven Trumpets 189

- First four Trumpets warns of natural disasters
- Fifth trumpet warns of evil's outcome
- Sixth trumpet warns of war.

12 Visions from the Seventh Trumpet 209

- Heavenly warfare
- Identification of the woman
- Identification of the male child
- Identification of the dragon
- Identification of the woman's offspring
- Description of the beast—an Anti-Christ?

CONTENTS

13 The Seven Bowls of God's Wrath 235

- Bowl one affects earth dwellers
- Bowl two turns the sea into blood
- Bowl three turns all rivers into blood
- Bowl four darkens the universe
- Bowl five unleashes evil
- Bowl six brings Armageddon
- Bowl seven splits the city into three parts.

14 The Destruction of the Beast 247

- Identifying the kings of the wicked empire
- Identifying the location of the wicked empire
- Three angels deliver proclamations of the fall of the beast
- Mourning of the wicked over the fall
- Rejoicing of the righteous over the fall

15 Consequences for Winners and Losers in "1,000 year" Theme 269

- Meaning of 1,000 years
- Satan is chained 1,000 years
- Some are resurrected to live and reign 1,000 years
- Those dead in sin remain dead 1,000 years
- Judgment of the dead
- Consequences experienced by winners and losers.

16 Victory in Jesus 285

- All things are made new for those who have overcome
- John describes the heavenly city, the redeemed

PREFACE

In 1987 my first edition of *Death of the Beast* was published to assist readers in grasping the meaning of John's *Revelation*. Because of the interest generated by the chapter over number symbolism, I wrote another book, *You Can Count On It,* published in 1988, to serve as a tool for decoding the symbolic numbers of the Bible, including the numbers in *Revelation*.

Through presentations and word-of-mouth, *Death of the Beast* sold out, and more were being requested. This alone would have prompted me to publish again, but another situation made the need even stronger. I had continued researching, and the testing of ideas through seminars and speeches led to parts of the book that needed revision. A new chapter was added to the 2nd edition to explore the imagery of Ezekiel used by John in *Revelation*. With so many changes having been made, I called the book, *Death of the Beast,* 2nd Edition.

Currently, four circumstances make it important for another printing of *Death of the Beast;*

- The second edition has now sold out, and once again we are receiving requests for more books.
- The learning process never ends; as I presented seminars and continued my study, I looked for better ways to explain complex concepts. Among the modifications made in this volume, a graphic can be found at the end of chapter 15 that compelled me to reprint.
- Along with these factors, the need for a third printing is important because many outlandish ideas continue flourishing throughout the religious world, and more will certainly come. An overwhelming number of bogus ideas come from mistaken concepts about the book of *Revelation*, and many people have been led astray by misunderstanding John's message. The need to have a book available using Scripture to analyze the meaning of *Revelation* is imperative.
- During the 23 years since the first printing, we have all watched America declining morally each year with increasing crime, drug addiction, and alcoholism, along with filth over television and the internet. Families are breaking apart and are absolutely at risk in this nation! Dishonesty among major company CEO's has hit the headlines all too often, and corruption and immorality have run

rampant among political leaders of the nation. This volume gives evidence that the Armageddon of *Revelation* occurred when Rome fell; however, many powers have collapsed over the past 2,000 years as each has faced its own "Armageddon." When Rome fell, the world was thrown into the dark ages for the next millennium. We won't go down alone; our nation has become significantly entangled and involved in multinational business around the world. This scenario could lead to a collapse unparalleled in world history. Many fear, and for good reason, that the United States of America is in danger of its "Armageddon." *Death of the Beast* is needed to address the question: What should Christians do as the nation's morality continues to sink into oblivion?

When I looked at the four reasons for revising *Death of the Beast*, there was no question – a new book was essential! Hopefully, this will help you understand my calling this the 3rd edition.

Death of the Beast is divided into three sections. When one begins reading *Revelation*, the reader must have some basic concept of where the book is going. There is only one chapter in the first section, and this one is a must for understanding the book of *Revelation*.

The reader has a choice as to which section to read next. This author suggests that the reader continue with section II to thoroughly prepare to comprehend the materials John wrote in *Revelation*. It is hard to understand the "revealed" if one does not first comprehend that which was "sealed." However, after reading section I, the reader may be eager to proceed immediately to section III. Regardless of where one reads after completing chapter one, section II will remain a good tool for clarification and additional research.

God has promised blessings to those who deal properly with the book of *Revelation*. *Revelation 1:3 Blessed is the one who reads the words of this prophecy, and blessed are those who hear it and take to heart what is written in it, because the time is near.*

May God bless your study and your understanding of John's visions penned in the book of *Revelation*. I believe God will act only as we submit and open ourselves to His mighty truth; I give God the glory and thanks for helping open doors for me to receive and accept clearer insights, knowing more will come after this volume is completed. May you always keep an open mind to expand your knowledge of the scriptures as God helps open doors of understanding.

SECTION I

Thesis of *Revelation*

Chapter One

The Thesis of *Revelation*

Are the events of John's *Revelation* about to take place in the near future? Many books on the market would have readers believe the battle of Armageddon is currently in the making. If this scenario is true, *Revelation* would have had no basic significance for the last 2 millenniums. It is amazing that every generation has had those who proclaimed that the events of their day were signals of Armageddon and the end of time.

On the other hand, there are those who claim John's visions came to pass during the first century and that *Revelation* has no relevance for the modern reader other than to understand the events of fulfillment.

There is a reason every generation has seen itself as being in *Revelation*'s "last days." This volume will explain why countless events have been interpreted as the prelude to Armageddon. It will give evidence that John's *Revelation* was understood by readers in the first century and that the message gave them strength to overcome the trials that came their way. Additionally, this volume will demonstrate that first century events established a philosophy that has repeated itself countless times since the original Armageddon as each generation has faced its own "Armageddon." ***Revelation* is a book written for every generation!**

All Truth is either "Sealed" or "Revealed"

It is useful for one to understand two basic principles concerning any revelation. Principle 1: A revelation makes something known that was previously unknown. Truth is truth whether or not it is presently known. The mold Penicillium notatum could have cured infections in the 19th Century, but no one knew this until Alexander Fleming's discovery in 1928.

What a great discovery when this information went from the hidden realm to the known! The "revelation" led to the use of penicillin in fighting infections.

> **To qualify as a revelation, the information must be previously unknown.**

Before the wheel was invented, it was already true round objects roll; however, before the invention, **this truth was in the unknown category.** After discovery, the truth became knowledge and was moved into the known realm. Knowledge of the wheel was a revelation because the information was new! Prophecies far into the future cannot be understood; thus, they are "concealed" until the time of fulfillment. This is why Daniel was told to "seal" his visions, and John was told to "reveal" his. When seals are removed, the resulting information is a revelation, understandable from that time forward!

> *Daniel 12:8,9 I heard, but I did not understand. So I asked, "My lord, what will the outcome of all this be?" He replied, "Go your way, Daniel, because the words are closed up and sealed until the time of the end."*

While Daniel was told to leave his visions in the realm of the unknown, John was told to "reveal" his information; in fact, he was commanded, **"Do not seal it"**!

> *Revelation 22:10 Then he told me, "Do not seal up the words of the prophecy of this book, because the time is near."*

To his reading audience, John gave new information, decoding truths Daniel had sealed some six hundred years earlier; thus, the name *Revelation.* John explains at the outset that it is the "revelation" of Jesus Christ, and at the end of his book John was given the order to leave the information in the known category, "Do not seal" the book. It is interesting to note the reason John was told not to conceal the information was that the events were to unfold in the near future.

Principle 2: Nothing is revealed if the information is not understandable! If one claims to be presenting a revelation but speaks in a language unknown to his audience, the communication simply cannot qualify as a revelation. In *Revelation 1:3*, John tells his readers they will be blessed if they read, hear, and obey the things written in the book. There could have been no blessing to the recipients of the letter if the book had been incomprehensible.

To qualify as a revelation, the information must be understandable!

Once truth is moved from the concealed area to the revealed area, it can be understood by the person who searches with discernment. The presence of so many varied interpretations of *Revelation* does not alter the fact that John gave a revelation and left it in the understandable domain in the first century. The diagram below will illustrate the difference in "sealing" and "revealing" by comparing various words that clarify the two concepts.

DANIEL	*REVELATION*
Sealed	Revealed
Concealed	Exposed
Hidden	Manifested
Unknown	Known
Closed	Opened

At the beginning of *Revelation*, John tells the readers he is revealing something to them:

> *Revelation 1:1 The revelation of Jesus Christ, which God gave him to show his servants what must soon take place. He made it known by sending his angel to his servant John ...*

For a modern author to claim he is making known that which was unknown means he is the revealer, not Jesus Christ through John. It also assumes the book was "sealed" for nearly 2,000 years, rather than being "revealed" as John claimed. JESUS DID THE REVEALING BY REMOVING ALL 7 SEALS. *Revelation* is what it claims to be — **REVELATION!!!**

The message was understandable to first century readers because the specific visions related to current events. However, the truth of the message has had tremendous significance for every generation since that time; namely, God brings an end to evil nations.

THE PRIMARY APPLICATION IS ROME

Seven reasons will clearly illustrate *Revelation* was written initially about the fall of Rome in the first century; these ideas will be critical not only in understanding this volume, but also in understanding the book of *Revelation*.

Reason 1

Revelation is a letter

Revelation is a letter written to people during the first century AD. This becomes apparent in *Revelation* 1:4 — *John, To the seven churches in the province of Asia ...* The seven churches were located in the Roman Empire at a time when great persecution was just around the corner. It is only logical that the direct relevance of the message would be for the intended audience. Although there are great truths in the letter that are significant for modern times, the letter was written to first century citizens. To study the letters to the Corinthians, one needs to understand the city of Corinth and the church in that location. To comprehend *Ephesians*, one needs to understand the nature of the city, its inhabitants, and some of the events of that era. Why should this letter be approached any differently? For some inexplicable reason, many ignore the original audience in trying to understand this truly significant letter. Why would the message be sent in the form of an epistle if it had no real significance to the named audience?

Reason 2

Blessings to the Reader

Revelation 1:3 Blessed is the one who reads the words of this prophecy, and blessed are those who hear it and take to heart what is written in it ...

When early Christians were told they would be blessed if they obeyed the truths of the book, one can conclude the book was comprehendible in the first century just as it can be today.

Reason 3

Timeframe

One needs to examine a timeframe comparison between *Daniel* and *Revelation*. John, without fail, claims the events of his book were to happen in the near future, while Daniel claims the events of his book were far into the future. The following passages were selected from each book because they give insights into the length of time from prophecy to fulfillment.

*Daniel 8:17 "Son of man," he said to me, "understand that the vision concerns the **time of the end**."*

*Daniel 8:26 seal up the vision, for it concerns the **distant future**."*

*Daniel 10:14 "Now I have come to explain to you what will happen to your people in the future, for the vision concerns a **time yet to come**."*

*Daniel 12:4 "But you, Daniel, close up and seal the words of the scroll until the **time of the end**.*

*Daniel 12:9 ... "Go your way, Daniel, because the words are closed up and sealed until the **time of the end**."*

*Revelation 1:1 The revelation of Jesus Christ, which God gave him to show his servants what must **soon take place**.*

*Revelation 1:3 . . . take to heart what is written in it, because the **time is near**.*

*Revelation 2:10 Do not be afraid of what **you are about to suffer**. I tell you, the devil **will put some of you in prison to test you, and you will suffer** persecution for ten days.*

*Revelation 3:10 I will also keep **you from the hour of trial** that is going to come upon the whole world to test those who live on the earth.*

*Revelation 22:6,7 The Lord ... sent his angel to show his servants the things that must **soon take place**. Behold, I am coming soon!*

*Revelation 22:10 "Do not seal up the words of the prophecy of this book, because the **time is near**."*

There is a significant difference in the two timeframes. Daniel's visions seem to be far into the future, but John's events carry the message of immediacy — **the events were imminent for the reader**

2,000 years ago! One of the worst persecutions Christianity has ever known occurred shortly after John wrote the letter. Each of the visions of John can be shown to relate directly to historical events occurring during the first century. This epistle, which was interpreted by first century readers as relating to their timeframe, was to prepare them for the tribulation coming soon. To further this point even more, consider the fact that *Daniel* was a sealed book and *Revelation* was an unsealed book.

> *Daniel 8:26 "The vision of the evenings and mornings that has been given you is true, but <u>seal</u> up the vision, <u>for</u> it concerns the **distant future**."*

> *Revelation 22:10 Then he told me, "<u>Do not seal</u> up the words of the prophecy of this book, because the **time is near**."*

Daniel was told the length of time until fulfillment was the reason why the book was to be sealed. The events described in that instance referred to the third kingdom, the Grecian empire about 161 BC; Daniel did his writing shortly after 600 BC. This means the vision was sealed because fulfillment would not occur for about 450 years; it is easy to see that one could not understand the prophetic message 450 years before completion. This underscores the principle that long term prophecy is not understood immediately; the message was concealed, or in biblical terms "sealed."

Doesn't it seem illogical for Daniel to seal his prophecy because 450 years is **far into the future**, and for John not to seal his prophecy because 2,000 years into the future is **near**? The conclusion would be non sequitur; it "does not follow!"

How interesting that Daniel and John are given opposite orders and opposite justifications based on opposite timeframes until fulfillment! Any claim the events of *Revelation* refer primarily to modern times, therefore, makes two mistakes: 1) the author is actually claiming to be the one doing the revealing. 2) The thesis denies the very title of *Revelation* by implying that John "sealed" his work until the current era in which the modern-day author is decoding the message.

THREE REASONS HAVE BEEN PRESENTED

* * *

ALL FOUR REMAINING REASONS POINT TO ROME

Perhaps after reading the first three points, the reader is still not convinced John's principle message was to the first century. John wrote a symbolic book in which he gave four tremendous clues concerning the identity of the kingdom that God would target for the fall in Armageddon; the kingdom is symbolized as a **10 horned beast.** He tells 1) when the beast was to exist, 2) who its kings had been and were to be, 3) what its identifying feature was, and 4) where it was located. If the principal character is identified, then it is reasonable the era in which it exists is the one where the primary application is to be made. The last four reasons all tie together to make the point clear — **the primary application concerns Rome.**

Reason 4

4th Kingdom

The beast seen by Daniel and by John refers to the fourth great empire on earth beginning with Babylon; this pinpoints the TIME of its existence. It is imperative to understand there is a vast difference between <u>kingdoms</u> and <u>kings</u>. Some of the confusion over these two prophetic books exists because of failure to distinguish clearly between the two. In *Daniel* the beast represents the 4th kingdom, and the 10 horns represent the kings of the kingdom. In *Revelation* the beast represents a kingdom, and the 7 heads represent the kings of the kingdom. In both books the beast represents a kingdom, not a king.

John made a statement in *Revelation* 17 that immediately identifies the kingdom as the Roman Empire when he indicated the 7 heads were symbolic of 7 kings. He stated that five of the kings had already fallen; one was on the throne at the time of the writing, and more were to come. When John was penning his work, Rome was the prevailing power of the world; if an existing king was the ruler of the kingdom in question, **the kingdom could be no other than Rome**. The identity of the 10 horned beast is established by this one phrase, but more evidence will follow to prove that the 10 horned beast symbolizes Rome.

The first step in analysis will be to prove the beasts are identical in both *Daniel* and *Revelation*. If this can be demonstrated, then it is clear the kingdoms symbolized by the beast are the same. Eleven comparisons of Daniel's beast with that of John's beast should suffice in making the point.

1. Both of the beasts have ten horns.

One can search the Bible from cover to cover and not find a 10 horned beast mentioned anywhere other than in *Daniel* and *Revelation*.

2. Both beasts were to say boastful things.

Daniel 7:20	*Revelation 13:5*
... the horn that looked more imposing than the others and that had eyes and a mouth that **spoke boastfully**.	The beast was given a mouth to **utter proud words** and blasphemies and to exercise his authority for forty-two months.

The wording of Daniel and John is so close in the King James Version that one cannot miss the connection between the two.

Daniel 7:20	*Revelation 13:5*
... and a **mouth that spake very great things** ...	... a **mouth speaking great things** and blasphemies.

The difference between the two passages comes when John reveals the "great things spoken" are actually blasphemous words. The edicts of the Roman emperors carried great weight in regulating world activities, but many of the edicts spoken by the Roman leader were absolutely against the Will of God. Furthermore, many of the caesars actually proclaimed themselves to be gods.

3. The beasts in both books originated from the sea.

Daniel 7:3 Four great beasts, each different from the others, ***came up out of the sea****.*

Revelation 13:1 ... And I saw a beast ***coming out of the sea*** *...*

The sea represents all the nations Rome controlled at the time of its power – a "sea" of people under its rule. It could also relate to the geographic significance of the Roman Empire; at the time of its zenith, Rome surrounded the Mediterranean Sea. The two viewpoints are not mutually exclusive; John may have been giving clues concerning both areas. When one examines the first three resemblances — both had ten horns, both boasted, and both originated from the sea — a strong picture begins to form. Study the maps on the next two pages to see the impact of the "beast coming up from the sea."

GROWTH OF THE ROMAN EMPIRE

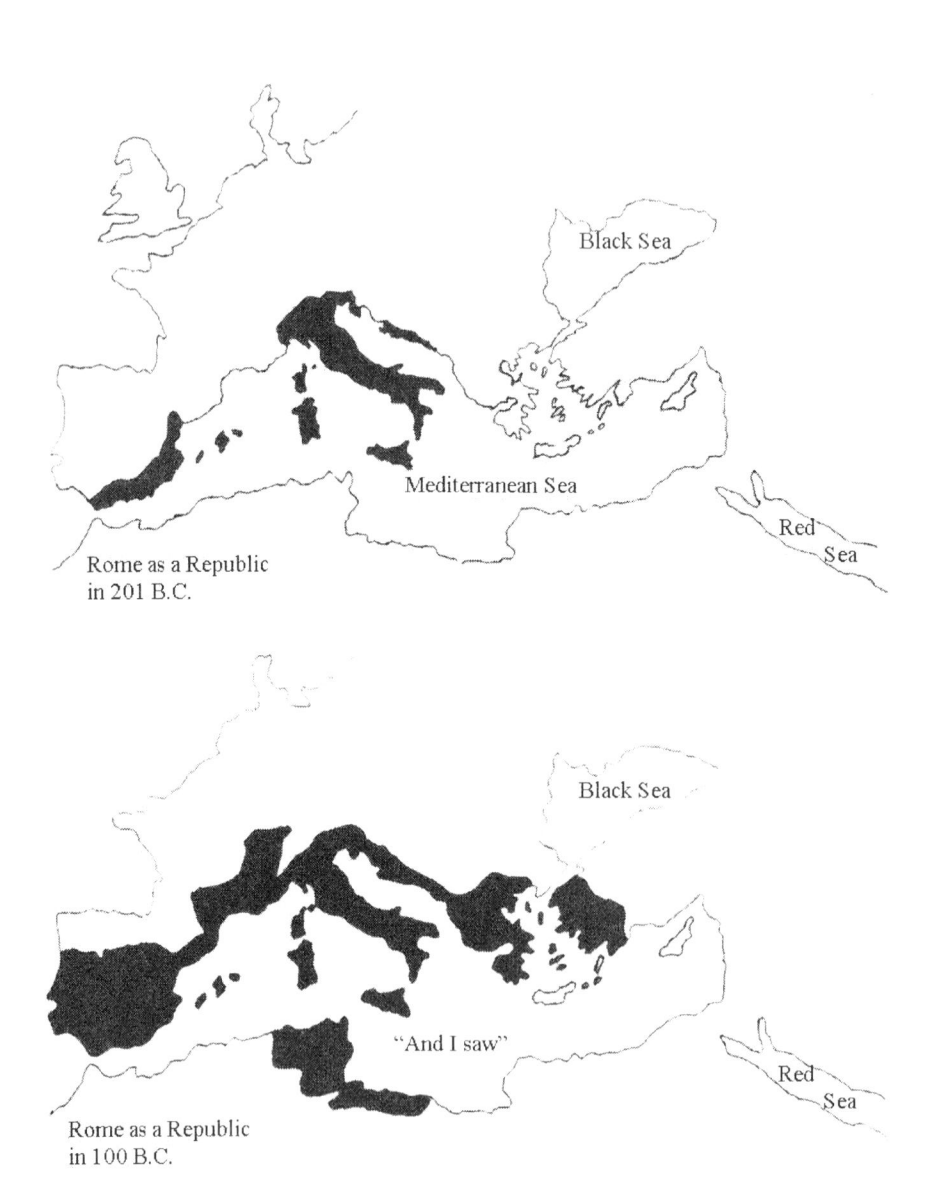

Rome as a Republic in 201 B.C.

Black Sea
Mediterranean Sea
Red Sea

Rome as a Republic in 100 B.C.

Black Sea
"And I saw"
Red Sea

"a beast"

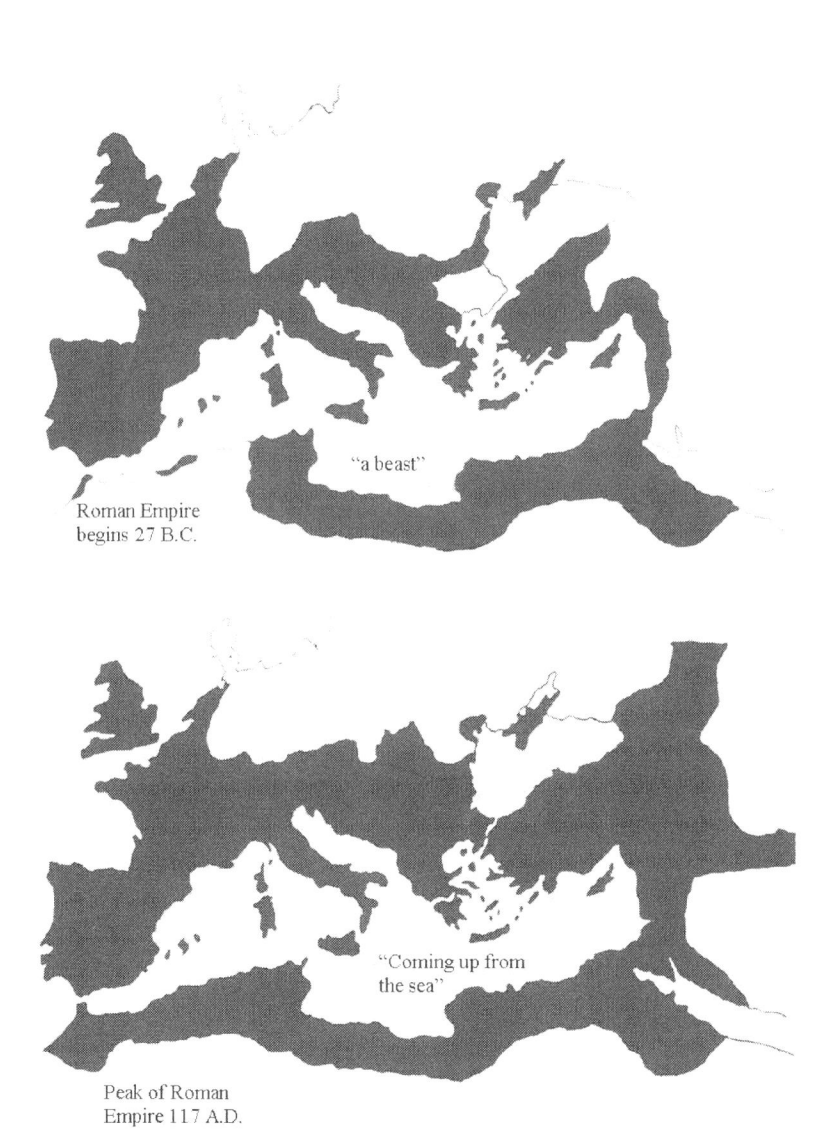

Roman Empire
begins 27 B.C.

"Coming up from
the sea"

Peak of Roman
Empire 117 A.D.

4. Both link the Beast to a lion, a bear, and a leopard.

Daniel's beast was to be preceded by a lion, followed by a bear, and finally by a leopard. On the other hand, John's description of the 10 horned beast had the appearance of a leopard, the feet of a bear, and the mouth of a lion.

John's description of the leopard, bear, and lion were in reverse order of Daniel's. Daniel's vision permitted him to see from Babylon into the future, and John's vision looked from his time back to Babylon. The 10 horned beast of *Revelation* had taken the appearance of the three kingdoms preceding it, looking like a leopard with the feet of a bear and the mouth of a lion.

Daniel 7:3-7 Four great beasts, each different from the others, came up out of the sea. "The first was like a **lion**, ... "And there before me was a second beast, which looked like a **bear**. ... " there before me was another beast, one that looked like a **leopard**. ... "After that, ... I looked, and there before me was a **fourth beast.** ... it had ten horns.	*Revelation 13:1-2* I saw a beast coming out of the sea. He had **ten horns.** ... The beast I saw resembled a **leopard**, but had feet like those of a **bear** and a mouth like that of a **lion**.

5. Both beasts were to be tremendously powerful.

Daniel 7:7 ... It had large iron teeth; it crushed and devoured its victims and trampled underfoot whatever was left.	*Revelation 13:7* He was given power to make war against the saints and to conquer them. And he was given authority over every tribe, people, language and nation.

Many powerful nations and empires have existed on this earth since the beginning of time, but none have exceeded the relative power of the Roman Empire. Daniel stresses its power by dwelling on its military might and its crushing of other nations. John illustrates the power with its authority over every tribe, people, language, and nation. Rome controlled the known world during its era.

6. The beast would battle saints.

When Christ came to earth, during the days of the Roman Empire, a great conflict was set in motion. It was the Roman Empire that crucified our Lord and Savior; today the Roman Empire is no more, but the people of God are still moving forward. This conflict between the two kingdoms is referred to in the following passages:

| *Daniel 7:25 He will speak against the Most High and oppress his saints and try to change the set times and the laws. The **saints will be handed over** to him for a time, times and half a time.* | *Revelation 13:7 He was given power to make **war against the saints** and to conquer them. And he was given authority over every tribe, people, language and nation.* |

7. The length of persecution is the same.

| *Daniel 7:25 The saints will be handed over to him for a **time, times and half a time**.* | *Revelation 12: The woman was given the two wings of a great eagle, so that she might fly to the place prepared for her in the desert, where she would be taken care of for a **time, times and half a time**, out of the serpent's reach.* |

Daniel stresses that the beast would persecute for **time, times, and half a time,** while John states that the woman would be protected for **time, times, and half a time** during the persecution by the beast. *Daniel* and *Revelation* are the only books in the Bible where this phrase occurs. What a clue!!!

> **Four ways the Bible states the same thing:**
> - 3 ½ years
> - 42 months
> - 1260 days
> - Time, times, and half a time
>
> Time = 1 year
> Times = 2 years
> Half a time = ½ year

Revelation 13:5 The beast was given a mouth to utter proud words and blasphemies and to exercise his authority for forty-two months.

The reasoning is clear — if the beast persecuted saints for time, times, and half a time, and if the beast exercised authority for forty-two months, this proves that the phrase "time, times, and half a time" symbolizes 42 months which is three and one-half years.

8. Judgment of the saints destroyed the beast.

Daniel 7:22 *Until the Ancient of Days came and pronounced **judgment in favor of the saints** of the Most High* *Daniel 7:22* *... and the time came when they possessed the kingdom.*	*Revelation 20:4* *I saw thrones on which were seated those who had been **given authority to judge ...*** *Revelation 20:4 ... They came to life and reigned with Christ a thousand years.*

In *Revelation 6*, John sees slain saints beneath the altar of God calling for vengeance on those who had persecuted them; their calls were not in vain. Vengeance will certainly come because the ones persecuted will possess the eternal kingdom. The following point will show the beast did fall — a result of the saints' judgment.

9. Despite their greatness, both beasts were to fall.

Daniel 7:26 "But the court will sit, and his power will be taken away and completely destroyed forever." *Daniel 7:11 Then I continued to watch because of the boastful words the horn was speaking. I kept looking until the beast was slain and its body destroyed and thrown into the blazing fire.*	*Revelation 19:20 But the beast was captured, and with him the false prophet who had performed the miraculous signs on his behalf. With these signs he had deluded those who had received the mark of the beast and worshiped his image. The two of them were thrown alive into the fiery lake of burning sulfur.*

10. When the beast falls, God's Kingdom survives.

Both authors claim the kingdom of God would last forever; there is no difference between an everlasting dominion and one whose king reigns for ever and ever. Both John and Daniel affirm the kingdom of God would survive the persecution and last eternally.

Daniel 7:14 His dominion is an everlasting dominion that will not pass away, and his kingdom is one that will never be destroyed.	*Revelation 11:15 ... there were loud voices in heaven, which said: "The kingdom of the world has become the kingdom of our Lord and of his Christ, and he will reign for ever and ever."*

11. Daniel foretold the kingdom in which John lived.

Daniel clearly identifies the "Beast Kingdom" for the reader who examines his entire prophecy. The first three kingdoms are explicitly named — Babylon, Medo-Persia, and Greece. In both Nebuchadnezzar's vision and Daniel's dream, the fourth kingdom experiences an identical event, the kingdom of God was established on earth. When one discovers which empire was in power when the King of kings arrived on earth to establish God's kingdom, he should have the necessary data to identify the name of the "Beast Kingdom."

Nebuchadnezzar's Dream	Daniel's Dream
Daniel 2:44 **"In the time of those kings, the God of heaven will set up a kingdom** *that will never be destroyed.*	*Daniel 7:13-14 there before me was one like a son of man, coming with the clouds of heaven. He approached the Ancient of Days and was led into his presence.* **He was given authority, glory and sovereign power;** *... his kingdom is one that will never be destroyed.*

Since the fourth kingdom of each vision experiences the same event, the coming of the King of kings to earth, it is only logical that the first three kingdoms of each vision are parallel as well. The following evidence will illustrate the line of the two visions from Babylon to Rome:

Babylon is the first kingdom

*Daniel 2:37-39 "You, O king, are the king of kings. ... **You are that head of gold.** After you, another kingdom will rise, inferior to yours.*

*Jeremiah 4:5-7 "Announce in Judah and proclaim in Jerusalem and say: ... **A lion has come out of his lair**; a destroyer of nations has set out. He has left his place to lay waste your land ...*

Although Daniel told Nebuchadnezzar he, king of Babylon, was the king of gold, he was distinct in pointing out that the image symbolized kingdoms rather than kings because the "gold" was to be replaced by a **kingdom** inferior to Nebuchadnezzar's rule. It is also interesting to discover that Jeremiah used the lion as a symbol for Babylon in his prophecy concerning Jerusalem's fall. Excavations in the Babylonian region indicate the lion was Babylon's ancient symbol.

Medo-Persia is the second kingdom

Nebuchadnezzar's vision indicated Babylon would be replaced by a kingdom inferior to itself, symbolized by silver. The 5th chapter of *Daniel* tells of the overthrow of Babylon by Medo-Persia. It only follows that if "golden Babylon" was to be overthrown by the "silver" kingdom, then Medo-Persia is the one of silver. Daniel had two dreams of this second kingdom; the first involved a bear; the other depicted a two-horned ram, symbolic of Medo-Persia.

Daniel 7:5 ... before me was a second beast, which looked like a bear. It was raised up on one of its sides, and it had three ribs in its mouth between its teeth ...

Daniel 8:3 ... before me was a ram with two horns, ... One of the horns was longer than the other but grew up later. Dan 8:20 The two-horned ram that you saw represents the kings of Media and Persia.

The bear had one side raised higher than the other; the two horned ram had one horn raised higher than the other. The message in both places refers to the two-fold kingdom of the Medes and Persians with

Persia's having more power than its counterpart. There is no doubt as to the name of the kingdom symbolized by the two horned ram; it is named in *Daniel* 8:20 as Medo-Persia.

Greece is the third kingdom

The third kingdom is explicitly named when Daniel saw a shaggy goat destroy the two horned ram that has been identified as Medo-Persia. Notice the name of the kingdom that overthrew the second great empire on earth:

Daniel 8:21 The shaggy goat is the king of Greece ...

Earlier it was established that Medo-Persia was the silver kingdom and that the silver would be overthrown by the bronze; since Medo-Persia was crushed by the bronze kingdom, also called the shaggy goat kingdom. The bronze empire and shaggy goat are obviously the same — **Greece**.

Rome is the fourth kingdom

Historically, the kingdom that followed Babylon, Medo-Persia, and Greece was Rome; however, Daniel did not leave this to conjecture. Daniel told of an event that would occur during the days of the fourth kingdom — God was to establish his kingdom on earth; **it is exciting to learn that during the days of the first Roman caesar, God chose to send His Son Jesus Christ to earth — the King of kings and Lord of lords!** When history records that the first king of the Roman Empire was Augustus, what an amazing scripture is found in Luke!

> *Luke 2:1-5 In those days Caesar Augustus issued a decree that a census should be taken of the entire Roman world. ... So Joseph also went up from the town of Nazareth in Galilee to Judea, ... He went there to register with Mary, who was pledged to be married to him and was expecting a child.*

What a clue Daniel gives as to the "nature of the beast!" Daniel's beast was Rome, and the beast of Daniel and John were one and the same. Conclusion: **THE BEAST OF *REVELATION* IS ROME!**

Reason 5

Rome's Kings

Daniel's and John's beasts both symbolized kingdoms, but each beast had features symbolizing kings. These kings relate too closely to the history of the Roman Empire to be mere chance. Daniel saw 10 kings, added one to arrive at 11, and then saw 3 destroyed to end with **8**. John began with 7 kings and added 1, also to end with **8**.

Daniel 7:23,24
... "The fourth beast is a fourth kingdom that will appear on earth. ... ***The ten horns are ten kings*** *who will come from this kingdom. After them another king will arise, different from the earlier ones; he will subdue three kings."*

Revelation 17:9-11 This calls for a mind with wisdom. The seven heads are seven hills on which the woman sits. ***They are also seven kings****. Five have fallen, one is, the other has not yet come; but when he does come, he must remain for a little while. The beast who once was, and now is not, is an eighth king. He belongs to the seven and is going to his destruction.*

After one horn was added and three had been broken off, Daniel's beast had only 8 horns. Why didn't John see an 8 horned beast? This would not have carried the same imagery as the 10 horned beast Daniel had seen; the beast was the same to show the kingdoms were identical. Rather than horns, John used 7 heads to represent the kings.

Where do we begin numbering the Roman kings? Julius Caesar was pulling the Roman Republic together and would have probably achieved the goal of making it an empire, but before he could get the job accomplished, he was assassinated in 44 BC. The Roman Republic was further divided with Lepidus controlling Asian territory, Mark Anthony controlling African territory, and Octavian controlling Europe for the next seventeen years.

It is only logical that we begin listing caesars once the Republic becomes the Roman Empire! In 27 BC Octavian gained control of all three areas to unify what would become known as the Roman Empire. Any credible Roman historian will date the beginning of the Roman Empire in 27 BC when Octavian was named Augustus Caesar. Augustus was followed by Tiberius, Gaius, Claudius, and Nero, before the civil war of 69 ended the Julio-Claudian dynasty.

Daniel used the 10 horns of the beast to symbolize kings; if one horn breaks off three horns, this indicates one king will overthrow three kings in the same kingdom. There was such a civil war in the year 69 AD in which three caesars were removed in what historians refer to as the "year of the four caesars." In the *Complete Works of Tacitus* p. 420, paragraph 2, a graphic picture of civil war is given.

> "I am entering on the history of a period rich in disasters, frightful in its wars, torn by civil strife, and even in peace full of horrors. Four emperors perished by the sword. There were three civil wars ..."

Nero died by his own sword when he committed suicide in the summer of 68 AD; afterwards, Rome experienced a year and a half of civil war. Civil upheaval began as Roman troops raised Galba to the throne only to see him defeated. Otho's followers placed him in power, but it didn't take long for him to be replaced by Vitellius who was soon assassinated. After the civil war, Vespasian and family began to rule Rome in what historians refer to as the Flavian dynasty.

Daniel said three horns (kings) were broken off, so John left them out. John saw a 10 horned beast, but the beast had seven heads that symbolized kings. It's easy to see why John left the losers of the civil war out — losers are never given official recognition. **Example:** Jefferson Davis' picture is not included on presidential calendars because he lost in the American Civil War! The charts on the following pages will help the reader to picture the kings of the Roman Empire.

ROMAN CAESARS in *DANIEL*
(Total who sat on the throne)

JULIO-CLAUDIAN DYNASTY

1. Augustus	27 BC
2. Tiberius	14 AD
3. Gaius (Caligula)	37
4. Claudius	41
5. Nero	54

CIVIL WARS

6. Galba	69
7. Otho	69
8. Vitellius	69

... shall ten kings arise:
And another shall arise after them ...
And he shall put down three kings.
Daniel 7:24

FLAVIAN DYNASTY

9. Vespasian	69
10. Titus	79
11. Domitian	81-95

ROMAN CAESARS in *REVELATION*
(Actual who were recognized)

JULIO-CLAUDIAN DYNASTY

1. Augustus	27 BC
2. Tiberius	14 AD
3. Gaius (Caligula)	37
4. Claudius	41
5. Nero	54

... and they are seven kings;
the five are fallen ...
Revelation 17:10

CIVIL WARS
69 AD
"Year of the Four Emperors"

3 had been removed in *Daniel*
The 3 were not considered in *Revelation*

FLAVIAN DYNASTY

9. Vespasian *... one is* 69
10. Titus ... *The other is not yet come* 79
11. Domitian ... *himself also an eighth,* 81-95
and is of the seven ... Revelation 17: 10,11

When one is attempting to decode information identifying the kingdom represented by the 10 horned beast, the answer must meet each of the four criteria established by John. The first two clues point very heavily to the Roman Empire because historically it was the fourth kingdom from Babylon's power, and its caesars correspond perfectly to the kings and the events of the Roman Empire. The last two clues also identify Rome as the 10 horned beast.

Reason 6

666

The number of the beast, a unique identifying feature, reveals it is Rome. In *Revelation 13:18*, John says the number of the name of the beast is **666**. Shortly before John wrote his letter to the seven churches, Rome had developed a new numbering system called "Roman Numerals."

Before the first century, numbering systems utilized all the letters of the alphabet. Every letter in the Greek alphabet and every letter of the Hebrew alphabet, according to Ethelbert Bullinger in *Number in Scripture* p. 48, also represented a numerical value. About two thousand years ago, the Romans chose only seven of their letters to represent numbers. If one needed to write the number 3, the Romans used three I's to do so; a 4 was made with the I and a V, etc. Greeks used the letter γ to express the number 3; The Hebrew symbol for the number 3 was their letter gimmel, ג. The differences in systems would surely encourage the early reader to examine the possibility of Roman Numerals being significant in forming the number 666. Notice the total of the first six Roman numerals when added:

$$
\begin{aligned}
I &= 1 \\
V &= 5 \\
X &= 10 \\
L &= 50 \\
C &= 100 \\
D &= \underline{500} \\
&\mathbf{666}
\end{aligned}
$$

No misspelling of names; no numerical juggling; no secret code to unravel the mystery — Rome can easily be identified by the number 666. It is also interesting to note that it takes the first 6 numerals to total 666. One might ask, "Weren't there seven Roman numerals; why count just the first six?" This is a fair question. But the first readers were looking at 6's, and six numerals total 666. Also, if all seven numbers are added, the 666 is still rather obvious because the total is 1,666. But the reader is thinking 6's all the way.

The first century reader would have seen this point much more rapidly than the modern reader for two reasons: 1) At that point in history many Christians were Jews living in Roman owned territory. The uniqueness in the Roman numeral system would have made the point even more obvious to Greek speaking citizens. If everything else is pointing to Rome, wouldn't the explorer examine a possible link to Rome? 2) From 500 B.C. to around 500 A.D., gematria was in every day use. Gematria was a game in which names were often coded by numbers. A person might write, "I am in love with number 457"; since numbers were also letters, the one dealing with Gematria would try to decode the message. First century citizens were simply aware of numbers.

Reason 7

7 Hills of Rome

John said the seven heads also represented seven mountains; this indicates location. Even if all six prior points were still questionable, reason seven could stand by itself in proving the beast to be Rome. Rome has always been known as the "City on 7 Hills." In fact, most books that address Rome to any degree of significance will list the names of the seven hills. Quoting *Rome of the Caesars* by Leonardo B. Dal Maso:

> The Palatine is the hill on which the city of Rome, the square city was born. And on this hill we can still see the very ancient traces which are identified with the origins of Rome.

Along with the Palatine, Dal Maso names the other hills of Rome: Aventine, Caelian, Esquiline, Viminal, Quirinal, and Capitoline.

What an indicator John gave his readers when he wrote of the 7 hills! If a writer were giving clues about a city and said the Empire State Building sat within the city, could anyone determine which city was meant without the name being spelled? **Of course!** When John gave this clue, he might as well have named the empire because this is the main topographical feature of the area known as ROME!

> *Revelation 17:9 This calls for a mind with wisdom. The seven heads are seven hills on which the woman sits.*

SUMMARY OF THE 7 POINTS

John gave four tremendous clues as to what the beast represents, and all four clearly say ROME; one might find another nation that fits one of these clues, but when one tries to find one nation to fit the four clues John gave as to the identity of the beast, **only one name emerges — ROME**! When one further realizes this is the very group to whom John was writing, Christians living in the Roman Empire, and that the events were to happen soon, there can be no other answer than Rome. The readers were to be blessed if they were faithful to Jesus during the persecution of the beast. What other nation ever persecuted Christianity more than Rome? These seven points become imposing when they are viewed together:

1. *Revelation* is a letter written to 1st century Christians.
2. The readers were to be blessed if they obeyed. (One must be able to understand.)
3. *Revelation's* events were to happen in the near future.
4. The fourth kingdom from Daniel's time was Rome.
5. The kings of the kingdom fit Roman history like a glove.
6. The number 666 is the total of the first 6 Roman numerals.
7. The empire sat on 7 hills — clearly referring to Rome.

Encircling these seven reasons is the meaning of the word revelation which indicates truth is being made known that previously was concealed.

Imagine being in the First Century

Once the thesis of *Revelation* has been explored by examining the "sealed" message of *Daniel*, the reader needs to imagine living in Rome during the first century. One day you learn of a unique scroll containing a message from John; it is obviously a letter because John uses the traditional greeting, "John, to the seven churches in Asia." You also learn from listening to the scroll's being read that blessings are promised to the one who reads, hears, and obeys the message of the letter, so you determine the letter will be understandable and important. As the reading continues, you learn the message concerns a vision presented to John by One dressed in linen, Who has a golden girdle, eyes like flaming fire, feet like burnished brass, and the voice of a multitude, and you remember that Daniel had a similar vision in the long ago. John leaves no doubt this person is Jesus Christ.

As the message unfolds, you hear warnings that the events in the letter are to happen in the near future. No wonder John is sending a letter of urgency to us! John writes that he saw God on His throne in heaven, holding a sealed book; you ask, "What book has God sealed in the past?" Knowing the Old Testament scrolls well, you recall that *Daniel* is the only Old Testament scroll God ever commanded to be "sealed."

As John continues telling about Jesus' removing the seals, you learn about a 10 horned beast just as Daniel had seen centuries before. You ask, "What did the 10 horned beast represent in *Daniel*?" You remember Daniel had envisioned four beasts symbolic of empires; a quick examination discloses the four kingdoms to be as follows: 1) Babylon 2) Medo-Persia, 3) Greece, and 4) Rome, the kingdom presently controlling your life. You also notice the fourth beast has taken on the appearance of the three preceding nations — the beast has the appearance of a leopard, the feet of a bear, and the mouth of a lion, the first three kingdoms mentioned in *Daniel.*

You also learn the number of the beast is 666. Because you live in the Roman Empire where Roman numerals were recently introduced, it is not a difficult task to see that the first six Roman numerals total 666. Further on, you learn that the beast has seven heads symbolizing seven kings, and you discover that the sixth one is on the throne as the book is being written. Another piece to the puzzle falls into place concerning the seven heads of the beast which also represent the seven mountains on which the city sits. This is Rome's nickname, and you even know the names of the seven hills. Living in the first century, what conclusion could you possibly draw? Suddenly you jump to your feet and exclaim, "I understand now! Two thousand years from now there will be a country by the name of Iraq; there will be another called the United States. The United States will join with Israel to ..." **There is no way you, a first century reader, could ever draw this conclusion; you would obviously conclude the message refers to Rome!!!**

SECONDARY APPLICATIONS

John's letter had immediate significance for the first century readers, but this does not mean there has been no relevancy for readers throughout the 2,000 years transpiring since the writing. *Revelation* conveys a relevant message to today's readers as well. One concept revealed in the book is that no earthly nation or kingdom is meant to last forever; only the kingdom of God is everlasting. This means all governments have a birth, a life, and a death. Before a nation crumbles, there are symptoms that can be observed signaling impending danger. These emerging signs are evident in the opening of the seals. As days pass and as evil of the nation worsens, warnings sound that a fall is imminent; these warnings are analogous to the trumpets of *Revelation*. God will not allow a nation to dabble in evil into infinity; the collapse of people and nations is the result of wickedness bringing the bowls of God's wrath. This truth became manifest in the days of Noah as evidenced in the following scripture:

> *Genesis 6:1-3 When men began to increase in number on the earth and daughters were born to them, the sons of God saw that the daughters of men were beautiful, and they married any of them they chose. Then the LORD said, "My Spirit will not contend with man forever, for he is mortal; his days will be a hundred and twenty years."*

History has recorded this truth with relentless consistency: Sodom, Gomorrah, Tyre, Sidon, Egypt, Assyria, Babylon, Jerusalem, Persia, Greece, Rome, Spain, Germany, Japan, Korea, the Soviet

Union, and others. One wonders which nation will be the next to experience its "Armageddon"; the United States is certainly not exempt. Scripture and history combine to present a basic truth: no nation or empire has ever been or will ever be strong enough to last forever! While John did not write **specifically** concerning the United States or any other modern country, the eternal truths he envisioned **apply today!** The removal of the seals revealed everlasting truths for all nations.

Are trumpets being sounded in America today? Which nations are already in the process of dying as the bowls are being poured? There have been many historical incidents paralleling the events of Rome's fall from power. This is why interpreters in virtually every generation have mistakenly seen John's prophecy applying specifically to their age, yet their observations of impending doom hold some truth because history repeats itself.

Another significant principle for today's readers relates to two phrases, "time of the end" and "end of time." When Daniel wrote about the end of Medo-Persia, he called it the "time of the end." When he wrote about the coming demise of Greece, he called it the "time of the end." When Jerusalem was pictured as falling, the author also called it the "time of the end." Finally, the fall of the fourth kingdom would signal a "time of the end." Simple logic makes it clear that time can end only once. However, any time an era closes, it is "a time of the end." John's "short term" prophecy refers primarily to the imminent destruction facing Rome; furthermore, it indicates victory in the future for all Christians even though earthly nations collapse. It also signals final victory when Jesus comes again to end all time. Toward the end of this volume, materials will be submitted to illustrate this great truth.

> **The philosophy
> of *Revelation* makes it
> a relevant message for all times**

Every generation since the time of Rome has viewed the message as relating directly to them, but they were actually perceiving the **recurring theme of God's destruction of evil.**

Many great truths from the book affect today's reader. Four will become clear when the text of *Revelation* is explored.

1) God controlled the universe in the first century, and God controls the universe today.
2) Man has always had a choice between good and evil, between following the ways of God or ways of the world.
3) Those choosing to follow God will have the ultimate victory through Jesus Christ.
4) Those choosing to follow the world will pay eternal consequences.

Other tools for understanding *Revelation* will be presented in the next seven chapters; these tools will be 1) *Daniel*, 2) *Ezekiel*, 3) ancient history, and 4) number symbols. Hopefully, this information will give the reader the background necessary to understand how the writings of Daniel, Ezekiel, and John, join in making *Revelation* known to all.

SECTION II

Tools for Understanding *Revelation*

Chapter Two

Daniel Prophesied the fall of Babylon

Three writers combined to bring readers the powerful message unveiled in the book of *Revelation*. Ezekiel and Daniel were exiles in Babylon when they wrote their prophetic messages. John was an exile (in person or in spirit) on the Isle of Patmos when Jesus Christ revealed to him the meaning of Daniel's and Ezekiel's messages. One cannot understand *Revelation* without having a grasp of *Daniel* and *Ezekiel*. The prophecies of Daniel and Ezekiel were long term prophecies; in fact, this volume will illustrate that John revealed what Daniel had sealed some six hundred years earlier. When a prophecy is fulfilled, it ceases to be sealed; the information is revealed through its taking place. After Babylon fell, Daniel exulted that he then understood what Jeremiah had spoken of in his prophecy. What had once been sealed became revealed through fulfillment.

> *Daniel 9:2 In the first year of his reign, I, Daniel, understood from the Scriptures, according to the word of the LORD given to Jeremiah the prophet, that the desolation of Jerusalem would last seventy years.*

Jeremiah's prophecy now looks very clear to the reader; however, when the prophecy was made, Judah had not yet fallen to Nebuchadnezzar, and Babylon was certainly a long way from its collapse.

> *Jeremiah 25:9-12 ... This whole country will become a desolate wasteland, and* **these nations will serve the king of Babylon seventy years. But when the seventy years are fulfilled, I will punish the king of Babylon and his nation, the land of the Babylonians, for their**

guilt," *declares the LORD, "and will make it desolate forever."*

In his book, Daniel prophesied about the fall of four kingdoms; he further prophesied about the everlasting nature of the kingdom of God. The four kingdoms for which he foretold disaster were Babylon, Medo-Persia, Greece, and Rome. As each of the empires collapsed, another part of prophecy was unsealed. The first three kingdoms had all fallen before John's lifetime; however, the fourth kingdom was in its power when John received his revelation from Jesus Christ. John revealed what Daniel had sealed.

Three prophecies relate to Babylon; two were made concerning a longer timeframe, and one was made about the relatively near future. The first came from Nebuchadnezzar's dream, the second from Daniel's vision, and the last by Belshazzar.

The Sealing and Revealing of the Fall of Babylon

First Prophecy about Babylon

Daniel foretold the fall of Babylon when he interpreted King Nebuchadnezzar's unusual dream of the metal man. In chapter 2 of *Daniel*, the king awoke one morning disturbed over a puzzling dream he had experienced during the night. He must have doubted the ability of his "wise men" to interpret dreams because he put them to the test. Rather than telling them his dream and having them explain the meaning, he demanded they first relate the dream and then tell its meaning. When astrology and magic failed to reveal the dream, Daniel was called upon for assistance. Through the help of God, Daniel explained the dream and its meaning.

Nebuchadnezzar had dreamed of a man made of metal; the man had a head of gold, an upper body of silver, a middle body of bronze, and a lower body (legs and feet) of iron and clay. The four parts he explained represented four kingdoms. As Daniel explained the vision, Nebuchadnezzar realized the head of gold symbolized Babylon.

> *Daniel 2:38 "In your hands he has placed mankind and the beasts of the field and the birds of the air. Wherever they live, he has made you ruler over them all. You are that head of gold."*

The "gold" part of the image indicates the grandeur of Nebuchadnezzar's kingdom; but the glory of the kingdom would end, and a new power would take its place.

Historians verify the greatness of Babylon under Nebuchadnezzar. *Encyclopedia Britannica* points out that Babylon was located in what is now known as Iraq, and almost all the palaces and temples excavated in Babylon date from Nebuchadnezzar's reign. The walls of the street were decorated with reliefs of lions, bulls, and dragons in colorful glazed bricks. The city had beautiful hanging gardens inside the exterior walls.

Ancient historian Herodotus claimed the wall was impenetrable; using modern measurements, the wall surrounding the city was 300 feet high and 80 feet thick. He also records that the River Euphrates ran beneath the wall, giving the city its necessary water supply. Even though many believe Herodotus exaggerated somewhat, it is clear that Babylon was the finest kingdom of its time.

A.E.R. Boak, Albert Hyma, and Preston Slosson in their book *The Growth of Western Civilization* tell about the Babylonian development in many areas. For instance, the Babylonians were advanced farmers, weavers, and traders. They had earlier developed a form of writing known as cuneiform which allowed them to keep official records of important events. Babylonians prepared the first known multiplication tables, which indicates a high degree of intelligence; they also developed formulas for calculating the areas of triangles, trapezoids, and irregular four-sided plots. With their mathematical genius, the Babylonians divided the circle into 360 equal parts or degrees — all of this shortly before the time of Daniel. Certainly the Babylonian empire was great for its time. The symbol of gold was perfect to represent the state of development and the power achieved by Babylon. Who would have ever thought Babylon would fall? But that is exactly what happened, just as Daniel had foretold.

Despite Babylon's greatness, both Isaiah in 13:17-22 and Jeremiah in 51:37-43 had prophesied its doom; Jeremiah, as observed earlier, even pin-pointed the time of its destruction, 70 years after Israel was taken into captivity.

Second Prophecy about Babylon

While chapter 2 of *Daniel* dealt with the interpretation of Nebuchadnezzar's dream concerning Babylon's coming doom, chapter 7 tells of Daniel's vision concerning the same event.

> *Daniel 7:1-4 In the first year of Belshazzar king of Babylon, Daniel had a dream, and visions passed through his mind as he was lying on his bed. He wrote down the substance of his dream. Daniel said: "In my vision at night I looked, and there before me were the four winds of heaven churning up the great sea. Four great beasts, each different from the others, came up out of the sea. The first was like a lion, and it had the wings of an eagle. I watched until its wings were torn off and it was lifted from the ground so that it stood on two feet like a man, and the heart of a man was given to it."*

Chapter one of this volume pointed out that the lion symbolizes Babylon. The lion, just as the head of gold, would indicate majestic facets of the Babylonian kingdom; it indeed was the grandest power of its time. The eagle's wings perhaps indicate not only the majesty of the empire, but also the speed with which the Babylonian kingdom under the king of Nebuchadnezzar rose to power. The author saw the king of land beasts with wings of an eagle, king of the air, symbolizing the nation in which he lived. However, Daniel learned the power of the beast was to be eroded; the beast would be given the heart of man and stand on two feet. Some have suggested this occurred during the time Nebuchadnezzar was insane, and it is amazing when Nebuchadnezzar was made into a beast, the kingdom of Babylon became more civil. Although the lion with eagle's wings created an imposing image, it would lose its power to another empire. Nebuchadnezzar saw the kingdom of gold fall to the silver kingdom; Daniel saw a bear, symbolizing Medo-Persia, replacing the lion of Babylon as the next world-power.

Third Prophecy about Babylon

Chapter 5 of *Daniel* deals with the last prophecy of doom and the actual fall of Babylon to the Medes and Persians, just as Daniel had prophesied about the silver overthrowing the gold and the bear replacing the lion. Babylon had continued to decline morally during the time Israel was being held captive. Nabonidas was king of Babylon from 555-536 B.C.; he had left his son Belshazzar in charge of the country on that fatal night. Belshazzar had the audacity to use the worship items of Israel in a drunken party honoring false gods of Babylon. His ancestor Nebuchadnezzar had made mistakes, but he had never stooped this low.

> *Daniel 5:1 King Belshazzar gave a great banquet for a thousand of his nobles and drank wine with them. While Belshazzar was drinking his wine, he gave orders to bring in the gold and silver goblets that Nebuchadnezzar his father had taken from the temple in Jerusalem, so that the king and his nobles, his wives and his concubines might drink from them. So they brought in the gold goblets that had been taken from the temple of God in Jerusalem, and the king and his nobles, his wives and his concubines drank from them. As they drank the wine, they praised the gods of gold and silver, of bronze, iron, wood and stone.*

For a long time, some questioned the historical existence of Belshazzar, noting official records of Babylon list Nabonidas as the last king of Babylon. Daniel actually lived through several Babylonian kings while in captivity — Nebuchadnezzar, 606-556 BC; Evil-Merodach, 561-560; Neriglissar, 559-556; Labash-Marduk, 556; and Nabonidas, 555-536 BC. Where then did Belshazzar come into the picture? In 1853 an archaeological discovery uncovered an inscription in a cornerstone of a Babylonian god:

> "May I, Nabonidas, king of Babylon, not sin against thee. And may reverence for thee dwell in the heart of Belshazzar, my first-born son."

Funk and Wagnalls Encyclopedia, 1983, explains:

> Nabonidas left the city of Babylon under control of his son Belshazzar and lived for a while in the city of Harran and later in the oasis of Teima, the Arabian Desert. In 539 BC the Babylonians were defeated by the Persian king Cyrus the Great, who had defeated Media. Nabonidas was captured at Sippar (near modern Baghdad, Iraq), and the Persians entered Babylon without resistance. Babylonia was then annexed to Persia and lost its independence for all time.

Remember what Belshazzar was doing in his father's absence? He was defiling the worship items brought from Jerusalem when the Jews were taken into captivity! Daniel says on that very night the king literally saw the "writing on the wall."

> *Daniel 5:5 Suddenly the fingers of a human hand appeared and wrote on the plaster of the wall, near the lampstand in the royal palace. The king watched the hand as it wrote.*

Verse 6 states that the king was so shaken his knees actually began to knock; he had lost his brazen composure exhibited in using the vessels of God. Just as his ancient predecessor Nebuchadnezzar had done, Belshazzar called in the magicians to interpret the inscriptions. He made a promise recorded in verse 7 that whoever interpreted the message would have a gold chain placed around his neck and be made ruler over one third of the Babylonian kingdom.

When the Babylonian magicians were unable to decipher the meaning, the queen remembered Daniel and relayed the information to Belshazzar. Some have tried to find difficulties in the fact that Nebuchadnezzar is referred to as Belshazzar's father in *Daniel 5:11*. However, relatives such as grandfathers and great-grandfathers were often referred to as father; Belshazzar came through Nebuchadnezzar's line — there is no problem. Daniel refused the king's gifts and began chastising Belshazzar with the following words:

> *Daniel 5:22-24 But you his son, O Belshazzar, have not humbled yourself, though you knew all this. Instead, you have set yourself up against the Lord of*

> heaven. *You had the goblets from his temple brought to you, and you and your nobles, your wives and your concubines drank wine from them. You praised the gods of silver and gold, of bronze, iron, wood and stone, which cannot see or hear or understand. But you did not honor the God who holds in his hand your life and all your ways. Therefore he sent the hand that wrote the inscription.*

Daniel indicated, then, that Belshazzar had overlooked the principle so frequently developed in Daniel's writing: GOD IS IN CONTROL OF THE UNIVERSE. Belshazzar was foolish enough to think he himself was actually in power and could do as he pleased. Nebuchadnezzar had learned the lesson through God-imposed insanity, but Belshazzar had failed to learn from his ancestor's experience. Daniel stated clearly that misuse of God's holy vessels brought the final judgment on this once great kingdom. Beginning with verse 25, after the condemnation from the lips of Daniel, Daniel gave the interpretation of the foreign handwriting as follows:

> *Daniel 5:25-28 This is the inscription that was written: MENE, MENE, TEKEL, PARSIN. "This is what these words mean: <Mene>: God has numbered the days of your reign and brought it to an end. <Tekel>: You have been weighed on the scales and found wanting. <Peres>: Your kingdom is divided and given to the Medes and Persians."*

Remember that Jeremiah had said this day was coming; the "handwriting was actually on the wall" long before Belshazzar ever saw it. The prophecy given to Belshazzar could also be classified as a revelation since the prediction was understandable before the foretold event occurred. There could have been no question as to what was about to transpire. Notice that it was God Who had numbered the kingdom's days and brought the proud city to an end; God controls who reigns and who falls. Wickedness was given as the reason for God's final judgment. The providence of God is also seen in the fact that the Medes and Persians didn't just take charge — **God gave them the kingdom Babylon once held.**

THE PROPHECIES ARE FULFILLED

The prophets had foretold Babylon's fall; several of the prophecies were made years before the fulfillment, but the last prophecy was certainly "at hand."

> *Daniel 5:30,31 That very night Belshazzar, king of the Babylonians, was slain, and Darius the Mede took over the kingdom, at the age of sixty-two.*

So ends the golden kingdom, the lion of all empires; this paves the way for Medo-Persia to make its entrance as the second empire. It would be inferior to Babylon, but it would control the known world for a period of time.

Chapter Three

Prophecies about Medo-Persia

The kingdom of silver came into power during Daniel's lifetime; Babylon, the kingdom of gold, had been deposed by God's will and had fallen to Medo-Persia.

Some writers try to make Media into the second kingdom and Persia into

> The sealing and revealing of the fall of Medo-Persia

the third. *Daniel* just won't permit this analysis. In *Daniel*, chapter 5, the interpretation of Belshazzar's vision indicated Babylon would be overthrown by the "Medes and Persians." Three times in chapter 6 he refers to the "law of the Medes and Persians." The following passages will clearly specify that the new kingdom was certainly a divided kingdom, a kingdom of the Medes and Persians.

> *Daniel 5:28 <Peres>: Your kingdom is divided and given to the **Medes and Persians**.*
>
> *Daniel 6:8 ... the laws of the **Medes and Persians**, which cannot be repealed.*
>
> *Daniel 6:12 ... with the laws of the **Medes and Persians**, which cannot be repealed.*
>
> *Daniel 6:15 ... according to the law of the **Medes and Persians** no decree or edict that the king issues can be changed.*

Boak, Hyma, and Slosson, in their book *The Growth of Western Civilization*, p. 48, state that the Medes' part of the kingdom was short lived. Persia took over completely three years after their alliance. Alone, the Medes never comprised an empire of any size or influence.

In fact Cyrus the Persian ordered Darius the Mede into action on the night Babylon fell from power. Daniel tied the two rulers together:

> *Daniel 6:28 So Daniel prospered during the reign of Darius and the reign of Cyrus the Persian.*

The meaning: Daniel was there when Darius took over and was still alive when Cyrus the Persian began his reign.

PROPHECIES ABOUT MEDO-PERSIA

First Prophecy about Medo-Persia

The first vision concerning the Medo-Persian kingdom was found when Nebuchadnezzar dreamed about the man made of metal.

> *Daniel 2:32 The head of the statue was made of pure gold, **its chest and arms of silver**, its belly and thighs of bronze.*

Daniel told the king the silver part of the body represented a kingdom that would rule after Babylon and would be inferior to Babylon, the golden empire. Daniel did not name Medo-Persia at that time; the reader has to wait until the overthrow of Babylon in chapter 5 to know it was Medo-Persia.

Second Prophecy about Medo-Persia

The second prophecy came through Daniel's dream in which he visualized four beasts representing four kingdoms; earlier evidence indicated the lion symbolized Babylon. The second beast, picturing Medo-Persia, was a bear.

> *Daniel 7:5 And there before me was a second beast, which looked like a bear. It was raised up on one of its sides, and it had three ribs in its mouth between its teeth. It was told, "Get up and eat your fill of flesh!"*

The symbolism of the bear raised up "on one of its sides" refers to the dual nature of the kingdom, with Persia being superior to the Medes.

The ribs in the teeth and the statement to the beast to "get up and eat your fill of flesh" refer to the militaristic nature of the empire.

Third Prophecy about **Medo-Persia**

The last vision about Medo-Persia leaves no doubt as to its name; the empire was symbolized by a ram with two horns. It is interesting that one of the horns stood taller than the other; earlier in this volume it was illustrated that "horns" represent kings. The difference in the length of the horns would indicate the Persians were more powerful and would outlast the Medes. This would also parallel the one side of the bear's being raised higher than the other. The following verses will illustrate the vast power of the Medo-Persian kingdom.

> *Daniel 8:3,4 I looked up, and there before me was a ram with two horns, standing beside the canal, and the horns were long. One of the horns was longer than the other but grew up later. I watched the ram as he charged toward the west and the north and the south. No animal could stand against him, and none could rescue from his power. He did as he pleased and became great.*

Daniel then told of another kingdom, symbolized by a goat with a significant horn that would attack the two horned ram (Medo-Persia).

> *Daniel 8:5-8 As I was thinking about this, suddenly a goat with a prominent horn between his eyes came from the west, crossing the whole earth without touching the ground. He came toward the two-horned ram I had seen standing beside the canal and charged at him in great rage. I saw him attack the ram furiously, striking the ram and shattering his two horns. The ram was powerless to stand against him; the goat knocked him to the ground and trampled on him, and none could rescue the ram from his power. The goat became very great, but at the height of his power his large horn was broken off, and in its place four prominent horns grew up toward the four winds of heaven.*

There need be no guesswork as to the symbolism in the passages because Daniel states explicitly that the ram with two horns represents Medo-Persia and that the goat represents Greece.

> *Daniel 8:19,20 He said: "I am going to tell you what will happen later in the time of wrath, because the vision concerns the appointed time of the end. The two-horned ram that you saw represents the kings of **Media and Persia**. The shaggy goat is the king of **Greece**, and the large horn between his eyes is the first king."*

The time of the fall of Medo-Persia is called "the appointed time of the end." Time did not end, but Medo-Persia's power did; it was the "time of the end of Medo-Persia." This additional information supplies the reader with another piece of the puzzle. The name of the third kingdom is Greece; therefore, the third part of the metal man, the bronze kingdom, symbolizes Greece, and the third animal that came up from the sea, the leopard, represented Greece.

Fourth Prophecy about Medo-Persia

The last prophecy given by Daniel concerning Medo-Persia is found in chapter 10. The Mede's part of the dual kingdom had disappeared; after all, it was represented by the lower side of the bear and by the shorter horn of the two-horned ram. Persia was in complete power until God determined to bring His wrath against this second kingdom by assisting Greece, the third empire spoken of by Daniel.

> *Daniel 10:20 So he said, "Do you know why I have come to you? Soon I will return to fight against the prince of Persia, and when I go, the prince of Greece will come."*

About the time of this vision, Daniel had been fasting and mourning for a period of three weeks; it apparently was because of his humility that Daniel was rewarded by a heavenly message. The prayers of Daniel assisted the heavenly messenger in reaching him at the end of the three week period.

> *Daniel 10:1-3 In the third year of Cyrus king of Persia, a revelation was given to Daniel (who was called Belteshazzar). Its message was true and it concerned a great war. The understanding of the message came to him in a vision. At that time I, Daniel, mourned for **three weeks.** I ate no choice food; no meat or wine touched my lips; and I used no lotions at all until the three weeks were over.*

When the heavenly messenger arrived, he told Daniel he had been trying to come to him for three weeks, "twenty-one days." This was the same length of time Daniel had been mourning and fasting.

> *Daniel 10:12-14 Then he continued, "Do not be afraid, Daniel. Since the first day that you set your mind to gain understanding and to humble yourself before your God, your words were heard, and I have come in response to them. But the prince of the Persian kingdom resisted me **twenty-one days.** Then Michael, one of the chief princes, came to help me, because I was detained there with the king of Persia. Now I have come to explain to you what will happen to your people in the future, for the vision concerns a time yet to come."*

The struggle of the heavenly messenger to reach Daniel constitutes a "battle in heaven" for several reasons: 1) An angel of God called "your chief prince Michael" assisted. 2) Michael is called "chief prince"; if angel = prince, then the "prince of Persia" would be an evil angel trying to thwart God's will. It is not logical that an earthly king could prevent a heavenly messenger from coming to Daniel. 3) *Daniel 4:35* talks about the "armies of God" in some versions and "powers of heaven" in others. In this sequence there is clearly a heavenly conflict that affects earthly outcomes.

This appears to be a Messianic vision; the "angel" certainly has the same appearance of Jesus Christ as revealed by John. The following passages compare the visions of Daniel and John.

Daniel 10:5,6	Revelation 1:13-15
... a man dressed in linen,	*... "like a son of man,"*
with a belt of the finest gold around his waist.	*dressed in a robe ...*
	with a golden sash around his chest.
His body was like chrysolite, his face like lightning,	*His head and hair were white like wool, as white as snow,*
his eyes like flaming torches,	*and his eyes were like blazing fire.*
his arms and legs like the gleam of burnished bronze,	*His feet were like bronze glowing in a furnace, and*
and his voice like the sound of a multitude.	*his voice was like the sound of rushing waters.*

Daniel 10:16 gives a strong link between the two visions — the messenger was one who looked "like a son of man"; Jesus often used this phrase to describe Himself. The NIV leaves out the words <u>son of</u>, but these words are in the original Hebrew manuscripts. John also saw one "like a son of man."

When the vision occurred, those around Daniel knew something was happening they could not explain, so they fled the scene; Daniel was so awe-stricken that he lost his strength and fell upon his face. Daniel was strengthened several times in this sequence. First, a hand touched him and strengthened him to the point of being lifted to his hands and knees.

> *Daniel 10:10,11 A hand touched me and set me trembling on my hands and knees. He said, "Daniel, you who are highly esteemed, consider carefully the words I am about to speak to you, and stand up, for I have now been sent to you." And when he said this to me, I stood up trembling.*

The message delivered to Daniel included the following: 1) Daniel's prayer and fasting had caused God to send the messenger. 2) The heavenly messenger was delayed because of a struggle with the "prince" or angel over the Persian kingdom. 3) The archangel Michael assisted the messenger in his quest to reach Daniel. 4) The events were to occur sometime in the distant future. In fact, the King James Version uses the phrase, "the latter days." With this wording one could think the end of time is indicated; however, it was merely the time of the end of Persia, because the prophecy was to be fulfilled when the Grecian empire gained control of the world.

> *Daniel 10:12-14 Then he continued, "Do not be afraid, Daniel. Since the first day that you set your mind to gain understanding and to humble yourself before your God, your words were heard, and I have come in response to them. But the prince of the Persian kingdom resisted me twenty-one days. Then Michael, one of the chief princes, came to help me, because I was detained there with the king of Persia. Now I have come to explain to you what will happen to your people in the future, for the vision concerns a time yet to come."*

Daniel was overwhelmed by the strength of the message, but the heavenly messenger strengthened him once again, this time by touching his lips. Daniel was so awed by the appearance of the being that he saw himself as being unworthy and too weak to communicate.

> *Daniel 10:15-17 While he was saying this to me, I bowed with my face toward the ground and was speechless. Then one who looked like a man touched my lips, and I opened my mouth and began to speak. I said to the one standing before me, "I am overcome with anguish because of the vision, my lord, and I am helpless. How can I, your servant, talk with you, my lord? My strength is gone and I can hardly breathe."*

The one with the appearance of a man touched Daniel and strengthened him again; after this, Daniel was ready to hear the message. Daniel learned from the vision that Persia was to fall to Greece, and he learned that the archangel Michael, along with the one bringing him the message, would assist in the turn of events.

> *Daniel 10:20 So he said, "Do you know why I have come to you? Soon I will return to fight against the prince of Persia, and when I go, the prince of Greece will come."*

The heavenly being went on to explain the beginning and end of the Medo-Persian kingdom with the following information: The messenger and Michael were there assisting when Darius the Mede took over at the beginning of the Medo-Persian kingdom. This change of kingdoms was not merely something that happened; God brought it about. After the messenger told Daniel the new kingdom would arrive because of Divine intervention, he next said the kingdom would also end because of God's will.

There would be four more kings in Persia before the Greek kings would begin having conflict with Persia; the one in power when Daniel received the message was Cyrus I, who ruled from 550 to 529 BC. 1) The king after Cyrus I was Cambyses II, 530 to 522 BC; 2) Gaumata was next in line, but only through deceit. According to *Funk and Wagnalls Encyclopedia* 1983, Smerdis was in line to be the next ruler, but he was murdered. The death was kept secret for seven months while Guamata took the place of Smerdis. 3) The third ruler was Darius the Persian, 522 to 486 BC. 4) The fourth was Xerxes, whose Hebrew name was Ahasuerus, the king who married Esther. Xerxes ruled from 486 to 465 BC; during his reign a great struggle began with Greece that lasted 140 years. Medo-Persia's fall was predictable because God had determined Greece to be the victor.

> *Daniel 10:21 ... (No one supports me against them except Michael, your prince. And in the first year of Darius the Mede, I took my stand to support and protect him.) "Now then, I tell you the truth: three more kings will appear in Persia, and then a fourth, who will be far richer than all the others. When he has gained power by his wealth, he will stir up everyone against the kingdom of Greece."*

Daniel lived long enough to see Medo-Persia come into power, but the actual fall of this empire came about 300 years after Daniel's foretelling the overthrow of this empire by Greece.

THE FULFILLMENT OF MEDO-PERSIA'S FALL

To study the fall of the Persian kingdom is to study the rise of the Grecian empire; Alexander the Great began his conquest of Persia in the spring of 334 BC and completed the job in 325 BC. The book of *Daniel* was probably written around 530 BC, about nine years after Cyrus the Persian and Darius the Mede overthrew Babylon. The dual kingdom of Medes and Persians continued for a few years before the Persian part of the kingdom took total control. Afterwards, the Persians lasted for nearly 200 years before the fulfillment of their fall and the coming of Greece, the kingdom symbolized by bronze, by the leopard, and by the shaggy goat. Daniel wrote about Greece and called it by name before it ever became a power, but the meaning of his visions would have been impossible to understand before Alexander the Great made his vast conquests; hence the vision was "sealed" until the "time of the end" of Persia.

Two of the empires envisioned by Nebuchadnezzar and Daniel have now passed with the coming of Greece. We will next examine the rise and fall of the third empire.

Chapter Four

Prophecies about Greece

Just as Daniel interpreted four visions concerning the fall of Medo-Persia, he also explained four visions about the rise and fall of the Grecian empire in chapters 2, 7, 8, 10 and 11. It is clear the third kingdom referred to by Daniel is Greece because of three factors: 1) Greece was the third kingdom from Babylon forward, 2) Greece is specifically named as the kingdom that overcame Medo-Persia in chapters 8 and 10, and 3) details of Grecian history are graphically depicted in chapters 8 and 11.

> The Sealing and Revealing of the fall of Greece

First vision of Greece

> *Daniel 2:39 After you, another kingdom will rise, inferior to yours. Next, a third kingdom, one of bronze, will rule over the whole earth.*

The first vision about Greece symbolized the empire as the middle part of the man made of metal. Greece was the bronze or brass part of the man, and it was to rule over the whole world. Alexander the Great was the ruler of Greece when it became an empire, and the empire controlled the known world at the time of Alexander's death in 323 BC. The sequence above does not name Greece as the kingdom, but this fact becomes crystal clear in chapter 8 when the Grecian empire is named in overcoming Persia to become the new world power.

Second vision of Greece

Daniel 7:6 After that, I looked, and there before me was another beast, one that looked like a leopard. And on its back it had four wings like those of a bird. This beast had four heads, and it was given authority to rule.

Daniel had previously seen a lion symbolizing Babylon and a bear representing Medo-Persia. The third beast was the leopard picturing Greece. The leopard had the wings of a bird; these most likely symbolize the speed with which Greece rose to power and conquered the world. The four heads represent the division of the Grecian empire after Alexander's death; each of the four generals of Alexander took a piece of the territory.

Third vision of Greece

Daniel 8:21 The shaggy goat is the king of Greece, and the large horn between his eyes is the first king.

In the third vision of Greece, Daniel pictures 6 leaders; he tells about Alexander, the first and greatest of all the Grecian kings. He then tells about the divided leadership that developed among the four generals after the death of Alexander. Finally, Daniel covers the most evil of all the kings of this third empire, Antiochus IV *Epiphanes*. The fact that Antiochus *Epiphanes* was the **6th** king listed in this vision highlights the evil nature of this despot. While there were many other kings in the empire, these six summarize the most important events in the history of this kingdom. Daniel refers to these six kings and fills in the rest of the historical detail in the fourth vision of Greece found in *Daniel*, chapter 11.

Alexander the Great's father Philip II, also known as Philip of Macedon, tried to conquer and rule the entirety of Greece. He did take over the rule of one of the Hellenic cities, Macedon, in 359 BC after his brother died. In 337 BC, Philip had all but subdued the individual city states located in Greece. It was now time for Philip to conquer Persia to solidify his power base, but he was assassinated before his dreams could become reality. Upon the death of Philip, the city states began to pull away from the new alliance with Macedon; however, Alexander used the base his father had won to assert his leadership over the Macedonian Empire. Before he could ever develop into the world conqueror of historical fame, he first had to unify Greece. Peter Connolly wrote in *Greece and Rome at War*, p. 66, concerning the unification of the Grecian forces under their new general Alexander.

> At the congress of Corinth a Greek confederacy was set up with Philip as its leader. The Macedonian now announced his long-cherished plans to invade the Persian empire, and the necessary forces were requisitioned. Before the enterprise could be realized, however, Philip was assassinated and his 20 year-old son Alexander came to the throne. On Philip's death the Greeks defected. Alexander's reaction was so fast that he re-conquered Greece without striking a blow.

Hannibal, the great Carthaginian general, was defeated by the Roman general Scipio Africanus in one of the greatest battles of all time. After his victory, Scipio Africanus asked the conquered Hannibal to name the greatest general in history. Hannibal didn't think long before naming Alexander the Great the best. Scipio didn't stop there; he asked Hannibal who he thought was second best. Hannibal responded, "Pyrrhus." Scipio asked next, "Who is third best?" He responded, "I am." One more question remained; Scipio asked, "What would have happened if you had defeated me?" Hannibal responded, "I would have been the best." Many today would still place Alexander at the top of the list; no wonder he is called Alexander the Great!

Alexander's life was extremely short, but he made tremendous impact on the world. After unifying Greece into a nation, his next goal was to develop an empire; standing between him and his goal was the ancient enemy Persia. Persia and Greece had fought for 140 years; until the time of Alexander, Persia had been successful partly because Hellenic cities were so divided. Unification had come through Alexander, and Persia's "time of the end" was not far away. The book of *Daniel* is compared with Connolly's writing about the fierce attack of Alexander upon the Persian forces:

Daniel 8:5-7 ... suddenly a goat with a prominent horn between his eyes came from the west, crossing the whole earth without touching the ground. He came toward the two-horned ram I had seen standing beside the canal and charged at him in great rage. I saw him attack the ram furiously, striking the ram and shattering his two horns. The ram was powerless to stand against him; the goat knocked him to the ground and trampled on him, and none could rescue the ram from his power.

Greece and Rome at War, p. 68: Beyond the Granicus river the Persian cavalry were drawn up in line backed by a phalanx of Greek mercenaries. In true Theban style, Alexander had strengthened one wing, which he led himself. The opening attack came from this wing; at the head of the companion cavalry he charged across the river and smashed through the lighter-armed Persian horsemen. The Persian cavalry broke and fled, leaving the Greek mercenaries to their fate.

Josephus, in his *Antiquities of the Jews*, Book XI, chapter 8, paragraph 5 states:

> And when the book of *Daniel* was showed him, [Alexander] wherein Daniel declared that one of the Greeks should destroy the empire of the Persians, he supposed that himself was the person intended.

Two hundred years earlier, Daniel had penned the words concerning the fall of Persia to a strong Grecian king; the time of the end had come for Persia during Alexander's rule. It is interesting to note that Alexander read the prophecy prior to its fulfillment; whoever showed him the book actually **revealed to him what had been hidden for all those years.** After Alexander conquered Persia, he began to expand his power-base through military conquest. Daniel foretold of Alexander's power, but he also foretold that Alexander would die at the height of his strength. The history as recorded by Connolly can once again be compared with Daniel's prophecy.

> *Daniel 8:8 The goat became very great, but at the height of his power his large horn was broken off, and in its place four prominent horns grew up toward the four winds of heaven.*
>
> *Greece and Rome at War*, p. 70: Alexander now advanced on Egypt which was quick to surrender. ... The Macedonian army returned to Syria and from here marched eastwards, fighting battles and founding cities. ... He pushed on into Russia to the end of the known world. ... In the early summer of 327 BC the army crossed the western spur of the Himalayas known as Hindu Kush and descended into the valley of the Indus. ... Two years later he was dead. He was not quite 33.

The previous prophecy tells that four prominent horns would take over after the great "horn" Alexander died. Horns are symbolic of kings; thus, four kings would rule the Hellenic empire after the death of Alexander. Connolly explained on page 77 that the four generals of Alexander divided the spoils; Daniel had foretold of these same events. Most of Asia was controlled by Seleucus, while Egypt came under the control of Ptolemy. Lysimachus controlled Thrace and northern and central Asia Minor; Cassander took over Macedon. This parallels the four prominent horns coming up in the place of the first king; it also parallels the four heads of the leopard image seen by Daniel in chapter 7.

Starting with *Daniel* 8:9, the author's vision turned to a persecuting leader who would take away the burnt-offering used in Jewish worship. Antiochus IV *Epiphanes* was king of Syria from 175 to 164 BC. From 171 to 168 BC, he was involved in a war with two Egyptian kings, and he ultimately captured Jerusalem, prohibited Judaism, and tried to establish the worship of Greek gods. A span of around 150 years occurred between the division of Alexander's kingdom to the time of Antiochus *Epiphanes*; Daniel explains the interim when he has another vision found in chapter 11.

ANTIOCHUS IV IS PICTURED AS GOD'S ENEMY

Daniel 8:9-12 Out of one of them came another horn, which started small but grew in power to the south and to the east and toward the Beautiful Land. It grew until it reached the host of the heavens, and it threw some of the starry host down to the earth and trampled on them. It set itself up to be as great as the Prince of the host; <u>it took away the daily sacrifice from him, and the place of his sanctuary was brought low</u>. Because of rebellion, the host [of the saints] and the daily sacrifice were given over to it. It prospered in everything it did, and truth was thrown to the ground.

Josephus, Book 1, Chapter 1, Paragraph 1: At the same time that Antiochus, who was called *Epiphanes*, had a quarrel with the sixth Ptolemy about his right to the whole country of Syria, a great sedition fell among the men of power in Judea, and they had a contention about obtaining the government; <u>he also spoiled the temple, and put a stop to the constant practice of offering a daily sacrifice of expiation</u> for three years and six months.

With historical information paralleled, scripture can be amplified — *Daniel 8:9* **Out of one of them** (one of the four generals of Alexander) **came another horn**, (Antiochus *IV*, a descendant of Seleucus) **which started small but grew in power to the south** (Antiochus had many battles with Ptolemy kings of Egypt) **and to the east and toward the Beautiful Land.** (Antiochus also attacked Israel; it is this conflict to which so much of Daniel's prophecy is devoted.) *Daniel 8:10* **It** (Antiochus IV) **grew until it reached the host of the heavens,** ("host of heavens" refers to angels; it seems this reference indicates another "war in heaven"; some of God's angels lost their place — see *2 Peter 2:4* and *Jude 1:6*) **and it threw some of the starry host down to the earth and trampled on them.**

With any interpretation it is clear that God's people lost in the conflict. *Daniel 8:11* **It** (the horn, King Antiochus IV) **set itself up to be as great as the Prince of the host**; (Daniel earlier referred to

Michael the archangel as the Prince of the host; this would further the idea of the heavenly struggle coinciding with the earthly battle) **it** (Antiochus IV) **took away the daily sacrifice from him**, (the historical information quoted earlier illustrated that Antiochus IV stopped the daily sacrifices for over three years) **and the place of his sanctuary was brought low.** (Antiochus also destroyed the temple) *Daniel 8:12* **Because of rebellion, the host [of the saints] and the daily sacrifice were given over to it**. (Antiochus used the altar to sacrifice pigs which he forced the Jews to eat) **It prospered in everything it did, and truth was thrown to the ground**. (Antiochus had a total disregard for God and His people.)

Daniel received information about the timeframe concerning Antiochus IV's devastation when he heard two angels, called "holy ones" discussing the matter.

> *Daniel 8:13 Then I heard a holy one speaking, and another holy one said to him, "How long will it take for the vision to be fulfilled — the vision concerning the daily sacrifice, the rebellion that causes desolation, and the surrender of the sanctuary and of the host that will be trampled underfoot?"*

Sacrifices were made daily in the evening and in the morning; therefore, 2,300 sacrifices would represent 1,150 days, approximating the three and one half years of persecution. *McGraw-Hill Encyclopedia of World Biography*, p. 203 states:

> Antiochus' policy proved disastrous in Judea, where confiscation of some temple funds and enforced worship of Zeus Olympius in place of Jehovah caused an uprising and guerrilla warfare by the Macabees from 167 to 164.

Daniel was confused about the vision he had seen.

> *Daniel 8:15 While I, Daniel, was watching the vision and trying to understand it, there before me stood one who looked like a man.*

The next verse indicates the angel who was to deliver the message was Gabriel; although the voice of the messenger was the "voice of a man," the reader understands the message was delivered by an angel.

> *Daniel 8:16 And I heard a man's voice from the Ulai calling, "Gabriel, tell this man the meaning of the vision."*

An interesting phrase, "time of the end," indicates the timeframe for the fall of Antiochus *Epiphanes*; when Antiochus fell, the vision entered the realm of the "revealed."

> *Daniel 8:17 As he came near the place where I was standing, I was terrified and fell prostrate. "Son of man," he said to me, "understand that the vision concerns the time of the end."*

As the message continues, it becomes obvious that Daniel does not refer to the end of time itself, but rather to the end of the specific time of prophecy. Time can only end once, but many nations have reached the "time of the end" of their dominance and existence. Daniel was so moved by the vision that he fell to the ground in a trance, but the angel continued his message to Daniel.

> *Daniel 8:19-22 I am going to tell you what will happen later in the time of wrath, because the vision concerns the appointed time of the end. The two-horned ram that you saw represents the kings of Media and Persia. The shaggy goat is the king of Greece, and the large horn between his eyes is the first king. The four horns that replaced the one that was broken off represent four kingdoms that will emerge from his nation but will not have the same power.*

Earlier in this chapter, historical data concerning Alexander's being the first king of the Grecian empire was presented; the earlier section also explains that his four generals (Seleucus, Ptolemy, Lysimachus, and Cassander) took control of the kingdom. The kingdom was never the same after Alexander's death.

EXPANDED PROPHECY ABOUT ANTIOCHUS IV

In *Daniel 8:9-13*, Antiochus was prophesied as being the wicked king who would devastate Israel. In the next three verses, this event is further explained.

> *Daniel 8:23-25 In the latter part of their reign, when rebels have become completely wicked, a stern-faced king, a master of intrigue, will arise. He will become very strong, but not by his own power. He will cause astounding devastation and will succeed in whatever he does. He will destroy the mighty men and the holy people. He will cause deceit to prosper, and he will consider himself superior. When they feel secure, he will destroy many and take his stand against the Prince of princes. Yet he will be destroyed, but not by human power.*

It is clear from the scriptures that Antiochus did not become strong by his own power, nor did he die because of human power. God used Antiochus' wickedness to punish the Jews for their unfaithfulness, and then God destroyed Antiochus for his evil ways. When Antiochus attacked Jerusalem and punished the Jews, he also destroyed many of Israel's finest. Daniel stated that the acts of Antiochus went so far as to oppose the "prince of princes." Chapter 10 of *Daniel* identifies the "prince of Israel" as Michael; this could also be a reference to Michael, the angel who watched over the affairs of the Jews. However, the "prince of princes" could also refer to Jesus Christ. God chose the Jewish nation through which to bring the redeemer of the world; Antiochus IV was threatening the very people who were to deliver the Savior. Antiochus' choosing to call himself "god on earth" sets him up as a perfect "anti-Christ" even before the arrival of Jesus nearly 200 years later. Polybius in Book 31, chapter 3, paragraph 9, says that Antiochus *Epiphanes* died "smitten with madness." In fact, Polybius said his countrymen referred to him not as *Epiphanes*, meaning "god with us," but rather as *Epimanes*, meaning "goon on earth." It was not the work of human hands that destroyed this maniac; God numbered the days of his kingdom.

When were these events to come? Daniel wrote his prophecy around 530 BC, and Antiochus *Epiphanes* ruled from 175 to 164 BC. From Daniel's time until fulfillment of this part of the vision would have been around 350 years.

> *Daniel 8:26 "The vision of the evenings and mornings that has been given you is true, but seal up the vision, for it concerns the distant future."*

> THE PURPOSE OF SEALING RELATES TO THE TIME OF FULFILLMENT

This principle of sealing a vision for the distant future is that although not presently understandable, it must be noted and anticipated! Daniel was to seal the vision because it was about 350 years into the future. John was not to seal the visions of *Revelation* because the events were in the "near future." This event was so far into the future that Daniel himself did not understand the vision he was receiving.

> *Daniel 8:27 I, Daniel, was exhausted and lay ill for several days. Then I got up and went about the king's business. I was appalled by the vision; it was beyond understanding.*

Fourth vision of Greece

After detailing the highlights of the sixth Grecian king in chapter 8, Daniel turned to other matters, but in chapter 11, beginning with verse 2, the prophet foresees the complete development of this kingdom beginning with Alexander the Great and his four generals who divided the kingdom.

> *Daniel 11:2-4 ... he will stir up everyone against the kingdom of Greece. Then a mighty king will appear, who will rule with great power and do as he pleases. After he has appeared, his empire will be broken up and parceled out toward the four winds of heaven. It will not go to his descendants, nor will it have the power he exercised, because his empire will be uprooted and given to others.*

The preceding information yields four prophecies about Greece:

1) Greece would overthrow Persia to become the third kingdom.
2) Alexander would be the Grecian king who would be tremendously powerful.
3) Alexander would die, and his kingdom would be divided into four parts (parceled out toward the four winds of heaven).

4) The Grecian empire would never have the power and influence it once held under the rule of Alexander.

Beginning with *Daniel 11:5*, most of the chapter treats the two strongest parts of the divided Grecian kingdom — Syria and Egypt; the two divisions were referred to by Daniel as the "north" and the "south." To understand the kings of the North and South, study the following genealogical chart and keep it handy for quick reference in understanding the materials that follow:

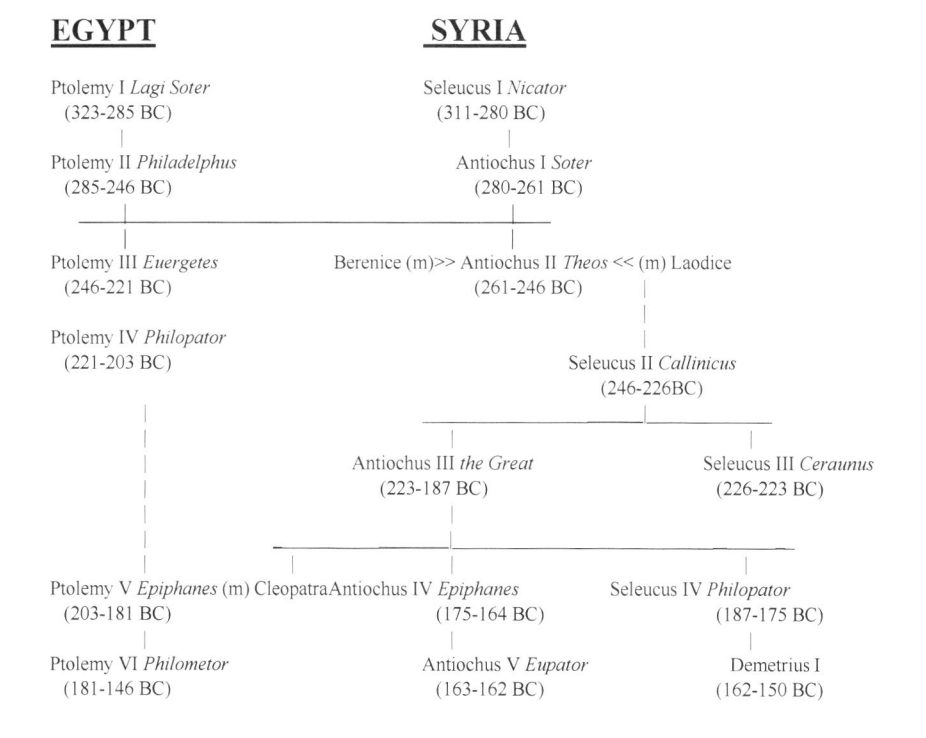

EGYPT SYRIA

Ptolemy I *Lagi Soter* (323-285 BC)
Seleucus I *Nicator* (311-280 BC)

Ptolemy II *Philadelphus* (285-246 BC)
Antiochus I *Soter* (280-261 BC)

Ptolemy III *Euergetes* (246-221 BC)
Berenice (m)>> Antiochus II *Theos* << (m) Laodice (261-246 BC)

Ptolemy IV *Philopator* (221-203 BC)
Seleucus II *Callinicus* (246-226BC)

Antiochus III *the Great* (223-187 BC)   Seleucus III *Ceraunus* (226-223 BC)

Ptolemy V *Epiphanes* (m) Cleopatra   Antiochus IV *Epiphanes* (175-164 BC)   Seleucus IV *Philopator* (187-175 BC)
(203-181 BC)

Ptolemy VI *Philometor* (181-146 BC)
Antiochus V *Eupator* (163-162 BC)
Demetrius I (162-150 BC)

PTOLEMY II AND ANTIOCHUS II

The events in verse 6 tell of a marriage arrangement that occurred between Ptolemy II of Egypt (king of the South) and Antiochus II of Syria (king of the North). Ptolemy II, who ruled from 285 to 246 BC, was also known as Ptolemy *Philadelphus*; Antiochus, who ruled from 261 to 246 BC, was called Antiochus *Theos*. Daniel's prophecy and historical fulfillment are listed in the following comparison:

Daniel 11:6	
After some years, they will become allies. The daughter of the king of the South will go to the king of the North to make an alliance, but she will not retain her power, and he and his power will not last. In those days she will be handed over, together with her royal escort and her father and the one who supported her.	*Hellenic History*, p. 393, Ptolemy persuaded Antiochus in 253 BC to put away his wife Laodice in favor of Ptolemy's daughter Berenice, with the understanding that Berenice's son should succeed to the throne. Berenice brought with her an immense dowry, but it was idle to hope that peace could be won by repudiating a Macedonian queen. *Legacy of Alexander* by M. Cary, p. 86, Antiochus, indeed, accepted the hand of Berenice and gave her to believe that a son who was presently born of the marriage should be the next king. ... Antiochus had been married for many years to his cousin Laodice I. ... Laodice worked hard for the recovery of her position, and in 246 BC induced Antiochus to visit her. During his stay in Ephesus, the king suddenly fell ill and died, but not before he had declared Seleucus II, his eldest son by Laodice, as his successor.

The passage can now be explained in this way: *Daniel 11:6* **After some years**, (toward the end of the reigns of Ptolemy II and Antiochus II) **they will become allies**. (This was done through a marriage arrangement between the two families.) **The daughter of the king of the South** (Berenice, daughter of Ptolemy II) **will go to the king of**

the North (Antiochus II, who divorced his first wife, Laodice) **to make an alliance,** (the marriage arrangement) **but she will not retain her power,** (Antiochus went back to Laodice.) **and he and his power will not last.** (*Encyclopedia Britannica* stated that Laodice had Antiochus poisoned in 246 BC.) **In those days she will be handed over,** (Berenice will lose her position of power; she and her son were murdered.) **together with her royal escort and her father and the one who supported her.** (Ptolemy II also died in 246 BC.)

PTOLEMY III AND SELEUCUS II

Daniel 11:7 prophesies about the brother of Berenice, Ptolemy III, also known as *Euergetes* and tells of Seleucus II, called *Callinicus*. Ptolemy reigned from 246 to 221 BC, and Seleucus was king of Syria from 246 to 227 BC. Study the comparisons:

Daniel 11:7,8 One from her family line will arise to take her place. He will attack the forces of the king of the North and enter his fortress; he will fight against them and be victorious. He will also seize their gods, their metal images and their valuable articles of silver and gold and carry them off to Egypt. For some years he will leave the king of the North alone.	*Polybius, Histories,* Book 5, paragraph 58 says that Prince Ptolemy *Euergetes* invaded Syria and seized Seleucia. *Hellenic History,* p. 393, Ptolemy decided to enforce arrangements which his predecessor had made and thus declared himself for Berenice. He captured Seleucia in Pieria... and continued to Antioch itself. In actual fact, Berenice and her son had been murdered in Antioch; this was kept secret, so that Ptolemy might appear not as an invader, but as one who had come on behalf of the legitimate heir to the throne.

The authors also point out that after the battle, Ptolemy went back to Egypt to settle down to his "habitual caution." This explains why Daniel prophesied that the king of the South would "leave the king of the North alone."

The passage can be illustrated as follows: *Daniel* 11:7 **One from her family line** (Berenice's brother Ptolemy III) **will arise to take her place.** (defend her memory and her cause) **He** (Ptolemy III) **will** attack the forces of the king of the North (Seleucus II) **and enter his fortress** (attack Seleucia); **he will fight against them and be victorious**. (Ptolemy will defeat Seleucus.) *Daniel 11:8* **He will also seize their gods**, (Ptolemy III captured several religious items.) **their metal images and their valuable articles of silver and gold and carry them off to Egypt. For some years he will leave the king of the North alone**. (Ptolemy would be cautious; he would not attack Syria.)

ANTIOCHUS III AND PTOLEMY IV

In the next sequence, the sons of Seleucus II were prophesied to war against Ptolemy IV, but ultimately, the conflict would boil down to trouble between Antiochus III, known as *The Great*, and Ptolemy IV, called *Philopator*. Ptolemy *Philopator* ruled from 221 to 204 BC, while Antiochus *The Great* was king from 223 to 187 BC.

Daniel 11:9-12
Then the king of the North will invade the realm of the king of the South but will retreat to his own country. His sons will prepare for war and assemble a great army, which will sweep on like an irresistible flood and carry the battle as far as his fortress. Then the king of the South will march out in a rage and fight against the king of the North, who will raise a large army, but it will be defeated. When the army is carried off, the king of the South will be filled with pride and will slaughter many thousands, yet he will not remain triumphant.

Encyclopedia Britannica, Seleucus *Callinicus*' oldest son, Seleucus III *Soter*, reigned from 227 to 223 BC. Antiochus III was *Callinicus*' younger son.
Hellenic History, p. 395, In 221 BC Antiochus set about the task of restoring his Empire by an attack on Egypt, where a new ruler, Ptolemy IV *Philopator* ... had become king. Antiochus had 68,000 men and 102 elephants, but he lost the battle of Raphia to Ptolemy's 55,000 men and 73 elephants. Antiochus lost because he delayed his attack. Ptolemy won the war, but he never had real power because of internal troubles back home.

With these historical events given, the passage can be explained:

Daniel 11:9 **Then the king of the North** (Seleucus II) **will invade the realm of the king of the South** (Ptolemy IV) **but will retreat to his own country.** *Daniel 11:10* **His** (Seleucus II) **sons** (Seleucus III and Antiochus III) **will prepare for war and assemble a great army, which will sweep on like an irresistible flood and carry the battle as far as his** (Ptolemy IV) **fortress.** *Daniel 11:11* **Then the king of the South** (Ptolemy IV) **will march out in a rage and fight against the king of the North,** (Antiochus III *The Great*) **who will raise a large army,** (68,000 men) **but it will be defeated.** (Ptolemy defeated the northern foe with a smaller army of 55,000 men.) *Daniel 11:12* **When the army is carried off, the king of the South will be filled with pride and will slaughter many thousands, yet he will not remain triumphant.** (Ptolemy had too much trouble at home for the success to be lasting.)

ANTIOCHUS III AND PTOLEMY V

Antiochus the Great has a new king of Egypt with whom to deal, the child Ptolemy V, also known as *Epiphanes*, who reigned from 205 to 181 BC; he was only four years old when he came to the throne. Below is the parallel; the right column will indicate the scripture number the historical references are explaining:

*Dan 11:**13-19** For the king of the North will muster another army, larger than the first; and after several years, he will advance with a huge army fully equipped.*
***14** In those times many will rise against the king of the South. The violent men among your own people will rebel in fulfillment of the vision, but without success.*
***15** Then the king of the North will come and*

13 *Hellenistic History*, p. 451 points out that Antiochus III opened the fifth Syrian War in 200 B.C. Philip of Macedon joined forces with Antiochus to increase his numbers.
JOSEPHUS gives the following details in Book 12, Chapter 3, Paragraph 3
14 "The Jews, of their own accord, went over to him, and received him into the city [Jerusalem], and gave plentiful provision to all his army, and to his elephants, and readily assisted him when he besieged the garrison which was in the citadel of Jerusalem. Wherefore Antiochus thought it but

build up siege ramps and will capture a fortified city. The forces of the South will be powerless to resist; *even their best troops will not have the strength to stand.*

16 The invader will do as he pleases; no one will be able to stand against him. He will establish himself in the Beautiful Land and will have the power to destroy it.

17 He will determine to come with the might of his entire kingdom and will make an alliance with the king of the South. And he will give him a daughter in marriage in order to overthrow the kingdom, but his plans will not succeed or help him.

18 Then he will turn his attention to the coastlands and will take many of them, but a commander will put an end to his insolence and will turn his insolence back upon him.

19 After this, he will turn back toward the fortresses of his own country but will stumble and fall, to be seen no more.

just to requite the Jews' diligence and zeal in his service."

This blessing didn't last long. It seems Jerusalem was a neat stop to release frustration for both the kings of the north and the south. After another battle with Egypt, Antiochus returned to Jerusalem.

15,16   Josephus wrote in Book 12, Chapter 5, Paragraph 3

"And when he had gotten possession of Jerusalem, he slew many of the opposite party; and when he had plundered it of a great deal of money, he returned to Antioch."

17 *Josephus* chapter 4, paragraph 1, reports that after this, Antiochus made a pact with Ptolemy, and gave him his daughter Cleopatra to wed.

18 Cary in *The Greek World* relates the following information: a) Hannibal had joined Antiochus and was overseeing the Seleucid Navy. b) Antiochus had built his forces to 75,000 troops, even greater than that used at Raphia. c) Scipio Africanus offered to mediate with Antiochus before the battle, but Antiochus would not agree. d) Rome won the battle because of tactical errors of Antiochus; then, Antiochus was forced to pay 15,000 talents — "the highest known to Ancient History." Antiochus was also forced to leave Asia Minor.

19 *Encyclopedia of Military History* by Dupuy and Dupuy, p. 87, tells that Antiochus died in 187 BC in Luristan, while he was attempting to recover the lost eastern provinces.

The prophetic information becomes clear when historical fulfillment is inserted. *Daniel 11:13* **For the king of the North** (Antiochus the Great) **will muster another army, larger than the first**; (Antiochus increased his numbers with the alliance of Macedon.) **and after several years,** (about 14 years after the Syrian War in 203 BC) **he will advance with a huge army fully equipped.** *Daniel 11:14* **In those times many will rise against the king of the South.** (Philip of Macedon was a confederate with Antiochus against Ptolemy V. Ptolemy the V, according to Cary in *The Legacy of Alexander*, had taken over for the deceased Ptolemy IV; he was only four years old at the time.) **The violent men among your own people will rebel in fulfillment of the vision, but without success.** (Several disloyal Jews aided Antiochus, but Antiochus ultimately turned on the Jews.) *Daniel 11:15* **Then the king of the North** (Antiochus III) **will come and build up siege ramps and will capture a fortified city.** (*The Encyclopedia of Military History*, p. 55, states that Antiochus' crowning victory was the Battle of Panium in 198 BC; this allowed Antiochus to occupy all Palestine and other Ptolemaic possessions in Syria and southeast Asia Minor except for Cyprus.) **The forces of the South will be powerless to resist; even their best troops will not have the strength to stand.** *Daniel 11:16* **The invader** (Antiochus III) **will do as he pleases; no one will be able to stand against him. He will establish himself in the Beautiful Land and will have the power to destroy it.** (Antiochus III will attack Jerusalem and control it.) *Daniel 11:17* **He** (Antiochus III *The Great*) **will determine to come with the might of his entire kingdom and will make an alliance with the king of the South.** (Antiochus gave Ptolemy his daughter Cleopatra in marriage to seal an agreement.) **And he will give him** (Ptolemy V, who was seven years old) **a daughter in marriage in order to overthrow the kingdom, but his plans will not succeed or help him.** *Daniel 11:18* **Then he will turn his attention to the coastlands** (The islands of Asia Minor became the target of Antiochus.) **and will take many of them, but a commander will put an end to his insolence and will turn his insolence back upon him.** (Scipio Africanus of Rome forced Antiochus to pay 15,000 talents in tribute to pay the cost of the war; Antiochus had intended to take money from the captured cities, but he himself had to pay the cost. Already, some 170 years from the establishment of the Roman Empire, the gears were in motion for the transfer of power from Greece to Rome.) *Daniel 11:19* **After this, he will turn back toward the fortresses of his own country** (Antiochus tried to regain lost Syrian territory.) **but will stumble and fall, to be seen no more**. (Antiochus died in 187 BC.)

SELEUCUS IV OF SYRIA

The next personage prophesied by Daniel is Seleucus IV *Philopator* of Syria, son of Antiochus III; Seleucus IV ruled from 187 to 175 BC. Below are the comparisons of biblical prophecy and historical fulfillment:

Daniel 11:20 *His successor will send out a tax collector to maintain the royal splendor. In a few years, however, he will be destroyed, yet not in anger or in battle.*	*Encyclopedia Britannica*, 1960, The Seleucid kingdom as Antiochus left it to his son, Seleucus IV *Philopator*, consisted of Syria, Mesopotamia, Babylonia, and Iran. Seleucus IV was compelled by financial necessities, created in part by the heavy war indemnity exacted by Rome, to pursue an unambitious policy, and was assassinated by his minister Heliodorus.

The amplified version would read: *Daniel 11:20* **His successor** (Seleucus IV) **will send out a tax collector** (his tax minister Heliodorus) **to maintain the royal splendor. In a few years, however, he will be destroyed, yet not in anger or in battle**. (Seleucus IV was killed by his own tax minister Heliodorus.)

ANTIOCHUS IV AND PTOLEMY VI

This is the third time Daniel has given details concerning Antiochus IV *Epiphanes*; the reason so much space is spent on this tyrant stems from his being the arch-enemy of Israel. Beginning with *Daniel 11:21* and continuing through verse 35, Daniel writes about Antiochus IV *Epiphanes* and Ptolemy VI *Philometor*. Antiochus IV reigned from 175 to 164 BC; Ptolemy VI ruled from 181 to 146 BC. The following materials present biblical text and historical parallels:

Daniel 11:21
He will be succeeded by a contemptible person who has not been given the honor of royalty. He will invade the kingdom when its people feel secure, and he will seize it through intrigue.
22 An overwhelming army will be swept away before him; both it and a prince of the covenant will be destroyed.
23 After coming to an agreement with him, he will act deceitfully, and with only a few people he will rise to power.
24 When the richest provinces feel secure, he will invade them and will achieve what neither his fathers nor his forefathers did. He will distribute plunder, loot and wealth among his followers. He will plot the overthrow of fortresses — but only for a time.
25 With a large army he will stir up his strength and courage against the king of the South. The king of the South will wage war with a large and very powerful army, but he will not be able to stand because of the plots devised against him.
26 Those who eat from the king's provisions will try to destroy him; his army will be swept away, and many will fall in battle.
27 The two kings, with their

21 *Encyclopedia Britannica*, 1960, The true heir, Demetrius, son of Seleucus, being detained in Rome, the kingdom was seized by the younger brother of Seleucus, Antiochus IV.
22 *Encyclopedia of Military History* by Dupuy and Dupuy, Antiochus IV *Epiphanes* twice successfully invaded Egypt (171 and also in 168 BC)
23 Cary, *Legacy of Alexander* Legal succession was set aside by Antiochus IV, who at that time was in favor with Rome and Pergamum.

24 Josephus, *Antiquities of the Jews*, book 12, chapter 5, "At which time Antiochus spared not so much as those that admitted him into it (Jerusalem), on account of the riches that lay in the temple... to plunder its wealth, he ventured to break the league he had made. He took away the golden candlesticks, and the golden altar (of incense), and table (shew bread), and the altar (burnt offering); and did not abstain from even the veils of linen and scarlet ..."
25 "Antiochus came with great forces to Pelusium, and circumvented Ptolemy *Philometor* by treachery, and seized Egypt."
26 Polybius in Book 28, chapter 20 says Antiochus deceived envoys into believing he had the right to receive Coele-Syria because of earlier arrangements between Egypt and Syria.
27 Polybius in Book 28, chapter 21 explains that Antiochus had all but

hearts bent on evil, will sit at the same table and lie to each other, but to no avail, because an end will still come at the appointed time.
28 *The king of the North will return to his own country with great wealth, but his heart will be set against the holy covenant. He will take action against it and then return to his own country.*
29 *"At the appointed time he will invade the South again, but this time the outcome will be different from what it was before.*
30 *Ships of the western coastlands will oppose him, and he will lose heart. Then he will turn back and vent his fury against the holy covenant. He will return and show favor to those who forsake the holy covenant.*
31 *His armed forces will rise up to desecrate the temple fortress and will abolish the daily sacrifice. Then they will set up the abomination that cause desolation.*
32 *With flattery he will corrupt those who have violated the covenant, but the people who know their God will firmly resist him.*
33 *Those who are wise will instruct many, though for a time they will fall by the sword or be burned or captured or plundered.*
34 *When they fall, they will*

convinced Ptolemy to give him Egypt before the events turned.
<u>28</u> *Encyclopedia of Military History* by Dupuy and Dupuy, p. 87: During his ignominious withdrawal from Egypt, he occupied Jerusalem, destroyed the city walls, and decreed the abolition of Judaism, causing a protracted Jewish revolt in 168 BC." Josephus says he entered Jerusalem by pretending peace.
<u>29</u> Dupuy and Dupuy, p. 87: "Antiochus IV twice successfully invaded Egypt." (171 & 168 BC)
<u>30</u> *Josephus*, book 12, chapter 5, section 3: "He came to the places about Memphis; and when he had taken them, he made haste to Alexandria, in hopes of taking it by siege, and of subduing Ptolemy. He was driven not only from Alexandria, but out of all Egypt, by the declaration of the Romans, who charged him to let that country alone. ...."
<u>31</u> *Josephus*, book 12, chapter 5, section 4: "And when the king had built an idol altar upon God's altar, he slew swine upon it, and so offered a sacrifice neither according to the law, nor the Jewish religious worship in that country."
<u>32-35</u> *Josephus*, book 12, chapter 5, section 4: "... many Jews there were who complied with the king's commands, either voluntarily, or out of fear of the penalty that was denounced. But the best men, and those of the noblest souls, did not regard him, but they paid a greater

receive a little help, and many who are not sincere will join them.
35 *Some of the wise will stumble, so that they may be refined, purified and made spotless until the time of the end, for it will still come at the appointed time.*

respect to the customs of their country than concerns as to the punishment which he threatened ... they every day underwent great miseries and bitter torments; for they were whipped with rods, and their bodies were torn to pieces, and were crucified, while they were still alive and breathed."

Historical information helps clarify the passage: *Daniel 11:21* **He** (Seleucus IV) **will be succeeded by a contemptible person** (Antiochus IV *Epiphanes* — Polybius in his 26th Book called him "*Epimanes*," meaning madman, because of his strange behavior) **who has not been given the honor of royalty**. (The expected heir was Demetrius I who was being held captive in Rome.) **He** (Antiochus IV) **will invade the kingdom when its people feel secure, and he will seize it through intrigue**. (Antiochus bargained with the Romans to help him establish his throne.) *Daniel 11:22* **Then an overwhelming army will be swept away before him**; (Antiochus was victorious in battle in 171-170 BC.) **both it and a prince of the covenant** (Jerusalem was a victim of Antiochus.) **will be destroyed**. *Daniel 11:23* **After coming to an agreement with him**, (Rome agreed to hold Demetrius and establish Antiochus on the Syrian throne.) **he will act deceitfully, and with only a few people he will rise to power**. (According to Polybius in Book VI, Rome did not expect Antiochus to have much power.) *Daniel 11:24* **When the richest provinces** (Coele-Syria and Phoenicia) **feel secure**, (Ptolemy was at peace) **he** (Antiochus) **will invade them and will achieve what neither his fathers nor his forefathers did. He will distribute plunder, loot and wealth among his followers. He will plot the overthrow of fortresses — but only for a time**. *Daniel 11:25* **With a large army he will stir up his strength and courage against the king of the South**. (Ptolemy VI) **The king of the South will wage war with a large and very powerful army, but he will not be able to stand because of the plots devised against him**. (Antiochus had tricked Ptolemy's envoys and had Egypt in a posture of virtual surrender; Antiochus certainly used deceit to undo the Egyptian ruler.) *Daniel 11:26* **Those who eat from the king's provisions will try to destroy him**; (Ptolemy's followers would be deceived and work against him.) **his army will be swept away, and many will fall in battle**. (Ptolemy VI *Philometor* lost major battles that reduced Egypt to a second-rate power.) *Daniel 11:27* **The two kings**, (Antiochus IV and Ptolemy VI) **with their hearts bent on evil, will sit at the same table and lie to each other, but to no avail, because an end will still come at the appointed time**. (Each would fall at the time God had determined for their "end." This "end" was not the end of time; it was the end of the era for Egypt and would later be the end for Syria.) *Daniel 11:28* **The king of the North** (Antiochus IV) **will return to his own country with great wealth, but his heart will be set against the holy covenant. He will take action against it and then return to his own country**. (Antiochus IV would return home to Syria, but not before attacking.) *Daniel 11:29* **At the appointed time** (This indicates God's will in earthly matters concerning the destruction of evil.) **he will invade the South again,** (The first confrontation with Egypt came in 171-170 BC; this battle occurred in 168 BC.) **but this time the outcome will be different from what it was before**. (This time another nation will intervene in the affair.) *Daniel 11:30* **Ships of the western coastlands will oppose him**, (Rome demanded that he turn from Egypt.) **and he will lose heart**. (Antiochus did not have enough power to counter Rome.) **Then he will turn back and vent his fury against the holy covenant**. (Antiochus once again attacked Jerusalem.) **He will return and show favor to those who forsake the holy covenant**. (Antiochus spared those Jews who turned against their beliefs.) *Daniel 11:31* **His armed forces will rise up to desecrate the temple fortress and will abolish the daily sacrifice**. (Antiochus took over the temple and sacrificed pigs on the altar; this is the same material covered below:)

> *Daniel 8:11 It set itself up to be as great as the Prince of the host; it took away the daily sacrifice from him, and the place of his sanctuary was brought low.*

Then they will set up the abomination that causes desolation. (The "abomination of desolation" or the final overthrow of Jerusalem came in 70 AD; Matthew and Mark link the final fall of Jerusalem to the desecration by Antiochus IV.)

> *Matthew 24:15 ... standing in the holy place 'the abomination that causes desolation,' spoken of through the prophet Daniel — let the reader understand.*
>
> *Mark 13:14 When you see 'the abomination that causes desolation' standing where it does not belong — let the reader understand — then let those who are in Judea flee to the mountains.*

Daniel 11:32 **With flattery he will corrupt those who have violated the covenant, but the people who know their God will firmly resist him.** (Some Israelites will follow after Antiochus IV, but the truly faithful of Israel would resist the Syrian king and remain faithful to God.) *Daniel 11:33* **Those who are wise will instruct many,** (The faithful of God would attempt to teach and instruct others to remain faithful.) **though for a time they will fall by the sword or be burned or captured or plundered.** (The protection of God would not necessarily keep faithful Jews from dying or being harmed in other ways; however, God would reward them through eternity.) *Daniel 11:34* **When they fall, they will receive a little help, and many who are not sincere will join them.** (This merely reiterates that some would be faithful to God, and some would fall for the flatteries of Antiochus.) *Daniel 11:35* **Some of the wise will stumble, so that they may be refined, purified and made spotless** (The persecution was to create other categories; (1) there were some who would completely go over to Antiochus, (2) there were some who would not move an inch away from God, (3) there were some who would serve Antiochus, but later would return to God.) **until the time of the end,** (This is not the end of all time; it refers to the end of the era.) **for it will still come at the appointed time.**

THE FOURTH SCENE INVOLVING ANTIOCHUS IV

Beginning with verse 36, controversy has been waged over who is referred to as "the king of the north." Some of the possible persons suggested are Herod, the Anti-Christ of *1st John* and *2nd John*, or a number of Roman emperors. The structure of the passage indicates that Daniel was simply extending the material on Antiochus IV, because it begins with "<u>And</u> the king of the north ..." Throughout the entire sequence of chapter 11, Daniel has referred consistently to the kings of the north and the south; Daniel has used these terms without fail to refer to Syrian and Egyptian leaders. Why should it suddenly change at this point, and especially without indication of the change? If the identity is to change to another empire, why is there no indication as to where the switch should occur? Anyone's guess would be as good as the next. The book of *Daniel* ends with reference to the removal of the daily sacrifices, the setting up of the abomination that makes desolate, and to the time of the end – these have all been discussed in the earlier materials about Antiochus *Epiphanes*. Daniel is merely giving a replay with additional information about Antiochus IV; the reason significant time and space is spent on Antiochus *Epiphanes* is that so much of Jewish history revolved around this tyrant and his oppression of the Jews.

As the historical correlations are presented, it becomes even clearer that the king of the north is none other than Antiochus IV.

Daniel 11:36 The king will do as he pleases. He will exalt and magnify himself above every god and will say unheard-of things against the God of gods. He will be successful until the time of wrath is completed, for what has been determined must take place.
37 He will show no regard for the gods of his fathers or for the one desired by women, nor will he regard any god, but will exalt himself above them all.
38 Instead of them, he will honor a god of fortresses; a god unknown to his fathers he

36 The name Antiochus chose for himself, *Epiphanes*, means "god on earth." *Josephus*, book 12, chapter 5, section 5, describes the false worship Antiochus imposed upon the Jews.
37 Polybius, *Histories*, 26th Book, tells that when Antiochus heard the younger men were at recreation, he would come in to display his effeminate nature. Polybius also reports the sacrifices and the honors he paid to the gods far exceeded that of his predecessors.
38 Botsford and Robinson, *Hellenic History*, relate that Antiochus tried to establish his own "divine monarchy." In 169 BC he removed the god Apollo in favor of the Olympian Zeus, and changed the legend "Of King Antiochus" to "Of King Antiochus, the god manifest." 38 *Josephus*, book 12,

will honor with gold and silver, with precious stones and costly gifts.
39 *He will attack the mightiest fortresses with the help of a foreign god and will greatly honor those who acknowledge him. He will make them rulers over many people and will distribute the land at a price.*
40 *At the time of the end the king of the South will engage him in battle, and the king of the North will storm out against him with chariots and cavalry and a great fleet of ships. He will invade many countries and sweep through them ...*
41 *He will also invade the Beautiful Land. Many countries will fall, but Edom, Moab and the leaders of Ammon will be delivered from his hand.*
42 *He will extend his power over many countries; Egypt will not escape.*
43 *He will gain control of the treasures of gold and silver and all the riches of Egypt, with the Libyans and Nubians in submission.*
44 *But reports from the*

chapter 5, section 4, tells of his using gold and silver in sacrificing to foreign gods in Jerusalem.

39 Polybius, *Histories*, book 28, section I, p. 1: "At this time Antiochus was in possession of Coele-Syria and Phoenicia. For ever since the father of this King Antiochus had defeated Ptolemy's generals in the battle of Panium, all the above districts yielded obedience to the kings of Syria."

40 Polybius, *Histories*, book 28, section I, p. 1: "Antiochus was struggling to defend the country as one belonging to him, while Ptolemy ... was not disposed to abandon these places to Antiochus. Meleager and his colleagues came, therefore, with instructions to protest to the senate that Ptolemy in defiance of all right had taken up arms first."

41-43 Botsford and Robinson, *Hellenic History* explain that Antiochus invaded Jerusalem and several other countries, but just as he was beginning to gain power, Rome intervened to spare some countries from his conquests. This occurred when a "Roman envoy drew a circle around him in the sand and told him not to step out until he had chosen whether to leave Egypt."

43 Polybius states that Antiochus gained an abundance of wealth in the victory over the young Ptolemy by breaking the pact

east and the north will alarm him, and he will set out in a great rage to destroy and annihilate many.
45 He will pitch his royal tents between the seas at the beautiful holy mountain. Yet he will come to his end, and no one will help him.

with the Egyptian king.
44 The *Fourth Book of Macabees* tells of two disturbing rumors about Antiochus, chapter 2, verse 32: "For when he was carrying on war with Ptolemy in Egypt and heard that the people of Jerusalem had rejoiced exceedingly over a report of his death, he immediately marched back against them."
45 This led Antiochus to turn on the Jews, and sealed his divine doom.

The explanation can now be made paralleling *Daniel 11:36* through the end of the chapter with historical data. *Daniel 11:36* **The king will do as he pleases. He will exalt and magnify himself above every god and will say unheard-of things against the God of gods**. (Who else could fit this better than Antiochus who called himself "god on earth"? He took it upon himself to oppose the Living God by stopping the sacrifices of the Jews for three and one-half years.) **He will be successful until the time of wrath is completed, for what has been determined must take place**. (God will allow Antiochus to have his way until God pulls the plug.) *Daniel 11:37* **He will show no regard for the gods of his fathers or for the one desired by women, nor will he regard any god**, (Antiochus was perverted in every way; not only did he turn from the gods of his fathers with Zeus Olympus, but he was also perverted in his desire for young men rather than the desire for women.) **but will exalt himself above them all**. *Daniel 11:38* **Instead of them, he will honor a god of fortresses; a god unknown to his fathers** (Antiochus placed himself as god and used gold and silver in his worship.) **he will honor with gold and silver, with precious stones and costly gifts**. (According to the *Fourth Book of Macabees*, chapter 2, verses 28-30, Antiochus established his own high priest by selling the office to Jason.) *Daniel 11:39* **He will attack the mightiest fortresses** (The strongest fortress refers to Jerusalem — God was their protection; Antiochus introduced false gods to the Jews and lured many of them into leaving the True, Living God.) **with the help of a foreign god and will greatly honor those who acknowledge him. He will make them rulers over many**

people and will distribute the land at a price. (Antiochus had substituted Zeus for Apollo and also had strengthened his position by granting favors to those who supported him.) *Daniel 11:40* **At the time of the end** (the end of Antiochus' despotic rule) **the king of the South** (Ptolemy VI) **will engage him in battle, and the king of the North will storm out against him with chariots and cavalry and a great fleet of ships.** (Some find difficulty here by claiming Ptolemy VI never attacked Antiochus IV. This is true in one sense, but the statement has historical backing; Polybius stated that Antiochus claimed Ptolemy pushed first; Antiochus then used this as an excuse to confront Ptolemy.) **He will invade many countries and sweep through them like a flood.** *Daniel 11:41* **He will also invade the Beautiful Land**. (Everything thus far points to Antiochus, as does this event. What better explanation than the invasion of Jerusalem by Antiochus IV?) **Many countries will fall, but Edom, Moab and the leaders of Ammon will be delivered from his hand**. (This came about because Rome forced Antiochus to go home.)

Daniel 11:42 **He will extend his power over many countries; Egypt will not escape**. (Polybius says Egypt would have probably been destroyed had it not been for Rome's intervention.) *Daniel 11:43* **He will gain control of the treasures of gold and silver and all the riches of Egypt, with the Libyans and Nubians in submission**. (Polybius states that Antiochus gained great wealth from Egypt and that the Libyans and Ethiopians, who bordered Egypt, did the bidding of Antiochus in fighting against Egypt.) *Daniel 11:44* **But reports from the east and the north will alarm him, and he will set out in a great rage to destroy and annihilate many**. (One cannot find a clearer parallel to this prophecy than the actual fulfillment found in chapter 2 of the *Fourth Book of Macabees*. Antiochus was greatly disturbed to hear rumors of his own death and even more disturbed to learn the Jews were rejoicing.) *Daniel 11:45* **He will pitch his royal tents between the seas at the beautiful holy mountain**. (Literally, this means between the seas — the Mediterranean and the Dead Sea, and not too far from Jerusalem — this permitted the attacks on Jewish worship; Josephus states that Antiochus absolutely hated the Jewish religion.) **Yet he will come to his end, and no one will help him**. (After Rome sent Antiochus home, he was virtually helpless and did nothing outstanding after his attacks on the Jews. This is another prediction of the fall of Antiochus *Epiphanes*.)

At this point it should be clear that verses 36 through the end of chapter 11 refer to Antiochus *Epiphanes*. The prediction of Antiochus *Epiphanes*' downfall continues with chapter 12 as the book of *Daniel* is finalized. As the book comes to a close, several important points are made concerning the "end times" of the third kingdom involved in Daniel's prophecy.

POINT 1) The archangel Michael would be instrumental in the fall of Antiochus *Epiphanes*.

> *Daniel 12:1 At that time Michael, the great prince who protects your people, will arise. There will be a time of distress such as has not happened from the beginning of nations until then. But at that time your people — everyone whose name is found written in the book — will be delivered.*

Michael consistently appears to defend, strengthen, and protect the people of God. The first time the Bible records information concerning the archangel Michael is *Daniel 10:13* when he assisted the angel who struggled to bring a message to Daniel. According to *Daniel 10:21*, Michael assisted in the Grecian overthrow of Persia. In chapter *12:1* above, Michael came to war against Antiochus *Epiphanes* in destroying Greece. The only other references to the archangel Michael are found in *Jude 1:9* and *Revelation 12:7*. In the first reference Michael contended with Satan over the body of Moses, and in the second, Michael assisted God's people in a conflict with Satan's forces. Without God's aid, it would have been impossible for the Jews to overthrow this despotic ruler; Jewish soldiers were untrained and poorly armed compared with their counterparts, the Syrian army. However, the atrocities of Antiochus IV led to the revolt of the Macabees and brought the tyrant's overthrow.

POINT 2) The Jews would make choices to follow God or Antiochus.

Daniel is told that consequences come based on human decision.

> *Daniel 12:1-3 ... But at that time your people — everyone whose name is found written in the book — will be delivered. Multitudes who sleep in the dust of the earth will awake: some to everlasting life, others to shame and everlasting contempt. Those who are wise will shine like the brightness of the heavens, and those who lead many to righteousness, like the stars for ever and ever.*

Prior references to Antiochus' invasion of Jerusalem indicated that many Jews were traitors to the cause; God knew who the faithful were and would reward them. They were the ones whose names were written in the Book of Life. For a period of three and one-half years, Israel's worship had been stymied, but at the "time of the end" Israel's worship would be restored. Verse 2 is probably the clearest reference to the resurrection that can be found in the Old Testament.

The verses concerning resurrection can be interpreted in two ways. First, it may be the resurrection when rewards and punishments will be determined. One group was to rise to everlasting life and to shine like stars because of their faithfulness. The other group was to rise to eternal shame. Second, Daniel could have used symbolic language of a resurrection to indicate the rebirth of spirituality in Jerusalem. Interpreted in this way, the scene would be similar to the rebirth of Jewish spirituality written of by Ezekiel in chapter 37 of his book. Ezekiel was shown a valley of dry bones that came to life before his very eyes to symbolize the rebuilding of spirituality.

> *Ezekiel 37:12-14 Therefore prophesy and say to them: "This is what the Sovereign LORD says: O my people, I am going to open your graves and bring you up from them; I will bring you back to the land of Israel. Then you, my people, will know that I am the LORD, when I open your graves and bring you up from them. I will put my Spirit in you and you will live, and I will settle you in your own land. Then you will know that I the LORD have spoken, and I have done it, declares the LORD."*

The latter viewpoint seems more credible; this view would point to a brighter day for God's people after the demise of Antiochus; God would destroy Antiochus and resurrect Israel. This approach can also be seen as pointing to the glory of the people of God caused by the fulfillment of all prophecy through the resurrection of Jesus Christ.

Although the return and renewal of God's people blends better with the overall theme, the first interpretation leaves a beautiful message also. The interesting thing is that both interpretations lead to truthful conclusions; the faithful of Israel were to be rewarded, and the unfaithful would be punished. Once again the theme of the omnipotence of God is advanced; it is God who determines rewards and punishment. Verse 10 extends the concept of the two choices in showing that knowledge and wisdom come to those who are faithful.

> *Daniel 12:10 Many will be purified, made spotless and refined, but the wicked will continue to be wicked. None of the wicked will understand, but those who are wise will understand.*

Perhaps this is similar to the issue made by John in presenting his revelation. The Romans certainly would not have understood, but those Christians living in Asia Minor under Roman rule could see the beasts of John and Daniel to be the same, and because the events were unfolding at the time, they could understand.

> *Revelation 1:3 Blessed is the one who reads the words of this prophecy, and blessed are those who hear it and take to heart what is written in it, because the time is near.*

POINT 3) Daniel was further instructed to "seal" the prophecy.

In verse 4 of the chapter Daniel was instructed to "... close up and seal the words of the scroll until the time of the end." Once again Daniel uses the phrase "time of the end" as it related to the END OF AN ERA, not to the end of all time. Daniel was then told that many "... will go here and there to increase knowledge." In other words, as time passed, people would understand the events that were at one time "sealed" because the incidents were about 400 years from occurrence. Remember the earlier principle: prophecy can only be understood after-the fact; this gives a perfect rationale for shutting up the words of prophecy — it simply was too far into the future for the readers to comprehend; thus, it was sealed. Verses 8 and 9 further clarify the purpose of sealing; even Daniel did not understand the meaning of the visions presented to him.

> *Daniel 12:8,9 I heard, but I did not understand. So I asked, "My lord, what will the outcome of all this be?" He replied, "Go your way, Daniel, because the words are closed up and sealed until the time of the end."*

The "time of the end" is the same event referred to in earlier references:

> *Daniel 11:35 Some of the wise will stumble, so that they may be refined, purified and made spotless until the **time of the end**, for it will still come at the appointed time.*

> *Daniel 11:40 At the **time of the end** the king of the South will engage him in battle, and the king of the North will storm out against him with chariots and cavalry and a great fleet of ships. He will invade many countries and sweep through them like a flood.*

> *Daniel 11:45 He will pitch his royal tents between the seas at the beautiful holy mountain. Yet he will **come to his end**, and no one will help him.*

Three other "times of the end" are presented in Daniel's prophecy:

1) The fall of the Persian kingdom was called "time of the end."

> *Daniel 8:17 As he came near the place where I was standing, I was terrified and fell prostrate. "Son of man," he said to me, "understand that the vision concerns the **time of the end**."*

> *Daniel 8:19 He said: "I am going to tell you what will happen later in the time of wrath, because the vision concerns the appointed **time of the end**."*

Verses 20 and 21 continue with the crushing of Persia by Alexander the Great to bring on the "time of the end" of Persia.

2) The fall of Jerusalem was labeled as the "time of the end."

> *Daniel 9:26,27   After the sixty-two `sevens,' the Anointed One will be cut off and will have nothing. The people of the ruler who will come will destroy the city and the sanctuary.* **The end will come** *like a flood: War will continue* **until the end**, *and desolations have been decreed. He will confirm a covenant with many for one `seven.' In the middle of the `seven' he will put an end to sacrifice and offering. And on a wing [of the temple] he will set up an abomination that causes desolation,* **until the end** *that is decreed is poured out on him.*

3) At the time Daniel's work was unsealed **(Rome)**, the period is called "time of the end." This occurred in chapters 6 through 8 of *Revelation* when Jesus removed the seven seals.

> *Daniel 12:4   But you, Daniel, close up and seal the words of the scroll until the **time of the end**.*

> *Daniel 12:9   He replied, "Go your way, Daniel, because the words are closed up and sealed until the **time of the end**."*

The end of time can come only once, but the "time of the end" of an era has occurred endless times.   Daniel dealt with four in his book.

POINT 4)   Daniel saw a vision that compares to an earlier view of Jesus Christ.

> *Daniel 10:5,6   I looked up and there before me was a man dressed in linen, with a belt of the finest gold around his waist. His body was like chrysolite, his face like lightning, his eyes like flaming torches, his arms and legs like the gleam of burnished bronze, and his voice like the sound of a multitude.*

> *Daniel 12:5,6   Then I, Daniel, looked, and there before me stood two others, one on this bank of the river and one on the opposite bank.*
> *One of them said to the man clothed in linen, who was above the waters of the river, "How long will it be before these astonishing things are fulfilled?"*

POINT 5) Daniel was apprised concerning the time for fulfillment to occur.

The length of time until completion is foretold in the next sequence, *Daniel 12:7*. This vision was brought by two angels and by the One clothed in linen who was pictured in *Daniel 10:5,6*. The question raised in *Daniel 12:6* dealt with the length of time until fulfillment. Fulfillment of what? Obviously it is the fulfillment of events Daniel has been envisioning concerning the "time of the end" of Antiochus IV *Epiphanes*.

> *Daniel 12:7 The man clothed in linen, who was above the waters of the river, lifted his right hand and his left hand toward heaven, and I heard him swear by him who lives forever, saying, "It will be for a time, times and half a time. When the power of the holy people has been finally broken, all these things will be completed."*

The phrase "time, times and half a time" is found in only two books of the Bible, *Daniel* and *Revelation*. The further study of John's vision will clearly show this puzzling phrase to mean three and one-half years. The "end" was said to be "When the power of the holy people has been finally broken, all these things will be completed." God would only permit Antiochus to abuse His people for a set period of time; earlier Josephus was quoted as saying that the daily sacrifices were stopped by Antiochus *Epiphanes* for a period of three and one-half years. Another proof the period refers to three and one-half years is found in verse 11.

> *Daniel 12:11 From the time that the daily sacrifice is abolished and the abomination that causes desolation is set up, there will be 1,290 days.*

The verse above states the time to begin counting: **when the daily sacrifice was abolished**. This is an obvious reference to the persecution of the Jews inflicted by Antiochus *Epiphanes*. As Daniel developed the theme of this third great kingdom on earth, Antiochus IV has been the central villain. The following passages all link to the abomination mentioned in the verse above.

> *Daniel 8:11,12 It set itself up to be as great as the Prince of the host; it took away the daily sacrifice from him, and the place of his sanctuary was brought low. Because of rebellion, the host [of the saints] and the daily sacrifice were given over to it. ...*

> *Daniel 8:24-26 ... He will destroy the mighty men and the holy people. He will cause deceit to prosper, and he will consider himself superior. When they feel secure, he will destroy many and take his stand against the Prince of princes. Yet he will be destroyed, but not by human power. The vision of the evenings and mornings that has been given you is true, but seal up the vision, for it concerns the distant future.*

> *Daniel 11:21 He will be succeeded by a contemptible person who has not been given the honor of royalty. 11:28 ... his heart will be set against the holy covenant. He will take action against it and then return to his own country. ... 11:31 His armed forces will rise up to desecrate the temple fortress and will abolish the daily sacrifice. Then they will set up the abomination that causes desolation.*

> *Daniel 11:41 He will also invade the Beautiful Land ...*

All of these verses point to the attack on Jerusalem, to the persecution of the Jews, and to the evil leader that perpetrated the events.

It is clear that the beginning point for counting time was Antiochus' violation of the altar in Jerusalem. What about the ending point? This is clarified in the last verse of the book when Daniel referred to "the end," referring to the end of Antiochus' encroachment on God's people.

> *Daniel 12:13 As for you, go your way till the end. You will rest, and then at the end of the days you will rise to receive your allotted inheritance.*

Daniel states that the length of time between the two events would be "a thousand two hundred and ninety days." The *Funk and Wagnalls Encyclopedia*, 1983, Vol. 5, states,

> The Jewish calendar is lunisolar, based on lunar months of 29 days alternating with 30 days. An extra month is intercalated every three years.

This addition of 30 days over the three year span would bring the total days in the Jewish calendar to 1269; one might question the difference between 1290 and 1269, but keep in mind that Josephus was not counting the exact number of days when he said Antiochus desecrated the temple for three and one-half years. The number of days, 1269, would certainly lead a person to say the time was "three and one-half years." Daniel is given the length of time Antiochus would violate God's will; this also indicates Divine guidance. The time had been set by the Almighty!

The statement found in verse 12, however, is a little more puzzling.

> *Daniel 12:12 Blessed is the one who waits for and reaches the end of the 1,335 days.*

John A. Copeland in *A Study of Daniel*, p. 64, explains from Josephus that a restraining wall was built around the temple to prevent further attempts to defile it. This may explain the additional month and one half to account for the length of time until all restraints were in place. Whatever explanation is given, however, the timeframe must relate in some way to the rule of Antiochus *Epiphanes* over Jerusalem because that is the context in which the verse is located.

An interesting sidelight to these final verses in *Daniel* is that Jesus made reference to Daniel's prophecies in His teachings. This is recorded in two of the gospels, *Luke* and *Matthew*.

> *Luke 21:20 When you see Jerusalem being surrounded by armies, you will know that its desolation is near.*

> *Matthew 24:15 So when you see standing in the holy place `the abomination that causes desolation,' spoken of through the prophet Daniel — let the reader understand.*

In the days of Antiochus *Epiphanes* there was an abomination of desolation when the Gentile Syrian army sacked the holy city; Jesus tied this to the abomination of desolation at the destruction of Jerusalem in 70 AD under the Gentile Roman legions led by Titus. In both occasions an ungodly man destroyed the "city of God." Desolation was the result of both of these invasions by "abominable" Gentile armies.

Daniel spoke of four earthly kingdoms; in earlier chapters we dealt with the fall of Babylon followed by the rise and fall of Medo-Persia. In this chapter we learned of the rapid rise of Alexander the Great as Greece rose to power, but we also observed his sudden death at the age of 33 and the eventual decay of the empire. In the next chapter we will explore Daniel's prophecies concerning the fourth kingdom — Rome.

Chapter Five

Prophecies about the Roman Empire

Now that materials have been covered pertaining to the rise and fall of the Babylonian empire, the Medo-Persian kingdom, and the Grecian empire, it is time to examine the fourth kingdom spoken of by Daniel. The fourth kingdom is viewed in two separate visions, the first in a dream of Nebuchadnezzar that was deciphered by Daniel; the other was a vision seen by Daniel.

> **The Sealing and Revealing of the fall of Rome**

The first vision of Rome

In chapter 2 of *Daniel*, Nebuchadnezzar had a dream of a four part image of a man formed of gold, silver, bronze, and a mixture of iron and clay. Chapter one of this volume clearly identified the four parts as the kingdoms of Babylon, Medo-Persia, Greece and Rome; although the fourth kingdom is not named in *Daniel*, all history testifies to the fact that Rome followed Greece. In Nebuchadnezzar's dream the fourth kingdom is seen as the legs and feet of the 'metal' man.

> *Daniel 2:33 Its legs of iron, its feet partly of iron and partly of baked clay.*

Verse 40 begins the explanation of the vision of the fourth empire.

> *Daniel 2:40 Finally, there will be a fourth kingdom, strong as iron--for iron breaks and smashes everything--and as iron breaks things to pieces, so it will crush and break all the others.*

Nothing could be more descriptive of Rome; in John's time, Rome controlled the known world in Europe, Africa, and Asia Minor. **Study the maps on pages 10 and 11 to see the full impact Rome had upon the world.** It consumed the land once controlled by each of the three kingdoms that had preceded it. Notice the information below:

> *Daniel 2:41 Just as you saw that the feet and toes were partly of baked clay and partly of iron, so this will be a divided kingdom; yet it will have some of the strength of iron in it, even as you saw iron mixed with clay.*

As the Roman Empire reached out and consumed more and more territory, it became harder to control the nations and people it had conquered. Loyalty can be fickle when the blood lines run thin; the mixture of people controlled by Rome was both a blessing and a curse to the nation. Rome built a fantastic system of roads throughout the empire to use for trade among the provinces, so Rome had all the goods it could possibly desire. However, this vastness later proved to be a curse when previously conquered territories turned on the Roman dynasty. This paradox of strength and weakness is explained in the next verse.

> *Daniel 2:42-43 As the toes were partly iron and partly clay, so this kingdom will be partly strong and partly brittle. And just as you saw the iron mixed with baked clay, so the people will be a mixture and will not remain united any more than iron mixes with clay.*

The Roman Empire would be tremendously strong; yet, it would have the weakness of not being able to totally assimilate those it had conquered. The failure to blend cultures would ultimately lead to a lack of loyalty and commitment.

Perhaps the most significant part of Nebuchadnezzar's vision relates to the kingdom of God being established during the tenure of the fourth earthly empire. Later when Daniel has his dream about four beasts, the kingdom of God was to be established in the days of the fourth empire.

> *Daniel 2:44 In the time of those kings, the God of heaven will set up a kingdom that will never be destroyed, nor will it be left to another people. It will crush all those kingdoms and bring them to an end, but it will itself endure forever.*

In *Daniel 7:14,21,22*, the author tells that during the days of the fourth beast the kingdom of God would be established; therefore, it is logical to conclude that the feet of iron and clay and the 10 horned beast are separate symbols of the same kingdom because the identical event was to occur within both. While the legs and part of the feet of the metal man were formed of iron for strength, the beast had iron teeth for the same purpose. It might also be significant that the first image had ten toes and the beast had ten horns; the ten horns represent ten kings of the fourth empire.

The second vision of Rome

Daniel spends more time explaining the fourth kingdom when he had his vision in chapter 7. He saw four beasts coming up from the sea; the fourth was described as follows:

> *Daniel 7:7 ... there before me was a fourth beast — terrifying and frightening and very powerful. It had large iron teeth; it crushed and devoured its victims and trampled underfoot whatever was left. It was different from all the former beasts, and it had ten horns.*

Daniel was puzzled by the vision as he indicates in the next verse.

> *Daniel 7:19,20 Then I wanted to know the true meaning of the fourth beast, which was different from all the others and most terrifying, with its iron teeth and bronze claws--the beast that crushed and devoured its victims and trampled underfoot whatever was left. I also wanted to know about the ten horns on its head and about the other horn that came up, before which three of them fell--the horn that looked more imposing than the others and that had eyes and a mouth that spoke boastfully.*

Notice that the fourth beast represents the fourth kingdom; never does Daniel deal with a fifth beast or a fifth part of the image or a fifth earthly empire, because he was concerned with the events that were to unfold with the coming of the fourth kingdom. During the days of the kings of the fourth kingdom, God would send the King of kings and Lord of lords to earth to establish an everlasting kingdom in the hearts of His followers.

The passage quoted on the previous page tells that the beast would say boastful things; the reader might recall the comparison in chapter one of this volume; both Daniel and John pictured beasts that said proud, boastful things.

After Daniel puzzled over the meaning, an explanation begins in verse 23 when the following truth is presented:

> *Daniel 7:23 ... The fourth beast is a fourth kingdom that will appear on earth. It will be different from all the other kingdoms and will devour the whole earth, trampling it down and crushing it.*

Rome is clearly pictured in two ways: 1) Rome was the fourth consecutive kingdom counting forward from Babylonian days; 2) all things considered, the Roman Empire was one of the most powerful nations ever to exist on earth.

The beast was obviously powerful, but what is the meaning of the symbolism of the 10 horns?

> *Daniel 7:8 ... there before me was another horn, a little one, which came up among them; and three of the first horns were uprooted before it. This horn had eyes like the eyes of a man and a mouth that spoke boastfully.*

The horns are symbolic of the kings of this fourth empire.

> *Daniel 7:24-26 The ten horns are ten kings who will come from this kingdom. After them another king will arise, different from the earlier ones; he will subdue three kings. He will speak against the Most High and oppress his saints and try to change the set times and the laws. The saints will be handed over to him for a time, times and half a time. But the court will sit, and his power will be taken away and completely destroyed forever.*

Four questions must be answered about the kings of this fourth kingdom:
    1) Who are the first ten kings?
    2) Who is the little horn that would be number 11?
    3) Who are the three who are broken off?
    4) Why is significant time spent on the eleventh horn?

> **Julio-Claudian Dynasty**
> 1. Caesar Augustus
> 2. Caesar Tiberius
> 3. Caesar Gaius
> 4. Caesar Claudius
> 5. Caesar Nero
>
> **Three broken off in the Civil War of 69 AD**
> 6. Galba
> 7. Otho
> 8. Vitellius
>
> **Flavian Dynasty**
> 9. Caesar Vespasian
> 10. Caesar Titus
> 11. Caesar Domitian

The first three questions can be answered quickly by using the chart above. The first eleven kings of Rome can easily be placed in three divisions: the Julio-Claudian Dynasty, the Flavian Dynasty, and those who tried to gain the throne during a year of turbulence in Rome. A clearer comparison of Roman kings seen by Daniel and John can be found on pages 18 and 19 of this volume. Most of the evils of the fourth empire are identified with the eleventh ruler of the kingdom.

More time was spent on ruler eleven, Domitian, since the great persecution and tribulation were to increase under him. This would be a time when Christians would be called on to make a choice between worshipping God through Jesus or worshipping Satan through the deified caesars of Rome. Daniel describes this ruler.

> *Daniel 7:25 He will speak against the Most High and oppress his saints and try to change the set times and the laws. The saints will be handed over to him for a time, times and half a time.*

The persecution would last for **time, times and half a time**; evidence earlier indicated this is the equivalent of three and one-half years. It might be noted that the three and one-half years do not correlate with the fifteen year reign of Domitian. However, Daniel is dealing with symbols. The Bible lists other instances where the opponents of God obstructed God's work for three and one-half years. Three and one-half is a broken seven; perhaps there is a strong message in this symbol.

The passages on the beast also reveal that the beast would fall, just as the beast of *Revelation* was to fall. Daniel earlier referred to the "time of the end" of Medo-Persia and Greece; at this point he refers to the final days of Rome

> *Daniel 7:11 Then I continued to watch because of the boastful words the horn was speaking. I kept looking until the beast was slain and its body destroyed and thrown into the blazing fire.*

The persecution could not last forever, as seen in the next verse.

> *Daniel 7:12 (The other beasts had been stripped of their authority, but were allowed to live for a period of time.)*

The first three kingdoms had all lost their power on earth, but their existence as people continued through and under the rule of the Roman Empire which had engulfed all others. Verse 26 refers to the end in this manner,

> *Daniel 7:26 But the court will sit, and his power will be taken away and completely destroyed forever.*

Daniel concludes the material on Rome with verse 28, indicating his uncertainty as to the meaning of the visions.

> *Daniel 7:28 This is the end of the matter. I, Daniel, was deeply troubled by my thoughts, and my face turned pale, but I kept the matter to myself.*

The revealing of the message did not occur until Jesus Christ took the sealed book from the right hand of God and began removing the seals in the sixth chapter of *Revelation*. While parts of *Daniel* were fulfilled before John wrote his book, the whole of *Daniel* was not understood until the revelation was made in the days of John.

After reading about the existence and collapse of four worldly kingdoms, let's remember that Daniel prophesied there would be a heavenly kingdom established in the days of the fourth empire. The next chapter will examine what Daniel had to say about the Kingdom of God.

Chapter Six

Daniel Writes about the Kingdom of God

While Daniel wrote about four earthly kingdoms, the most significant kingdom addressed in his book is the kingdom of God. This chapter will deal with when the kingdom was to be established, who the king was to be, how the kingdom was to be persecuted by the Roman Empire, how the Roman Empire would be destroyed, and how the kingdom of God would be an eternal kingdom.

> Kingdoms of the earth are temporary, but the kingdom of God will last forever!

1. WHEN WAS GOD'S KINGDOM TO BE ESTABLISHED?

Daniel tells the reader in two different sections that the kingdom of God would be established during the days of the fourth kingdom; this concept was discussed in chapter 1 and in chapter 5 of this volume. God's kingdom has actually gone through many stages throughout the existence of time. **God has always been King of the universe**. To Abraham the kingdom came through promise; from Moses to the birth of Jesus the kingdom was localized in Israel during the time of preparation for the coming of the King of kings. When Jesus was born, the King had arrived; after his death, Christ claimed all power was His. On Pentecost the earthly phase of the kingdom was established; when Christ comes again to end all time, the earthly phase of God's kingdom will end.

The first vision of the kingdom of God

Daniel 2:34,35   While you were watching, a rock was cut out, but not by human hands. It struck the statue on its feet of iron and clay and smashed them. Then the iron, the clay, the bronze, the silver and the gold were broken to pieces at the same time and became like chaff on a threshing floor in the summer. The wind swept them away without leaving a trace. But the rock that struck the statue became a huge mountain and filled the whole earth.

This might be very puzzling to the reader if it were not for the interpretation found in verses 44 and 45.

Daniel 2:44-45   In the time of those kings, the God of heaven will set up a kingdom that will never be destroyed, nor will it be left to another people. It will crush all those kingdoms and bring them to an end, but it will itself endure forever. This is the meaning of the vision of the rock cut out of a mountain, but not by human hands--a rock that broke the iron, the bronze, the clay, the silver and the gold to pieces. The great God has shown the king what will take place in the future. The dream is true and the interpretation is trustworthy.

The first thing discovered in the interpretation is that the kingdom of God would be established during the time of the fourth kingdom from Daniel's era. Dating from Daniel's days, one can easily count these kingdoms; namely, 1) Babylon, 2) Medo-Persia, 3) Greece, and 4) Rome. The spiritual kingdom arrived on earth with the coming of the King of kings and Lord of lords. From these verses one also learns that the kingdom of God would destroy earthly kingdoms; the point is, the kingdom of God will survive eternally although earthly kingdoms perish. A further point is that nations opposing the kingdom of God have only one possible outcome — destruction.

The second vision of the kingdom of God

Daniel 7:13,14   In my vision at night I looked, and there before me was one like a son of man, coming with the clouds of heaven. He approached the Ancient of Days and was led into his presence. He was given authority, glory and sovereign power; all peoples, nations and men of every language worshiped him. His dominion is an everlasting dominion that will not pass away, and his kingdom is one that will never be destroyed.

The spiritual kingdom of God on earth began when the King of kings took the throne; Jesus came during the days of the fourth empire and claimed to have all authority.

Matthew 28:18   Then Jesus came to them and said, "All authority in heaven and on earth has been given to me."

More evidence of the origin of God's spiritual kingdom is presented when Daniel actually pinpoints the year Christ was to be anointed.

The third vision of the kingdom of God

Daniel 9:25,26   Know and understand this: From the issuing of the decree to restore and rebuild Jerusalem until the Anointed One, the ruler, comes, there will be seven `sevens,' and sixty-two `sevens.' It will be rebuilt with streets and a trench, but in times of trouble. After the sixty-two `sevens,' the Anointed One will be cut off and will have nothing. The people of the ruler who will come will destroy the city and the sanctuary. The end will come like a flood: war will continue until the end, and desolations have been decreed.

Daniel gives a starting point, an ending point, and the length of the interval between the two. The starting point is the "decree to restore and to rebuild Jerusalem." This order was given by Artexerxes in 457 BC. The ending point was the arrival of the Anointed One. Jesus' personal ministry began in the year 26 AD; this would be **483 years** from the starting point. The time for fulfillment was 7 weeks plus 62 weeks, totalling 69 weeks or **483 days**. By taking a day for a year, 483 years from the year 457 BC would pinpoint the year 26 AD. Today we know the Gregorian calendar used in the West is off from 4 - 6 years. Jesus was actually born in 4 BC; He began His personal ministry at the age of thirty, the age when priesthood began for the Jews. This may be one of the most amazing prophecies in the entire Bible. **Jesus was anointed with the Holy Spirit in 26 AD, 483 years after the command was issued by Artaxerxes to restore and rebuild Jerusalem!**

> *Matthew 3:16 As soon as Jesus was baptized, he went up out of the water. At that moment heaven was opened, and he saw the Spirit of God descending like a dove and lighting on him.*

2. WHO IS THE KING OF GOD'S KINGDOM?

The material above has already identified Jesus as King. Daniel gives Messianic visions throughout his prophecy; these will now be examined as the focus shifts to the King of kings.

First vision of Jesus

> *Daniel 7:13,14 In my vision at night I looked, and there before me was one like a son of man, coming with the clouds of heaven. He approached the Ancient of Days and was led into his presence. He was given authority, glory and sovereign power; all peoples, nations and men of every language worshiped him. His dominion is an everlasting dominion that will not pass away, and his kingdom is one that will never be destroyed.*

Jesus came to this earth to establish His kingdom; He reigns today, and **Christians reign with Him**.

> *Romans 5:17 For if, by the trespass of the one man, death reigned through that one man, how much more will those who receive God's abundant provision of grace and of the gift of righteousness reign in life through the one man, Jesus Christ.*

It would be impossible for people to reign with Christ today if Christ were not reigning.

Second Vision of Jesus

Daniel has already informed us that Jesus was to come to earth to become King of God's eternal kingdom. In the following section of his prophecy, Daniel details seven things the arrival of Jesus was to accomplish. The passage below begins relating significant purposes for the coming of Jesus to earth.

> *Daniel 9:24 Seventy 'sevens' are decreed for your people and your holy city to finish transgression, to put an end to sin, to atone for wickedness, to bring in everlasting righteousness, to seal up vision and prophecy and to anoint the most holy.*

FIRST PURPOSE

The first purpose given for the arrival of Jesus Christ was stated in two ways — "to finish transgression, to put an end to sin." For years the Jews had a system of sacrifices to atone for sins, but the Hebrew writer states that Jesus died once to accomplish that purpose for all times. While sin is inevitable, forgiveness of sin is possible through Jesus Christ; therefore, He came to finish transgression, to bring forgiveness of sins.

SECOND PURPOSE

Jesus came "to atone for wickedness." Man was separated from God in the Garden of Eden because he chose the knowledge of good and evil over a life of serving God. From that moment, God planned to send His Son to reconcile man to Himself by the atoning blood of Jesus. This great plan of God was fulfilled after Jesus came to this planet.

> *Romans 5:11 Not only is this so, but we also rejoice in God through our Lord Jesus Christ, through whom we have now received reconciliation.*

THIRD PURPOSE

The third purpose accomplished in Jesus' coming to earth was "to bring in everlasting righteousness." Everlasting righteousness exists, not because man is perfect, but because the blood of Jesus brings continual cleansing and forgiveness.

> *I John 1:7 But if we walk in the light, as he is in the light, we have fellowship with one another, and the blood of Jesus, his Son, purifies us from all sin.*
>
> *Romans 3:21-23 ... righteousness from God comes through faith in Jesus Christ to all who believe.*

Man cannot achieve righteousness on his own, but he can achieve righteousness through Jesus Christ because Christ was willing to come to earth to fulfill that purpose.

FOURTH PURPOSE

A fourth objective reached by Christ was to end the time "to seal up the vision and the prophecy." Two other versions make this point even clearer. The Jerusalem Bible says that seventy weeks remained for "setting the seal on vision and prophecy." The New American Version states that seventy weeks remained until vision and prophesy were ratified; thus, Jesus would end the sealing of prophecy by fulfilling or ratifying it. Jesus ended the sealing of vision and prophecy in three ways:

1) He fulfilled the prophets to end the lack of understanding.

> *Matthew 5:17 Do not think that I have come to abolish the Law or the Prophets; I have not come to abolish them but to fulfill them.*

In reading the Old Testament prophets, one can find countless prophecies relating to Jesus Christ. The arrival of Jesus, His life and death on earth, and His ascension into heaven all fulfilled prophecy.

2) Jesus ended the sealing of prophecy by opening the seals of *Revelation*.

> *Revelation 5:9,10 ... "You are worthy to take the scroll and to open its seals, because you were slain ...*

3) Jesus ended the sealing of prophecy by ordering John to leave the book open. Jesus had removed all 7 seals!

> *Revelation 22:10 ... "Do not seal up the words of the prophecy of this book, because the time is near."*

FIFTH PURPOSE

Jesus came to "anoint the most holy." The anointing was done to officially recognize the king, and Jesus was to be the King of kings, the Lord of lords over God's kingdom. At the time Jesus was born on earth, Herod had heard rumors about the King of the Jews being born, and he tried to stop the occasion by killing male Jewish babies. When Jesus died on the cross, an inscription was placed above His head, KING OF THE JEWS; some had wanted to place the words above His head, "He said he is king of the Jews," but Pilate refused to let this occur. **Jesus rules over God's kingdom!**

After Daniel detailed the first five purposes of Jesus' tenure on earth, he predicted two events that were to occur sometime after seven 7's plus sixty two 7's. Sixty nine 7's totaled 483 days; prophetically, a day symbolizes a year, so we have 483 years. Earlier evidence indicated that this prophecy pointed to the year 26 AD when Jesus began His personal ministry. The two events are evident in purposes 6 and 7.

SIXTH PURPOSE

Jesus came to earth to die for the world. Notice that this event was to occur in the middle of the last 7. Not only did Daniel foretell when Jesus would be anointed, he also foretold the time of his death! Jesus' personal ministry lasted 3½ years, exactly half of 7. His death ended the old sacrificial system.

> **SEVENTY SEVENS**
> **69 7's needed to accomplish:**
> 1. Finishing transgression
> 2. Atoning for wickedness
> 3. Bringing eternal righteousness
> 4. Ending the sealing of prophecy
> **5. Anointing Jesus Christ in 26 AD**
>
> **(69 X 7 days = 483 prophetic years)**
>
> **The 70th 7 was to accomplish the following:**
> 6. Jesus' death in the middle of the week
> **(middle of 7 days = 3½ prophetic years)**
> 7. The destruction of Jerusalem
> **(Jesus announced coming destruction)**

Daniel 9:26,27 After the sixty-two 'sevens,' the Anointed One will be cut off and will have nothing. The people of the ruler who will come will destroy the city and the sanctuary. ... He will confirm a covenant with many for one 'seven.' In the middle of the 'seven' he will put an end to sacrifice and offering.

Notice that Jesus did away with ceremonial sacrifices when the "written code" was nailed to the cross.

Colossians 2:14 Having canceled the written code, with its regulations ... he took it away, nailing it to the cross.

SEVENTH PURPOSE

Daniel 9:27 On a wing [of the temple] he will set up an abomination that causes desolation, until the end that is decreed is poured out on him.

In *Daniel 9:24* we learned that "Seventy 'sevens' are decreed for your people and your holy city." Titus, leading a Gentile army, became the abomination that caused the desolation of Jerusalem 40 years after Jesus was crucified. This was essential because the seat of God's kingdom was changed from Jerusalem to new Jerusalem (the church). In *Matthew 24*, Jesus told His followers the temple would be destroyed before the end of the generation. Jesus came to proclaim the end of Jerusalem.

> *Matthew 24:34 ... this generation will certainly not pass away until all these things have happened.*

Third vision of Jesus

> *Daniel 10:5,6   I looked up and there before me was a man dressed in linen, with a belt of the finest gold around his waist. His body was like chrysolite, his face like lightning, his eyes like flaming torches, his arms and legs like the gleam of burnished bronze, and his voice like the sound of a multitude.*

Point 1 dealt with when the kingdom of God would be established; point 2 answered the question about who was to be King.

3. THE KINGDOM OF GOD WOULD BE PERSECUTED

> *Daniel 7:21 As I watched, this horn was waging war against the saints and defeating them,*
>
> *Daniel 7:25 He will speak against the Most High and oppress his saints and try to change the set times and the laws. The saints will be handed over to him for a time, times and half a time.*

Herod attempted to kill the new King by killing all Jewish male boys under the age of two, but he failed. The Romans killed Jesus on the cross, but even this did not destroy the King; instead, His death and resurrection ushered the kingdom into being. After this, the Romans persecuted the kingdom and tried to force worship of deified caesars, but God was not going to let this continue.

4. HOW WOULD ROME BE DESTROYED?

God was to come in judgment of the Roman Empire, and the saints were to take part in the judgment; their godly lives would stand as evidence that one could live for God in an evil world.

> *Daniel 7:22 Until the Ancient of Days came and pronounced judgment in favor of the saints of the Most High, and the time came when they possessed the kingdom.*

The opening of the fifth seal in *Revelation* revealed saints beneath the altar, asking God to vindicate them. When saints pray for "the death of the beast," God listens! The 20th chapter of *Revelation* shows saints sitting on thrones of judgment. God has the ultimate victory, and those who serve Him will share in that victory. This leads to the last point in this chapter — the kingdom of God is to be eternal.

5. GOD'S KINGDOM WILL BE ETERNAL

> *Daniel 2:44 In the time of those kings, the God of heaven will set up a kingdom that will never be destroyed, nor will it be left to another people. It will crush all those kingdoms and bring them to an end, but it will itself endure forever.*

> *Daniel 7:27 Then the sovereignty, power and greatness of the kingdoms under the whole heaven will be handed over to the saints, the people of the Most High. His kingdom will be an everlasting kingdom, and all rulers will worship and obey him.*

How can one know God's kingdom will last forever? Because God, through Daniel, accurately prophesied when four successive earthly kingdoms would rise and fall and when His kingdom would be established; God controls the universe. This is the same point made in *Revelation 3* when John envisions God upon His throne, the center of the entire universe. The eternal nature of the kingdom is emphasized when John saw 144,000 sealed on earth and a numberless band of those who had already come through tribulation to inherit heaven. The point: the kingdom of God carries a Christian from this life to the next without affecting his citizenship; the kingdom of heaven and its citizens are eternal. *Revelation 22:5* also states that saints "shall reign forever."

Daniel is an awesome book with a glorious message — God is eternal and so is His kingdom. By first understanding the meaning of *Daniel*, the reader will be able to proceed to the book of *Revelation* with great expectation of understanding. Once readers understand the sealed material, they have experienced a true "revelation." Those who received the letter in the first century were told they would be "blessed if they read, understood, and took to heart" the message of the book. Two thousand years ago John's material was truly a "revelation" to those early readers.

Having explored Daniel's sealed message, look with excitement as we proceed to discover many images and visions in the book of *Ezekiel* that will appear in *Revelation*.

Chapter Seven

John used the Imagery of Ezekiel

Earlier evidence linked John, the author of *Revelation*, with Daniel and Ezekiel as "authors in exile." Some prophets who wrote concerning the captivity of Israel in Babylon did their writing before Nebuchadnezzar's time. Other prophets were post-exilic authors, meaning their prophecies came after Israel's captivity had ended. Two prophets, Daniel and Ezekiel, wrote while they were exiled in Babylon. John, while exiled on the Island of Patmos, used the imagery of Ezekiel as he wrote concerning the opening of the seals Daniel had placed on his prophecy. The previous chapters of this volume explained the link between Daniel's and John's visions; this chapter will explore the connection between John and Ezekiel.

John and Ezekiel Wrote While in Exile

Ezekiel 1:1 In the thirtieth year, in the fourth month on the fifth day, while I was among the exiles by the Kebar River, the heavens were opened and I saw visions of God. On the fifth of the month — it was the fifth year of the exile of King Jehoiachin.

Revelation 1:9 I, John, your brother and companion in the suffering and kingdom and patient endurance that are ours in Jesus, was on the island of Patmos because of the word of God and the testimony of Jesus.

Both Prophets Saw Four Living Creatures

Ezekiel 1:5 And in the fire was what looked like four living creatures.
Ezekiel 10:12 Their entire bodies were completely full of eyes ...
Ezekiel 1:6 ... each ... had four faces and four wings.
Ezekiel 1:10 ... Each ... had the face of a man, and on the right side ... the face of a lion, and on the left the face of an ox; each also had the face of an eagle.
Ezekiel 1:14 The creatures sped back and forth like flashes of lightning.

Revelation 4:6
... In the center, around the throne, were four living creatures, and they were covered with eyes, in front and in back.
Revelation 4:7 The first living creature was like a lion, the second was like an ox, the third had a face like a man, the fourth was like a flying eagle.
Revelation 4:8 Each of the four living creatures had six wings and was covered with eyes all around, even under his wings ..."

There are more similarities than differences when the two visions are paralleled. Both saw living creatures, and each author saw four. The appearance of both sets included a lion, ox, eagle, and man; Ezekiel saw each creature with four faces because he was watching the creatures in motion as they travelled back and forth. John saw the creatures as he viewed a circle surrounding God; he saw all four creatures but mentioned only one face on each. The living creatures seen by both authors were full of eyes, and both prophets saw the creatures in connection with a vision of God. Ezekiel in chapter 10 identifies the living creatures as being Cherubim (high ranking angels).

John and Ezekiel Saw God's Appearance like a Rainbow

*Ezekiel 1:27,28 I saw that from what appeared to be his waist up he looked like glowing metal, as if full of fire, and that from there down he looked like fire; and brilliant light surrounded him. Like the appearance of a **rainbow** in the clouds on a rainy day, so was the radiance around him. This was the appearance of the likeness of the glory of the LORD.*

*Revelation 4:2 At once I was in the Spirit, and there before me was a throne in heaven with someone sitting on it. And the one who sat there had the appearance of jasper and carnelian. A **rainbow**, resembling an emerald, encircled the throne.*

John and Ezekiel Saw Visions While "in the Spirit"

*Ezekiel 2:2 As he spoke, **the Spirit came into me** and raised me to my feet, and I heard him speaking to me.*

*Revelation 1:10 On the Lord's Day **I was in the Spirit**, and I heard behind me a loud voice like a trumpet.*

John and Ezekiel Were Both Given Open Scrolls to Eat

Ezekiel 2:9-3:5
... a hand stretched out to me. In it was a **scroll, which he unrolled** *before me. On both sides of it were written* <u>words of lament and mourning and woe</u>. *And he said to me, "Son of man,* **eat what is before you, eat this scroll**; *then go and speak to the house of Israel." So I opened my mouth, and he gave me the scroll to eat. Then he said to me, "Son of man, eat this scroll I am giving you and fill your stomach with it." So I ate it, and* **it tasted as sweet as honey in my mouth**. *He then said to me: "Son of man,* **go now to the house of Israel and speak my words** *to them. ..."*

Revelation 10:8
"... take the **scroll that lies open** *in the hand of the angel who is standing on the sea and on the land." So I ... asked him to give me the little scroll. He said to me,* **"Take it and eat it**. <u>It will turn your stomach sour</u>, *but* **in your mouth it will be as sweet as honey."** *I took the little scroll from the angel's hand and ate it. It tasted as sweet as honey in my mouth, but when I had eaten it, my stomach turned sour. Then I was told,* **"You must prophesy again** *about many peoples, nations, languages and kings."*

The similarities are astounding. Both Ezekiel and John were given scrolls by a heavenly being. Ezekiel's scroll was unrolled as it was given to him; the first time John saw the scroll it was in the hands of God and secured with seven seals. Jesus had removed all seven seals by the time this scene arrived; thus, it was an open scroll John received. The scroll John saw in the hands of God had writing on both sides; the same is true with the scroll given to Ezekiel. The commandment was given to both writers to eat the scrolls, and both did as instructed. Both prophets experienced a contrast in taste. Ezekiel's scroll was full of mourning and woe, but it tasted sweet; John's scroll tasted sweet, but it turned his stomach sour. The recipients were to internalize the Word of God to the extent it would be a part of them. Both prophets were commissioned to preach what they had ingested. The difference is that Ezekiel was to preach only to Israel; John was to send his message to the entire world, symbolized by four components — peoples, nations, languages, and kings.

John and Ezekiel Were Both Transported from Exile

*Ezekiel 8:3 He stretched out what looked like a hand and took me by the hair of my head. The Spirit lifted me up between earth and heaven and in visions of God he took me to **Jerusalem**, to the entrance to the north gate of the inner court, where the idol that provokes to jealousy stood.*

*Revelation 21:1,2 Then I saw a new heaven and a new earth, for the first heaven and the first earth had passed away, and there was no longer any sea. I saw the Holy City, the **new Jerusalem**, coming down out of heaven from God, prepared as a bride beautifully dressed for her husband.*

Ezekiel was in Babylonian captivity when the visions were given to him; for part of his visions, he was taken by the Spirit to Jerusalem to witness the corruption to which the people of God had succumbed. He was shown four visions of defilement: 1) through a gate, he viewed the "idol of jealousy" that was causing Israel to leave God and drive Him from His sanctuary; 2) he then saw vile paintings on a wall, along with seventy elders who were offering incense to false gods; 3) next he was shown Israelite women weeping over Tammuz, the Babylonian god who was supposedly resurrected every year; 4) lastly, Ezekiel saw twenty-five men in the inner court of the Lord's house who were worshipping the sun. The visions combined utilize the number 4 to further highlight the sinful condition of the Jewish nation.

In the first chapter of *Revelation*, John tells in verse 9 that he was located on Patmos Island because of his testimony about Jesus Christ. In the next verse he relates he was in the Spirit when the visions began to appear. While Ezekiel was transported to Jerusalem to see God's people in degradation, John was given a vision of new Jerusalem to see God's people glorified. Ezekiel saw the sinful condition into which Jerusalem had drifted, highlighting the need for the Redeemer; John saw the beauty of God's people, cleansed by the blood of the Redeemer.

Visions of Jerusalem and New Jerusalem

1. New Jerusalem is another name for the church.

*Hebrews 12:22,23 But you have come to ... the **heavenly Jerusalem**, the city of the living God. You have come to ... **the church** of the firstborn ...*

Not only are the terms heavenly Jerusalem and church used interchangeably, but also the timeframe for heavenly Jerusalem is in the present tense. The scripture above uses the verb have come to indicate that new Jerusalem is in existence now. The same point is made in the *Galatian* letter; notice the present tense verb is.

Galatians 4:26 But the Jerusalem that is above is free, and she is our mother.

John saw new Jerusalem coming down out of heaven as a "bride adorned for her husband." "The Bride of Christ" is another name for new Jerusalem and for the church.

Ephesians 5:25-27 Husbands, love your wives, just as Christ loved the church and gave himself up for her to make her holy, cleansing her by the washing with water through the word, and to present her to himself as a radiant church, without stain or wrinkle or any other blemish, but holy and blameless.

II Corinthians 11:2 I am jealous for you with a godly jealousy. I promised you to one husband, to Christ, so that I might present you as a pure virgin to him.

The Jews were chosen for a purpose — for Jesus Christ to come into the world. Once Jesus died, the emphasis changed from a national kingdom to a spiritual one; part of the change was in the seat of government. Under the old law, Jerusalem was the capitol city, but Jesus Christ placed His followers in a heavenly kingdom.

Philippians 3:20 But our citizenship is in heaven. And we eagerly await a Savior from there, the Lord Jesus Christ.

2. Jerusalem's citizens were Jews; spiritual Jerusalem's citizens are those born into the kingdom of God.

Jesus' death not only brought a shift of emphasis from physical Jerusalem to spiritual Jerusalem, but also a shift in the citizens from those born as Jews to those who are born into the spiritual kingdom of God. Jesus informed Nicodemus that a man cannot enter the kingdom of God until he is born again.

> *John 3:3-5 In reply Jesus declared, "I tell you the truth, no one can see the kingdom of God unless he is born again." "How can a man be born when he is old?" Nicodemus asked. "Surely he cannot enter a second time into his mother's womb to be born!" Jesus answered, "I tell you the truth, no one can enter the kingdom of God unless he is born of water and the Spirit."*

According to Jesus' words in the scripture above, when one is born again, he enters the kingdom of God; this places one's citizenship in "new Jerusalem." If one is a citizen of "spiritual Jerusalem," what does this say about his status?

> *Romans 2:28,29 A man is not a Jew if he is only one outwardly, nor is circumcision merely outward and physical. No, a man is a Jew if he is one inwardly; and circumcision is circumcision of the heart, by the Spirit, not by the written code. Such a man's praise is not from men, but from God.*

Paul furthered the concept of "spiritual Israel" in the third chapter of *Galatians*. God made a promise to Abraham that the entire world would be blessed by his offspring. Jesus Christ was to come through the family line of Abraham to bless the whole world through His sacrifice for sin. Whoever is in Jesus Christ partakes of this promise and is, therefore, a child of Abraham.

> *Galatians 3:6-9 Consider Abraham: "He believed God, and it was credited to him as righteousness." Understand, then, that **those who believe are children of Abraham**. The Scripture foresaw that God would justify the Gentiles by faith, and announced the gospel in advance to Abraham: "All nations will be blessed*

through you." So those who have faith are blessed along with Abraham, the man of faith.

To those who are victorious over the pressures of the world, God has made a beautiful promise indicating the change of status or the new birth into "spiritual Jerusalem."

Revelation 3:12 Him who overcomes I will make a pillar in the temple of my God. Never again will he leave it. I will write on him the name of my God and the name of the city of my God, the new Jerusalem, which is coming down out of heaven from my God; and I will also write on him my new name.

3. The Jewish system of worship was a picture of worship in the church today.

Inspired writers claim the events that affected Israel and the pattern of worship prescribed for Jewish worship were pictures of Christian worship today.

Colossians 2:17 These are a shadow of the things that were to come; the reality, however, is found in Christ.

Hebrews 8:5 They serve at a sanctuary that is a copy and shadow of what is in heaven. This is why Moses was warned when he was about to build the tabernacle: "See to it that you make everything according to the pattern shown you on the mountain."

4. The old Jewish system and the spiritual Jewish system represent God's people throughout time.

Jesus came to bring the two groups into one body; His blood completed the sacrifices that were performed under the Old Law, and His one-time sacrifice was all needed for the rest of earth-time. The first passage below indicates Christ's blood was shed for those under the Old Law; the second proves He needed to die only once for all sins to be forgiven.

> *Hebrews 9:15 ... Christ is the mediator of a new covenant, that those who are called may receive the promised eternal inheritance — now that he has died as a ransom to set them free from the sins committed under the first covenant.*
>
> *Hebrews 9:28 So Christ was sacrificed once to take away the sins of many people; and he will appear a second time, not to bear sin, but to bring salvation to those who are waiting for him.*

There was a time God favored Israel as the chosen people through whom Jesus would enter the world, but for God to favor national Israel today would be contrary to the message received by Peter before going to the household of Cornelius.

> *Acts 10:34,35 Then Peter began to speak: "I now realize how true it is that God does not show favoritism but accepts men from every nation who fear him and do what is right."*

Either God favors physical Israel, OR He favors spiritual Israel, the redeemed of every nation and culture who are united in God's spiritual kingdom; the two positions are mutually exclusive. Physical Jerusalem fell in 70 AD because of its rejection and execution of the Messiah. It is apparent God's chosen people today are those who have accepted Jesus Christ to become part of God's eternal kingdom. To conclude the point, the blood of bulls and goats was replaced with the one time sacrifice of Jesus Christ. Jerusalem is no longer the center of God's religion; Jerusalem was replaced by new Jerusalem, the church. God used Jesus to bless the entire world by coming through the Jewish nation; Jesus was born 70 – 80 years before John wrote the book of *Revelation*. From all evidence, the collapse of Jerusalem and the writing of *Revelation* came within ten years of each other. Jerusalem fell in 70 AD, and as earlier indicated, *Revelation* was written between 69 AD and 79 AD during the reign of Vespasian.

John and Ezekiel Foresaw the Sealing of God's People

*Ezekiel 9:2-5 And I saw six men coming from the direction of the upper gate, ... With them was a man clothed in linen who had a writing kit at his side. ... Then the LORD called to the man clothed in linen who had the writing kit ..."Go throughout the city of Jerusalem and put a **mark on the foreheads** of those who grieve and lament over all the detestable things that are done in it." As I listened, he said to the others, "Follow him through the city and kill, without showing pity or compassion."*

*Revelation 7:2-3 ... Then I saw another angel coming up from the east, having the seal of the living God. He called out in a loud voice to the four angels who had been given power to harm the land and the sea: "Do not harm the land or the sea or the trees until we put a **seal on the foreheads** of the servants of our God."*

Marking the people of God identified and protected them from approaching disaster. Ezekiel envisioned harm coming from the sword; John observed winds of destruction. God knows each and every one of His followers; none will face ultimate harm. More will follow about the 144,000 John saw marked with the seal of God.

John and Ezekiel Envisioned Death from Four Means

*Ezekiel 14:21 "I send against Jerusalem my four dreadful judgments — **sword** and **famine** and **wild beasts** and **plague** — to kill its men and their animals!"*

*Revelation 6:8 Death, and Hades ... were given power over a fourth of the earth to kill by **sword**, **famine** and **plague**, and by the **wild beasts** of the earth.*

John and Ezekiel Both Used the Vine As an Analogy

*Ezekiel 15:2-6 ... is the wood of a vine better than that of a branch on any of the trees in the forest? Is wood ever taken from it to make anything useful? Do they make pegs from it to hang things on? And after it is thrown on the fire as fuel and the fire burns both ends and chars the middle, is it then useful for anything? If **it was not useful for anything** when it was whole, how much less can it be made into something useful when the fire has burned it and it is charred? ... As I have given the wood of the vine among the trees of the forest as fuel for the fire, so will I treat the people living in Jerusalem.*

*Revelation 14:18-20 Still another angel, who had charge of the fire, came from the altar and called in a loud voice to him who had the sharp sickle, "Take your sharp sickle and gather the clusters of grapes from the **earth's vine**, because its grapes are ripe." The angel swung his sickle on the earth, gathered its grapes and threw them into the great winepress of God's wrath.*

The imagery of the vine is another link between the Old and New Testaments. Since Jesus came through the Israelite nation, the vine is a perfect picture to explain the connection. Israel was a degenerate vine, but when it ushered in the King of kings and Lord of lords, a new vine was introduced into the world. Jesus is the true vine, and He claims Christians are the branches of that vine.

John 15:5 I am the vine; you are the branches. If a man remains in me and I in him, he will bear much fruit; apart from me you can do nothing.

Both Authors Wrote about the Cup of God's Wrath

Ezekiel 23:32,33
*This is what the Sovereign LORD says: "You will drink your sister's cup, a cup large and deep; it will bring scorn and derision, for it holds so much. You will be filled with drunkenness and sorrow, the **cup of ruin and desolation,** the cup of your sister Samaria."*

*Revelation 14:9,10 A third angel followed them and said in a loud voice: "If anyone worships the beast and his image and receives his mark on the forehead or on the hand, he, too, will drink of the wine of God's fury, which has been poured full strength into the **cup of his wrath**. He will be tormented with burning sulfur in the presence of the holy angels and of the Lamb."*

Ezekiel and John Both Wrote Concerning an Evil City

1. Both cities had allies who discarded them.

As long as Tyre and Rome were powers and were flourishing, all those who had a part with them thrived and enjoyed the good times. But when the collapse began, former friends began to depart like "fleas off a dead dog." They may have mourned the fall, but the grieving was done from a distance. They did nothing to prevent the occurrence.

Ezekiel 26:16-18
*... all the **princes of the coast** will ... lament ...*
*27:29-32 All who handle the oars will abandon their ships; the **mariners and all the seamen** will stand on the shore. ... they will take up a lament ... "Who was ever silenced like Tyre, surrounded by the sea?"*
*Ezekiel 27:35,36 .... The **merchants** among the nations hiss at you; you have come to a horrible end and will be no more.*

*Revelation 18:9,10 ... the **kings of the earth** ... will weep and mourn over her. "Woe! Woe, O great city, O Babylon, city of power!*
*18:15-18 The **merchants** ... will weep and mourn ... Every sea captain, and all who travel by ship, the sailors, and all who **earn their living** from the sea, will stand far off. When they see the smoke of her burning, they will exclaim, 'Was there ever a city like this great city?'*

2. Both cities thought themselves to be invincible.

*Ezekiel 27:3 ... You say, O Tyre, "**I am perfect in beauty**." Ezekiel 28:2 In the pride of your heart you say, "**I am a god; I sit on the throne of a god in the heart of the seas.**" But you are a man and not a god...*

*Revelation 18:7 Give her as much torture and grief as the glory and luxury she gave herself. In her heart she boasts, "**I sit as queen; I am not a widow, and I will never mourn**"*

Each of these cities was the showcase of its time; their geographic location gave them military superiority because they were not land locked and surrounded by enemies. Tyre was an island, and Rome was located on a peninsula. Not only were they militarily superior, but they also controlled international trade; other nations became dependent upon them. The collapse of either nation was never considered as a possibility. **As the old adage goes, "The bigger they are, the harder they fall!"**

3. Both cities were destroyed.

Ezekiel 28:19 All the nations who knew you are appalled at you; you have come to a horrible end and will be no more.

Revelation 18:18 When they see the smoke of her burning, they will exclaim, "Was there ever a city like this great city?"

4. Both cities had an extensive list of goods lost in trade.

Ezekiel 27:12-24
Tarshish — exchanged silver, iron, tin and lead ... Greece, Tubal and Meshech exchanged slaves and articles of bronze ... Beth Togarmah — work horses, war horses and mules ... Rhodes — ivory tusks and ebony. Aram — turquoise, purple fabric, embroidered work, fine linen, coral and rubies ... Judah and Israel — wheat from Minnith and confections, honey, oil and balm ... Damascus — wine from Helbon and wool from Zahar. Danites and Greeks from Uzal — wrought iron, cassia and calamus ... Dedan — saddle blankets ... Arabia — lambs, rams and goats. Sheba and Raamah — the finest of all kinds of spices and precious stones, and gold. Haran, Canneh and Eden and merchants of Sheba, Asshur and Kilmad — beautiful garments, blue fabric, embroidered work and multicolored rugs with cords twisted and tightly knotted.

Revelation 18:11-13
... merchants of the earth will weep and mourn over her because no one buys their cargoes any more — Cargoes of gold, silver, precious stones and pearls; fine linen, purple, silk and scarlet cloth; every sort of citron wood, and articles of every kind made of ivory, costly wood, bronze, iron and marble; ... cinnamon and spice, of incense, myrrh and frankincense, of wine and olive oil, of fine flour and wheat; cattle and sheep; horses and carriages; and bodies and souls of men.

Both Authors Envisioned Destruction of God's Enemy

*Ezekiel 32:21-31 From within the grave the mighty leaders will say of Egypt and her allies, They have come down and they lie with the uncircumcised, with those killed by the sword. Assyria is there ... Elam is there ... They bear their shame with those **who go down to the pit**; they are laid among the slain. Meshech and Tubal are there ... You too, O Pharaoh, will be broken and will lie among the uncircumcised, with those killed by the sword. Edom is there ... All the princes of the north and all the Sidonians are there ... Pharaoh — he and all his arm — will see them and he will be consoled for all his hordes that were killed by the sword, declares the Sovereign LORD.*

*Revelation 19:19-21 Then I saw the beast and the kings of the earth and their armies gathered together to make war against the rider on the horse and his army. But the beast was captured, and with him the false prophet who had performed the miraculous signs on his behalf. With these signs he had deluded those who had received the mark of the beast and worshiped his image. The two of them were **thrown alive into the fiery lake of burning sulfur**. The rest of them were killed with the sword that came out of the mouth of the rider on the horse, and all the birds gorged themselves on their flesh.*

Each Prophet Tells of a Resurrection of God's People

Ezekiel saw a valley of bones so dry there could be no hope of life. He was asked, "Can these bones live?" This seemingly futile situation was reversed when God brought the bones to life before Ezekiel's eyes. The purpose of this vision is explained below:

Ezekiel 37:13,14 Then you, my people, will know that I am the LORD, when I open your graves and bring you up from them. I will put my Spirit in you and you will live, and I will settle you in your own land. Then you will know that I the LORD have spoken, and I have done it, declares the LORD.

John saw the two witnesses of God lying slain in the street; the witnesses are symbolized by "candlesticks," which chapter 1 of *Revelation* identifies as churches. These witnesses were also brought back to life to prove God's people are protected.

> *Revelation 11:11 But after the three and a half days a breath of life from God entered them, and they stood on their feet, and terror struck those who saw them. Then they heard a loud voice from heaven saying to them, "Come up here." And they went up to heaven in a cloud, while their enemies looked on.*

Jesus Was Seen as King by Both Writers

Luke 1:32 He will be great and will be called the Son of the Most High. The Lord God will give him the throne of his father David.

Ezekiel had prophesied the information confirmed in *Luke 1:32* connecting Jesus to David. John and Ezekiel make similar statements in the following comparison.

Ezekiel 37:24 My servant David will be king over them, and they will all have one shepherd. They will follow my laws and be careful to keep my decrees.	*Revelation 17:14 ... Lamb will overcome them ... he is Lord of lords and King of kings ...* *Revelation 19:16 he has this name written: KING OF KINGS AND LORD OF LORDS.*

Gog and Magog Play a Role for Both Ezekiel and John

Ezekiel 38:2 Son of man, set your face against Gog, of the land of Magog ... *Ezekiel 38:15 ... all of them riding on horses, a great horde, a mighty army.*	*Revelation 20:8 ... to deceive the nations in the four corners of the earth —Gog and Magog — to gather them for battle. In number they are like the sand on the seashore.*

Ezekiel saw Gog as a person and Magog as a place; John's vision could be interpreted that both are persons or that both are places, but they belong in the same category. Because of the shift in meaning, Gog and Magog are obviously symbolic; information will be covered in future chapters to interpret the meaning of these important symbols.

Both Saw the Temple Measured for Perfection

Ezekiel 40:3 ... I saw a man whose appearance was like bronze; he was standing in the gateway with a linen cord and a measuring rod in his hand.

Revelation 21:15 The angel who talked with me had a measuring rod of gold to measure the city, its gates and its walls.

Both Writers Saw Beautiful Cities

*Ezekiel 40:2
In visions of God he took me to the land of Israel and set me on a very high mountain, on whose south side were some buildings that looked* **like a city**.

*Revelation 21:16
The city was laid out like a square, as long as it was wide. He measured the city with the rod and found it to be 12,000 stadia in length, and as wide and high as it is long.*

Ezekiel gives great clues that the temple he describes is one that will never be built on earthly soil. The description of the city, temple, worship items, and people of God are covered in *Ezekiel*, chapters 40 through 48. There is nothing in history to indicate this physical temple was ever constructed. The imagery is so close to that in *Revelation* that one can conclude Ezekiel saw the same vision seen by John about six hundred years later. The vision of both writers applies to a spiritual city; "new Jerusalem" is being pictured in the visions. Perhaps Ezekiel's greatest clue of all is in the name of the city. The last verse of *Ezekiel* states that the name of the city is — **THE LORD IS THERE**. Several comparisons will establish the link between the two cities:

1. The gates of both cities symbolize the twelve tribes.

Ezekiel 48:31-34 The gates of the city will be named after the tribes of Israel. The three gates on the north side will be the gate of Reuben, the gate of Judah and the gate of Levi. On the east side, which is 4,500 cubits long, will be three gates: the gate of Joseph, the gate of Benjamin and the gate of Dan. On the south side, which measures 4,500 cubits, will be three gates: the gate of Simeon, the gate of Issachar and the gate of Zebulun. On the west side, which is 4,500 cubits long, will be three gates: the gate of Gad, the gate of Asher and the gate of Naphtali.

Revelation 21:12,13 It had a great, high wall with twelve gates, and with twelve angels at the gates. On the gates were written the names of the twelve tribes of Israel. There were three gates on the east, three on the north, three on the south and three on the west.
Revelation 21:15 The angel who talked with me had a measuring rod of gold to measure the city, its gates and its walls.

2. The focal point in each city was the temple of God.

Ezekiel 44:4 Then the man brought me by way of the north gate to the front of the temple. I looked and saw the glory of the LORD filling the temple of the LORD, and I fell facedown.

Revelation 21:22 I did not see a temple in the city, because the Lord God Almighty and the Lamb are its temple.

Only one passage was selected from *Ezekiel* for the comparison, but much time is spent in the measuring of the temple. In fact most of the last nine chapters are dedicated to the temple itself. The detailed plans given to Ezekiel were never used to build an earthly temple; John says there is no need for an earthly temple today; God is the temple in His spiritual city. The spiritual city, as clarified earlier, is "new Jerusalem"! Ezekiel was looking forward to its coming; John wrote about its existence.

3. Ezekiel and John saw a river flowing from the temple.

Ezekiel 47:1 ... I saw water coming out from under the threshold of the temple toward the east (for the temple faced east). Ezekiel 47:6 ... he led me back to the bank of the river.

Rev 22:1 Then the angel showed me the river of the water of life, as clear as crystal, flowing from the throne of God and of the Lamb.

4. Ezekiel and John saw eternal trees on each side of the river.

Ezekiel 47:12 Fruit trees of all kinds will grow on both banks of the river. Their leaves will not wither, nor will their fruit fail. Every month they will bear, because the water from the sanctuary flows to them.

Revelation 22:2 Down the middle of the great street of the city. On each side of the river stood the tree of life ...

5. The leaves of the trees were for healing.

*Ezekiel 47:12 ... Their fruit will serve for food and their leaves for **healing**."*

*Revelation 22:2 ... the leaves of the tree are for the **healing** of the nations.*

The imagery taken from Ezekiel's visions is used by John to tell of the opening of the seals of Daniel; the three exilic prophets are brought together in a beautiful way. So far, background material has been presented concerning *Daniel*, *Ezekiel*, and ancient history. Along with these valuable tools, having a background concerning number symbols in the Bible will prove to be extremely valuable in understanding the book of *Revelation*. This will be our next task as we proceed to chapter 8 and number symbols.

Chapter Eight

Number Symbols in *Revelation*

A second major tool that must be understood deals with the symbolism of numbers. Upon reading *Revelation*, one becomes aware that numbers play a significant role. Vincent Hopper in his book *Medieval Number Symbolism* quotes Augustine:

> Concerning now the science of number, it is clear to the dullest apprehension that this was not created by man, but was discovered by invention ... It is not in man's power to determine at his pleasure that 3 X 3 are not 9, or do not make a square, or are not the triple of 3 ... By investigation, therefore, man may discover the mysteries of God which are set down in Scripture. Tertullian once charged Marcus with the statement that Christ, in calling himself the Alpha and Omega, authorized the search for numerical values. This could be claimed because Greek letters each had numerical value.

Hopper wrote that *Revelation* was tremendously popular through the fourth century because the numbers throughout the book encouraged and demanded study and thought.

It is rather interesting when one learns the study of number symbols had its roots in Babylon — the very place where Daniel lived when his prophecies were made. Herbert G. May in *Studies in Biblical and Semitic Symbolism* said on p. 94:

> In fact, one may safely say that ... Pythagoras, who is usually looked upon as the father of symbolism of numbers was really the heir of a science which had its origin in Southern Babylonia some 3,000 years ago.

The *Funk and Wagnall's Encyclopedia* estimates that Pythagoras lived somewhere between 582 and 500 BC; this would have been during the very time Israel was exiled in Babylon. Isn't it amazing how history and the Bible come together! Pythagoras did not create number symbolism; he simply discovered what was already there, begun by Moses some 1,000 years earlier in writing the Pentateuch.

Jesus underscored the symbolic nature of numbers when he asked his disciples a question demanding a numerical answer. As the following scripture is read, one should become aware that the last question Jesus asked would have been absolutely meaningless if numbers had no symbolic meaning.

> *Mark 8:18-21 "Do you have eyes but fail to see, and ears but fail to hear? ... When I broke the five loaves for the five thousand, how many basketfuls of pieces did you pick up?" "Twelve," they replied. "And when I broke the seven loaves for the four thousand, how many basketfuls of pieces did you pick up?" They answered, "Seven." He said to them, "Do you still not understand?"*

Throughout the Bible, the number <u>40</u> appears too many times to be mere coincidence — the flood lasted 40 days; Moses was on the Mount of God for 40 days to receive the Law; Jonah preached to Nineveh for 40 days; Israel wandered in the wilderness for 40 years; Jesus fasted for 40 days; Jesus was on earth 40 days between the resurrection and the ascension into heaven.

Revelation uses numbers almost as a second language. If numbers had not been used symbolically before the writing of *Revelation*, the reader would have been somewhat handicapped in understanding the message; however, this is not the case. *Genesis* has its share of symbolic numbers with a 7 day creation, a 40 day flood, 10 plagues, 10 commandments, 12 tribes, and many more. When the number is stated explicitly, the reader can see it and analyze it much more easily; however, sometimes the number is found within a list and is much more subtle in nature.

How, one may ask, can a person determine the symbolic meaning of numbers? When certain numbers are used in connection with the same concepts, the conclusion can be drawn by the link between the number and the concept, item, or symbol. This is much the same way one arrives at words to symbolize objects. If a person sees an eight inch long object that is four inches wide and two inches thick, he may not know what to call it at first because of lack of familiarity. However, if he hears enough people call the object "brick," he can soon link the object with the word. Through the years, many persons have analyzed numbers and their symbolic value.

Number symbols are important, but a warning needs to be issued. Just as words are sometimes literal and sometimes symbolic, numbers can be used in the same way. Jesus at one time spoke of tearing down the literal "temple" of Jerusalem, but He also spoke of rebuilding the "temple," referring to His bodily resurrection. In one sense it was literal and in the other it was figurative. At times a number may indicate a fact, but at other times the number may be symbolic. **One needs to pray and learn to discern!** Chapter 9 of this volume will begin the chapter-by-chapter analysis of *Revelation,* and many comments will be made concerning number symbols involved in certain passages. This material will establish the basis for the analysis of numbers in *Revelation* to assist the reader in having a more complete understanding of the book.

The number [1]

The number 1, according to a fifth century writer, Martianus Capella in *De Nuptiis*, is the monad; it is the principle number. There is one Father of all, one God, one world, one sun. Pythagoreanism said everything proceeded from the One. In recent years the great physicist Stephen Hawkings stated, "Everything began with a singularity." I wonder if he realized what that statement suggests. Just as all numbers come from the one, all of creation came from God.

> *Deuteronomy 6:4   Hear, O Israel: The LORD our God, the LORD is one.*

Since the time man chose to walk a path away from God, God's plan has been designed to bring everything back to the unity of one.

> *I Corinthians 15:28 When he has done this, then the Son himself will be made subject to him who put everything under him, so that God may be all in all.*

God's plan is summed up in one name — **Jesus**! It is through Jesus Christ that all are to be brought back to God, and in the end all will return to one.

> *Galatians 3:28 There is neither Jew nor Greek, slave nor free, male nor female, for you are all one in Christ Jesus.*

The number [2]

The number 2, according to Capella, was the dyad and was considered evil because it created division. It probably isn't significant, but it is rather interesting that in *Genesis*, the second day of creation was the only one in which God did not say, "It is good."

Unclean animals went into the ark in 2's while the clean animals went into the ark in groups of 7.

Two is the first number that can be divided; the Bible has many examples of this divisibility. On the second day of creation God separated the water in the firmament from the water on the earth.

Division can also be seen in struggles between famous Bible pairs such as Cain and Abel, Saul and David, Esau and Jacob, etc. There is the choice between light and darkness, and judgment will separate the sheep from the goats. Some have asked about the two divisions of the Bible — Old Testament and the New Testament; both are good. That is true, but the covenants were in effect one at a time; in writing about the two covenants, the writer of *Hebrews* had this to say:

> *Hebrews 10:9,10 Then he said, "Here I am, I have come to do your will." He sets aside the first to establish the second. And by that will, we have been made holy through the sacrifice of the body of Jesus Christ once for all.*

The number [3]

The number 3, according to Capella, was the triad and was the first to have a beginning, middle, and end. It is considered one of the four perfect numbers and is the ideal form. Hopper says the 3, by its relation to the godhead, becomes a number of perfection. The number 3 appears quite frequently in *Revelation* and relates to the three-fold nature of the godhead. God has 3 major functions fulfilled through His 3 roles as Father, Son, and Spirit; God has 3 great characteristics — omniscience (all knowing), omnipresence (presence everywhere), and omnipotence (all powerful). Ethelbert W. Bullinger wrote in *Number in Scripture,* p. 107:

> All things that are especially complete are stamped with this number three. God's attributes are three: omniscience, omnipresence, and omnipotence. There are three great divisions completing time — past, present, and future. Three persons, in grammar, express and include all the relationships of mankind. Thought, word, and deed complete the sum of human capability. Three degrees of comparison complete our knowledge of qualities. ... Three kingdoms embrace our ideas of matter — mineral, vegetable, and animal.

Jesus holds three offices — Prophet, Priest, and King; the statement "King of the Jews" was written above the cross in three languages. In emphasizing the work of the trinity in the writing of the book of *Revelation,* John uses many sets of 3 in chapter 1.

The number [4]

The number 4 represents the world. Capella called it the tetrad and said it deals with solidity; he claimed man has four ages, four vices, and four virtues. Hopper, in *Medieval Number Symbolism*, says on p. 84:

> Four by the known analogues of the four winds, the four elements, the four seasons, and the four rivers is specifically the number of the "mundane sphere."

Four, therefore, is the number of the world. The number 4 is used frequently in *Revelation*; when this occurs, it refers to the world, worldliness, or worldly people. Aristotle said there are 4 great elements — earth, air, fire, and water. In *Genesis* the 10th chapter, the generations of the families of the sons of Noah were numbered with a four-fold criterion in the first census taken in the world. In verse 5 the criteria is listed as lands, tongues, families, nations. In verse 20 it is called families, tongues, countries, and nations. Then in verse 31 it is called families, tongues, lands, and nations. This sounds much like the worldly people referred to in *Revelation* as nations, tongues, tribes, and peoples. When the world or worldliness is involved, other labels are used in *Revelation*, but the clusters are listed in groups of 4. Earlier material has already covered the 4 great powers from the time of Daniel to the time of John.

LARGE NUMBERS MUST BE STUDIED BY ANALYZING THEIR COMPOSITION

Before going any further, it is important to understand relationships that numbers have to each other. Hopper, in *Medieval Number Symbolism*, says on p. 82:

> All large numbers are reduced to their roots for explanation. Strictly speaking, adding numbers sums up their significance into a single unit. Multiplying diffuses a property into a given number of directions or objects. Squaring gives extension. Cubing either produces solidity, or, more often, gives height or godliness.

Therefore, when numbers occur like 144,000, the analyst must look to its roots — 12 X 12 equals 144, and 10 X 10 X 10 equals 1,000 which will be multiplied by 144. To understand the number, one must understand the 12 and the 10. To understand the 12, one must understand the 3 and the 4. Numbers gain more power when added, multiplied, squared, or cubed, and in that order.

The number [5]

Five is an interesting number; Ethelbert W. Bullinger on p. 135 of *Number in Scripture* discusses the number 5 by explaining that 5 is symbolic of God's Grace. He notes that the promise made to Abraham by God was sealed with 5 sacrifices: a heifer, a goat, a ram, a dove, and a pigeon (*Genesis* 15:9), and he further states that the tabernacle had 5 as its all pervading number; nearly every measurement was a multiple of 5.

The holy anointing oil of *Exodus* 30:23-25 was composed of 5 parts — four spices including myrrh, cinnamon, calamus, and cassia, along with one hin of olive oil. The incense also was composed of 5 parts — four were spices such as stacte, on'ycha, gal'banum, and frankincense, along with one measure of salt. These were all ways of receiving the grace of God. In the seventh chapter of *Revelation*, four angels held back destructive winds until the fifth angel arrived from the East with the seal of God to identify His followers.

The number [6]

Since man was created on the 6th day, the number of humanity is 6. This will be tremendously important to remember when analyzing the number of the beast, 666. The number 6 is derived by multiplying the 2 and the 3. Philo Judaeus, who lived between 30 BC and 50 AD, wrote in *De Opificio Mundi*,

> For among things that are, it is the odd that is male, and the even female. Now of odd numbers 3 is the starting point, and of even numbers 2, and the product of these two is 6.

Goliath was 6 cubits tall; he had 6 pieces of military equipment, and his armor weighed 600 shekels. Nebuchadnezzar created a gold idol that was 600 cubits tall and 6 cubits wide. When 6 types of instruments were played, people were to fall down and worship the image. Solomon imported 666 talents of gold into his kingdom each year (II *Chronicles 9:13*). Satan was called by 6 different names in *Revelation*, and in *Revelation 13:18* the number of the beast is said to be a man's number; the number of the beast is 666. The meaning of the number 6, will help clarify this controversial passage later in this volume. Mankind's failures stem from his own humanity; the number 6 highlights the finite nature of man. I find it disconcerting that some Bible versions remove God's numbers when they resort to feet and inches rather than cubits. I believe this to be a mistake; God's numbers are important!

The number [7]

The number 7 is the second of the perfect numbers. The 3 symbolizes the perfectness of the godhead; the 7 symbolizes the perfection of man gained through the forgiveness of God. In *II Kings 5*, Naaman was required to dip in the Jordan River seven times to cure the unclean disease of leprosy. Jesus told His followers to forgive their brothers seven times in *Luke 17:4*; when Peter tried to take the 7 literally, Jesus told Peter to forgive 70 X 7. Man, because of his human nature, cannot live a perfect life; however, he can be perfected through forgiveness, symbolized by the number 7.

In *Revelation* this number is used quite frequently — there are 7 stars, 7 churches, 7 angels, 7 letters, 7 thunders, 7 spirits, 7 seals, 7 trumpets, and 7 vials.

The number [8]

Eight is the first number to be reached by a cube — 2 X 2 X 2. Hopper on p. 85 of *Medieval Number Symbolism* said about the number 8:

> [There is significance in the] seven-fold nature of the world and the resurrection of Christ on the eighth day,

> the day of circumcision and the first day of the second week ... Rest was appointed to the Sabbath, and Regeneration to the number eight.

To illustrate that 8 is the number of rejuvenation and regeneration, it might be noted that the number 8 was significant in the flood. According to *I Peter 3:20*, eight souls survived the destruction of the flood to begin a new world. Circumcision was to be performed on the eighth day as stated in *Genesis 17:12*. *Exodus 22:29,30*, states that the first-born was to be given to Jehovah on the eighth day. Augustine said in *Contra Faustura*, XVI, p. 29:

> Since the universe is constituted in the number 7, the number 8 is the number of immortality.

When Abraham was promised the Messiah would come through his family line, the covenant was sealed with three 8's. In *Genesis 17*, God confirmed the agreement by adding one letter to Abram's name, the Hebrew letter ה, which is also the symbol for the number 8. Sarai's name was changed by the addition of the letter ה — once again, the number 8. To finalize the agreement, God established the ordinance of circumcising all male children on the 8th day after birth. **What better way to tell Abram that 888 would come through his family line than to seal the covenant with three 8's!!!** *You Can Count On It* explains that the number of Jesus' name is 888; each Greek letter is also a Greek number. By adding each number within the name of Jesus, one arrives at the number 888.

Isaac and David are linked with Christ because of the number 8. Abraham had 8 sons. Seven of these were born under normal circumstances. One stands out among the **8**, **Isaac**; he came through promise and had a miraculous birth. Isaac is a perfect symbol of Christ, being the only begotten son of Sarah and Father Abraham. He was also a sacrifice and was the promised seed through whom the world would be blessed. Jesus was to take the throne of David; **David was the 8th** son of Jesse. Since the number 7 constitutes completeness, the number 8 begins the next set. Having risen from the dead on the first day of the week, it can be said Jesus rose from the dead on the eighth day.

The number [9]

Bullinger, on p. 235, states that the 9 is the number of finality or judgment; furthermore, he states:

> The numerical value of the word <u>Dan</u>, which means judge, is 54 (9 X 6) ... the sieges of Jerusalem have been 27 in number, or three times nine.

The number <u>9</u> is powerful because it is composed of the number of the godhead, 3, squared. It is also intriguing because when 9 is multiplied by any single digit number, the sum of the product totals nine.

9 x 2 = 18;	1 + 8 = **9**	9 x 3 = 27;	2 + 7 = **9**
9 x 4 = 36;	3 + 6 = **9**	9 x 5 = 45;	4 + 5 = **9**
9 x 6 = 54;	5 + 4 = **9**	9 x 7 = 63;	6 + 3 = **9**
9 x 8 = 72;	7 + 2 = **9**	9 x 9 = 81;	8 + 1 = **9**

It is no coincidence that Jesus died in the ninth hour!

The judgments of God prophesied by Haggai are enumerated in 9 ways:

> *Haggai 1:11   I called for a drought on the (1) fields and the (2) mountains, on the (3) grain, the (4) new wine, the (5) oil and (6) whatever the ground produces, on (7) men and (8) cattle, and on the (9) labor of your hands."*

The number [10]

Ten is the third of the perfect numbers. The number <u>3</u> is the perfectness of the godhead; the <u>7</u> is the perfection of man through God's forgiveness; the number <u>10</u> is a combination of the <u>3</u> and the <u>7</u>; it signifies completeness or totality. Pythagoras saw the number 10 as a natural expression of totality; it is a total of the first four numbers — 1+2+3+4. Maurice Farbridge in *Studies in Biblical and Semitic Symbolism* states on p. 143:

> The symbolism of "ten" has been accounted for in many ways. As we have already noted, according to some scholars its symbolic importance arose because it is the basis of the decimal system; according to others because it is the sum of the two numbers three and seven, themselves symbolical.

God sent 10 plagues on Egypt, and He gave 10 commandments at Mount Sinai. Tithing requested one-tenth of the Jews' wealth to be contributed. Ten virgins trimmed their lamps in *Matthew 25*.

The number 10, when cubed, yields the powerful number 1,000. When the Bible says that God will be faithful to 1,000 generations, it means ALL OF THEM. The passages below illustrate the power of the number 1,000.

> *I Chronicles 16:15 He remembers his covenant forever, the word he commanded, for a thousand generations ...*
>
> *Psalms 105:8 He remembers his covenant forever, the word he commanded, for a thousand generations ...*

The number 12

The number 12 is the fourth of the perfect numbers. The 3 signifies the perfectness of the godhead; 7, the perfection of forgiven saints; 10, the number of completeness and totality. The number 12 relates to God's reaction with and interrelation to man; similar to the 7, the 12 is formed by the interaction of the numbers 3 and 4. Augustine in *On John* XLIX, p. 8, stated:

> For 12, rightly considered, is merely another form of 7 since both are composed of 3 and 4. Christ chose 12 disciples to indicate himself and the Spiritual Day and to make known His Trinity through the 4 parts of the world.

Jesus' choice of 12 apostles is no coincidence. This was God's ordained number for working with Israel under the Old Covenant, and it would be His ordained number for apostle selection under the New.

As stated above, the organization of the Old Covenant was based on the number 12. Jacob had 12 sons, and his family formed the 12 tribes of Israel. It would have been simple for each son to father the tribe that bore his name and for the name of that tribe to be used for all occasions; however, this was not always the case. When tribes were assembled for various purposes and Joseph was listed as a tribe, the obvious listing of the twelve sons was used. However, when it came to the distribution of land, Levi was not included in the land dispersion; the number 12 was important enough that Joseph's two sons, Ephraim and Manasseh, were listed in place of Joseph to retain the number 12. When spies were sent into Canaan, Levi was not included in the tribes; therefore, Ephraim and Manasseh each sent a representative to make the number 12.

In both covenants God established with His people, 12 was the symbolic number — 12 tribes in the Old and 12 apostles in the New. The number 12 manifests itself in many ways in the book of *Revelation*. In chapter 22 the 12 gates of the city of God symbolize the 12 tribes, and the 12 foundations of the city symbolize the apostles. When the heavenly city is measured, it is 12,000 stadia in length, width, and height; the walls were 144 cubits thick — 12 x 12. It is also seen in the 24 elders — 12 + 12 and the number 144,000 who were sealed in the 7th chapter of *Revelation* — 12 x 12 x 1,000.

Much time and space have been spent in this volume establishing background for understanding John's *Revelation*. Hopefully, the reader is now ready to move into chapter 9 and an explanation of one of the most intriguing books in the Bible, *Revelation*.

SECTION III

Analysis of *Revelation*

Chapter Nine

The Beginning of the Letter

It is important at this point to review the seven points in chapter one of this volume to confirm that *Revelation* was a book written primarily about first century Rome, but the book contains a philosophy relating to all nations and all generations from that time forward.

1. *Revelation* is a letter written to first century Christians.

2. Readers were blessed if they obeyed; one cannot obey the unintelligible.

3. Revelation's events were to happen "in the near future."

4. The 10 horned beast symbolizes the kingdom in power when John wrote *Revelation*. It was the fourth kingdom envisioned by Daniel and had consumed the territory of the three kingdoms before it — Babylon, Medo-Persia, and Greece.

5. The 6th king of the 4th kingdom was sitting on the throne when John wrote the letter; it could be no other nation but Rome.

6. The first 6 Roman numerals total 666.

7. The wicked city sits on 7 hills — Rome's nickname.

Additionally, chapter 1 of this volume explains the meaning of the word revelation is to make known something previously concealed. John "revealed" the material "sealed" by Daniel some 600 years earlier; he did this by using the imagery of Ezekiel to link the three exiled writers.

Five major ideas are interwoven throughout John's message: 1) Jesus is the true author of the book; 2) the church was about to undergo great tribulation; 3) the church would be protected during the times of persecution; 4) evil would be punished; and 5) the events described were to happen in the near future. As these ideas emerge in the study of the book, they will be identified and further explored.

Revelation is divided into three major sections — the seals, the trumpets, and the vials or bowls; however, before these are presented beginning with *Revelation 6*, John set up the book with certain basics to prepare the reader for the main message. To interpret *Revelation 1*, one must become aware of the prevalence of the number 3 which emphasizes that the message was coming through John from 1) God, 2) Jesus, and 3) the Holy Spirit.

WHO IS THE AUTHOR?

John penned the letter

> *Revelation 1:1,2 The revelation of Jesus Christ, which God gave him to show his servants what must soon take place. He made it known by sending his angel to his servant* **John, who testifies to everything he saw —** *that is, the word of God and the testimony of Jesus Christ.*
>
> *Revelation 1:4* **John**, *To the seven churches in the province of Asia: Grace and peace to you from him who is, and who was, and who is to come, and from the seven spirits before his throne ...*
>
> *Revelation 1:9* **I, John, your brother and companion** *in the suffering and kingdom and patient endurance that are ours in Jesus, was on the island of Patmos because of the word of God and the testimony of Jesus.*
>
> *Revelation 22:8* **I, John, am the one who heard and saw these things** ...

It is clear that John penned the letter, but which person named John did the writing? Several church leaders bore the name John, but most today believe the book to have been written by the apostle John; virtually all of the early writers accepted this position, including Justin Martyr, Irenaeus, Tertullian, Clement of Alexandria, Origen, and Hippolytus of Rome.

The true authorship is divine, evidenced by the number [3]

While John did the physical writing of the book, the true authorship is divine. This is one of the five major concepts considered in *Revelation*. That the Trinity authored the book will be established by verbal means as well as by the use of the number 3. The three-fold message of the work of the trinity is found as 1) God sends the message through 2) Jesus Christ, through 3) his angel.

> *Revelation 1:1 The revelation of **Jesus Christ**, which **God** gave him to show his servants what must soon take place. He made it known by sending his **angel** to his servant John ...*

The work of the Trinity is further accentuated when a three-fold blessing is placed upon those receiving the message.

> *Revelation 1:3 Blessed is the one who **reads** the words of this prophecy, and blessed are those who **hear** it and **take to heart** what is written in it, because the time is near.*

All books of the Bible are a blessing to those who read and follow their precepts; however, this letter gives specific blessings to those who work with the message. John's letter concerned the survival of Christians during the coming onslaught of the Roman Empire, but today's readers who comprehend, and act upon the message are blessed as well. If those first readers were expected to obey the words of the letter, the message must have been understandable. These readers were about to undergo one of the most severe persecutions ever inflicted upon the people of God; it was necessary for them to be prepared for what was coming by realizing the protection God affords those who follow Him.

The number 3 once again emphasizes the authorship of the message as coming from God, Jesus, and the Spirit. The seven spirits simply indicate the "perfect" Spirit of God. It is one of the many instances where the number 7 plays an important role in *Revelation*.

> *Revelation 1:4,5 ... from **him** who is, and who was, and who is to come, and from the **seven spirits** before his throne, and from **Jesus Christ** ...*

In verse 4, God is shown to be eternal because He lives in all three timeframes — the past, present, and future.

> *Revelation 1:4 ... from him who **is**, and who **was**, and who **is to come** ...*

In verse 5, Jesus serves three important functions in operating as mediator between God and man.

> *Revelation 1:5 And from Jesus Christ, who is the **faithful witness**, the **firstborn from the dead**, and the **ruler of the kings of the earth** ...*

Because of His love, Jesus has done three things for humanity.

> *Revelation 1:5,6 ... To him who **loves us** and has **freed us** from our sins by his blood, and has **made us** to be a kingdom and priests to serve his God and Father — to him be glory and power for ever and ever! Amen.*

Verse 8 returns to characteristics of God, emphasized by a cluster of three.

> *Revelation 1:8 "I am **the Alpha** and **the Omega**," says the Lord God, "who is, and who was, and who is to come, **the Almighty**."*

In the same verse, God is once again said to live in all three timeframes.

> *Revelation 1:8 ... the Lord God, "who **is**, and who **was**, and who **is to come** ..."*

The significance of the number 3 is again a factor when John enumerates the ways in which he was a brother and companion of others who were persecuted for the cause of Christ.

> *Revelation 1:9 I, John, your brother and companion in the **suffering** and **kingdom** and **patient endurance** that are ours in Jesus ...*

Three more statements are made concerning Jesus Christ in *Revelation 1:17, 18*.

> *... I am the **First and the Last**.*
>
> *I am the **Living One** ...*
>
> *... **I hold the keys of death and Hades**.*

The statement "I was dead, and behold I am alive for ever and ever!" merely expands the earlier point that Jesus is the "Living one."

Within the last set of three, John was commissioned to write concerning three timeframes:

Revelation 1:19 Write ... **what you have seen**, **what is now** *and* **what will take place later**.

If you have been counting incidences of three so far in chapter 1, there have been eleven. In addition to the number <u>3</u> sending a message of the letter's coming from God, John also saw a vision of the Messiah, a vision very similar to the one seen by Daniel.

| *Revelation 1:13 And among the lampstands was someone "like a son of man," dressed in a robe reaching down to his feet and with a golden sash around his chest. His head and hair were white like wool, as white as snow, and his eyes were like blazing fire. His feet were like bronze glowing in a furnace, and his voice was like the sound of rushing waters.* | *Daniel 10:5,6 I looked up and there before me was a man dressed in linen, with a belt of the finest gold around his waist. His body was like chrysolite, his face like lightning, his eyes like flaming torches, his arms and legs like the gleam of burnished bronze, and his voice like the sound of a multitude.* |

There is no question that John saw Jesus Christ because of the phrase "like a son of man." This was one of Jesus' most frequently used phrases to describe Himself. The passage above gives seven descriptive features making Jesus the focal point of the vision:

1. He looked "like a son of man."
2. He was dressed in a robe reaching down to His feet.
3. A golden sash was around His chest.
4. His head and hair were white like wool.
5. His eyes were like blazing fire.
6. His feet were like bronze glowing in a furnace.
7. His voice was like the sound of rushing water.

John adds to the description of Jesus in verse 16 with the following characteristics.

> *Revelation 1:16 In his right hand he held seven stars, and out of his mouth came a sharp double-edged sword. His face was like the sun shining in all its brilliance.*

Each part of the description reveals something about the nature of Jesus Christ. The whiteness represents His purity; the eyes of fire indicate His all knowing function; the feet like burnished bronze symbolize His ability to carry out those things He sets out to do; the voice of many waters shows the power of the Word of God.

The last verse of chapter 1 explains that the stars are symbolic of angels; Jesus' holding of the seven stars shows the authority He has over the angels and the churches.

The two-edged sword coming from the mouth of Jesus symbolizes the strength of His word; Jesus has the power to war against and destroy His enemies. These characteristics are used by John in chapters 2 and 3 to reveal that Jesus is the true author of each of the seven letters. One part of the description, the two-edged sword, will be used in other parts of *Revelation* as Jesus deals with the faithless and with His opponents.

WHERE WAS JOHN WHEN HE WROTE?

John says he wrote the book while on the Isle of Patmos, just off the coast of Asia Minor where the seven churches of Asia were located; he explains he was there "because of the word of God and the testimony of Jesus." The location of the writing ties closely with the timeframe in which the book was written. Some claim John was exiled by Domitian around 90 AD, and this may be possible because Domitian did his fair share of exiling those in disfavor. However, John's vision came during the 6th ruler, Vespasian 69-79 AD. There is no evidence Vespasian exiled anyone during these years.

Ezekiel was taken "in spirit" from Babylon to Jerusalem to see the apostasy of God's people. John was on Patmos "because of the word of God and the testimony of Jesus," but what does this mean? It could simply mean John was there to receive the information to write in his letter. John says on the Lord's Day he was "In the Spirit"; perhaps God took John in Spirit from Jerusalem to Patmos to see the coming tribulation of God's people. Furthermore, John could have been there "in spirit" to taste the future with Domitian's reign of terror. Since no further clarification is given, anything beyond this is mere conjecture.

> *Revelation 1:9-10* ***I, John ... was on the island of Patmos because of the word of God and the testimony of Jesus. On the Lord's Day I was in the Spirit. ...***

WHEN DID JOHN WRITE THE LETTER?

John tells the reader the book was written during a ten year timeframe. How did he "nail down" the timeframe of his revelation? When John wrote about the kings of the wicked empire, he said five were "past history." The sixth king of the realm was on the throne at the time of the writing. When the reader learns that the 6th king of the 4th empire was on the throne during the time John was penning *Revelation*, two conclusions become necessary. 1) The beast could be no other than Rome since Rome was in control at the time John was writing the letter. 2) **The letter would have been written between 69 and 79 AD** since the sixth caesar, Vespasian, was on the throne when John wrote the letter. This information is highlighted on pages 20-21 of this volume. The number 6 highlights the human nature of the kingdom in question.

The primary audience: The 7 churches of Asia

Early in the letter, John identifies a specific target audience to whom the letter was being written.

> *Revelation 1:4   John, To the seven churches in the province of Asia: Grace and peace to you ...*

When a letter is written to a specific group of people, one of the best tools for evaluation is audience analysis. With any other epistle in the New Testament, scholars try to discover information about the audience, the date the letter was written, and the prevailing conditions at the time; these valuable principles are often neglected with analysis of *Revelation*. The primary audience specified by John is the seven churches of Asia.

> *Revelation 1:4   John, To the seven churches in the province of Asia ...*
>
> *Revelation 1:11 "... send it to the seven churches: to Ephesus, Smyrna, Pergamum, Thyatira, Sardis, Philadelphia and Laodicea."*

Historical records show other congregations of the Lord existed in Asia Minor; *Colossians 1:2* permits readers to know Colossae had a church; *Colossians 4:13* further indicates that Hierapolis had a congregation. In reading *Acts 20:5* we learn that the church existed in Troas. Ignatius, who wrote around 115 AD, refers to churches located at Magnesia and Tralles.

Did the Lord just arbitrarily pick seven of the locations to receive the message? This is not likely; remember once again the significance of the number 7. It seems this letter would have been written to all members of God's family living under the control of the Roman Empire. The descriptions of each church give a cross-section of Christianity throughout the world at that time. Just knowing *Revelation* is a letter written to first century Christians living in Asia Minor is strong proof the book concerns itself with the tribulation already taking place by the time John began writing the letter.

Message: Prepare for tribulation

Revelation 2 and *3* present mini-letters to each of the congregations, letters designed to prepare the churches for the impending tribulation. These chapters stress two concepts: 1) the church was to undergo tremendous persecution and 2) the persecution would occur shortly after the letter was completed. Consistently throughout the letter, the author tells the reader the events were coming soon; they were "at hand." Promises were made in each of the letters to those who overcame the persecution. The number 7 is significant in these letters; not only were the letters written to seven churches, but also each letter contained seven parts, either explicit or implicit. The seven parts are as follows: 1) salutation, 2) description of Christ as the true author, 3) commendations for strengths, 4) condemnations for weaknesses, 5) appeals or warnings, 6) exhortations to listen, 7) and a promise for those who overcame.

1 - Salutation to Ephesus

Revelation 2:1 "To the angel of the church in Ephesus write ..."

Jesus Christ	[ ]
Through John	
	To the Angel
	Church at Ephesus
	Asia Minor

According to *Peloubet's Bible Dictionary*, p. 695, Ephesus was the seat of worship to Diana. Portable shrines to Diana were manufactured and sold in Ephesus. Ephesus had one of the largest theaters ever built by the Greeks, possibly able to seat over 21,000. Paul worked in Ephesus for over two years and wrote a letter to the Ephesians. The place where Ephesus existed is now in vast ruins.

Is it possible congregations have angels watching over their welfare? The Bible does allude to angels ministering to Christians.

Hebrews 1:14 Are not all angels ministering spirits sent to serve those who will inherit salvation?

Another plausible idea is that the angel represents the leadership of the congregation. Other Scriptures and ancient church history indicate that each city had a bishop overseeing the flock; the angel could be symbolic of someone in this position. The main point is that the letter is being transcribed by John from Jesus Christ and is to be delivered to the congregation.

2 - Christ is the true author

Revelation 2:1 ... These are the words of him who holds the seven stars in his right hand and walks among the seven golden lampstands.

In chapter 1 John gave this glimpse of Jesus as a part of the overall description; now he uses this part of the depiction as proof of divine authorship of the letter to Ephesus. According to the last verse of chapter 1, the seven golden candlesticks were symbolic of the seven churches; Christ was in the presence of the churches, a comfort to those who were about to undergo a severe time of tribulation.

3 - Commendations and praise for strengths

> *Revelation 2:2,3 I know your deeds, your hard work and your perseverance. I know that you cannot tolerate wicked men, that you have tested those who claim to be apostles but are not, and have found them false. You have persevered and have endured hardships for my name, and have not grown weary.*

Jesus knows these things because He walks among the churches (candlesticks), a part of God's omnipresence. One can gather from these commendations that the church at Ephesus was a vibrant congregation because of the words <u>work</u> and <u>toil</u>. Another meritorious factor was their perseverance or patience, mentioned twice in brief span. It was going to take steadfastness to withstand the pressures approaching this Christian family; they were being encouraged to continue developing perseverance. This congregation had also overcome the problem of false apostles, apparently by using the Word of God to test the authenticity of those making the claim.

This was a diligent congregation indeed; further praise was given the group in verse 6:

> *Revelation 2:6 ... You hate the practices of the Nicolaitans, which I also hate.*

The Nicolaitans were a heretical religious sect that attempted to make their ideas look better by calling themselves after Nicolas, one of the seven selected in *Acts 6:5* to look after the affairs of the widows. The Ephesian church did not tolerate wickedness under any name. With all of these strengths, it would seem this church surely could make it through the persecution to come; however, they also had some weak areas to set right before they could withstand the coming tribulation.

4 - Condemnation for faults

Revelation 2:4 Yet I hold this against you: You have forsaken your first love.

The indictment indicates they were going through the motions of serving Christ, but their hearts were not really in it. *I Corinthians 13* says Christians can give their bodies as a sacrifice and can give all their goods to the poor, but if these actions do not come from love, there is no benefit from the action.

5 - Warnings, admonitions and advice

Revelation 2:5 Remember the height from which you have fallen! Repent and do the things you did at first. If you do not repent, I will come to you and remove your lampstand from its place.

Tribulation was near; if this group did not change their motivation, Rome could destroy them eternally. The test of Christianity is not based on what happens in good times; anyone can be enthusiastic and faithful during good times. The true test is based on what happens when circumstances are gloomy and when persecution is the rule of the day. The Ephesians were warned they could lose their very identity as a church; if they did not correct their present path, the candlestick, representative of the church, was to be removed. **They would no longer be recognized as the people of God!**

6 - Command to listen

Revelation 2:7 He who has an ear, let him hear what the Spirit says to the churches ...

While the admonition was specifically to the readers at Ephesus, the exhortation carries over to readers today. There is a difference between hearing and listening; Jesus is not imploring the audience simply to "hear" his words. Jesus desires His followers pay attention to the message and take it to heart.

7 - Rewards for those who overcome

Revelation 2:7 ... To him who overcomes, I will give the right to eat from the tree of life, which is in the paradise of God.

Failure is inevitable in times of distress if one does not have his heart set upon Jesus; each church was given a promise symbolizing everlasting life — the tree of life. The will to resist was going to be difficult when Romans offered Christians the right to live if they renounced the name of Jesus, but for those who overcame, eternal life was to be granted. The tree of life is symbolic of the cross and the blessings coming from Jesus' death, burial, and resurrection for those who are victorious in the face of persecution.

1 - Salutation to Smyrna

Revelation 2:8 "To the angel of the church in Smyrna write ..."

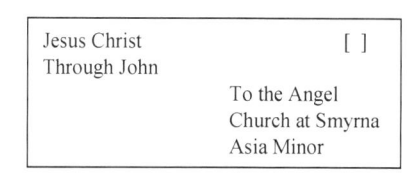

Jesus Christ	[ ]
Through John	
	To the Angel
	Church at Smyrna
	Asia Minor

Smyrna is described in *Peloubet's Bible Dictionary,* p. 696, as a city on the Aegean Sea, 40 miles north of Ephesus. The city, which has always been susceptible to earthquakes, is located in Turkey.

2 - Jesus is the true author

Revelation 2:8 "These are the words of him who is the First and the Last, who died and came to life again."

The reference to the One who was dead and lived again clearly points to Jesus as the author, but another interesting statement is made as well — Jesus is the "first and the last." This is a statement usually reserved for God. It is another expression of omnipresence because Jesus is God! John presents this great truth in his Gospel:

John 1:1-3 In the beginning was the Word, and the Word was with God, and the Word was God. He was with God in the beginning. Through him all things were made; without him nothing was made that has been made.

> *John 1:14 The Word became flesh and made his dwelling among us.*

3 - Commendations and praise for strengths

> *Revelation 2:9 I know your afflictions and your poverty — yet you are rich! I know the slander of those who say they are Jews and are not, but are a synagogue of Satan.*

It may seem the commendations are on the slim side after reading the letter to Ephesus, but one needs to consider the underlying message. This congregation lived in an area where many falsely professed to be Christians. Material presented in the chapter dealing with *Ezekiel* demonstrated that the emphasis today is not on national Israel, but rather on the spiritual kingdom of Christ. The problem was not about people claiming to be physical Jews; rather, it involved people claiming to be Christians but not walking the talk.

> *Romans 2:28,29 A man is not a Jew if he is only one outwardly, nor is circumcision merely outward and physical. No, a man is a Jew if he is one inwardly; and circumcision is circumcision of the heart, by the Spirit, not by the written code. Such a man's praise is not from men, but from God.*

Apparently these Christians had put to test those who claimed to be "Jews" or Christians and had found their claims false. They also lived in physical poverty, a condition the Roman government controlled; however, even though they were poor in worldly goods, they were commended for being rich — obviously spiritual riches are indicated. This one brief statement indicates strength through and through. This church was ready to handle the coming turmoil.

4 - Condemnations for faults

No condemnation is given for weaknesses, thus emphasizing the previously mentioned strengths of this church. Although no blame is placed on two of the churches, the very absence of condemnation still speaks to the point — **none existed**.

5 - Warnings, admonitions and advice

> *Revelation 2:10 Do not be afraid of what you are about to suffer. I tell you, the devil will put some of you in prison to test you, and you will suffer persecution for ten days. Be faithful, even to the point of death, and I will give you the crown of life.*

One of the main concepts of the book is found in the passage above — the suffering was "about" to occur. A wave of persecution had already run its course through Nero; Vespasian and Titus persecuted to a degree, but Domitian was on the way. In fact, this suffering was to be so severe they were told if they were faithful in the face of death, they would be awarded the crown of life. The persecution was to last "ten days"; this is not a literal ten days but is symbolic of a total period of time. They must remain faithful throughout the persecution's entirety. Christians were about to be forced to worship caesars and Roman gods; imprisonment and possible death awaited those who refused. The letter's purpose was to prepare readers to receive the promises of victory in Jesus.

6 - Command to listen

> *Revelation 2:11 He who has an ear, let him hear what the Spirit says to the churches.*

7 - Rewards for those who overcome

> *Revelation 2:11 ... He who overcomes will not be hurt at all by the second death.*

If one is not harmed by the second death, he has everlasting life. This reverse promise of eternal life was emphasized because of the threat of physical death in the coming persecution. Those who faced death without recanting their faith in Christ would not be hurt by the second death or eternal condemnation. When one compares the two results, it seems clear which goal should be sought, but often during the heat of the moment, one's values become blurred.

1 - Salutation to Pergamum

Revelation 2:12 "To the angel of the church in Pergamum write ..."

Jesus Christ Through John	[ ]
	To the Angel Church at Pergamum Asia Minor

According to *Peloubet's Bible Dictionary*, p. 696, Pergamum is a city of Mysia, about 3 miles to the north of the river Caicus. It was founded at the time of Alexander the Great about 335 BC. The city was noted for its vast library, with only the library at Alexandria being larger. Temples existed in Pergamum to many gods such as Zeus, Athene, Apollo, and Aesculapius. Emperor worship was significant in Pergamum. The modern name of the city is Bergama.

2 - Jesus is the true author

Revelation 2:12 To the angel of the church in Pergamum write: These are the words of him who has the sharp, double-edged sword.

In *Revelation 1*, John saw a vision of Christ with a sharp two-edged sword proceeding from His mouth. When John describes the author of this letter having a sharp, double-edged sword, the reader knows it refers to Jesus. The significance of this symbol is made clear in verse 13 when Jesus warned that a failure to change would bring Him into war against those guilty, and His weapon would be the two-edged sword. The sword is usually indicative of the Word of God; this image is intensified by the fact that the sword in chapter 1 came from the mouth of Jesus.

3 - Commendations and praise for strength

Revelation 2:13 I know where you live — where Satan has his throne. Yet you remain true to my name. You did not renounce your faith in me, even in the days of Antipas, my faithful witness, who was put to death in your city — where Satan lives.

The omniscience of the godhead is reiterated with the phrase "I know." It is hard to remain faithful in the face of adversity, and in hardships true Christians are separated from mere pretenders. Two circumstances indicate the adverse conditions under which Pergamum Christians were working — first, it was called the place where Satan's throne exists. This shows wickedness to which each of the Christians must have been subjected daily, yet they had remained faithful. The second indicator was the death of Antipas through martyrdom; this disciple is not mentioned anywhere else in the New Testament, but information given suggests he was a leader in the congregation. The tribulation had begun with Nero a few years earlier, but more was to come! These Christians had remained faithful even when their leaders were slain in their presence — WHAT A COMMENDATION! Even with these strengths, there were still certain weaknesses to be addressed.

4 - Condemnations for faults

> *Revelation 2:14,15 Nevertheless, I have a few things against you: You have people there who hold to the teaching of Balaam, who taught Balak to entice the Israelites to sin by eating food sacrificed to idols and by committing sexual immorality. Likewise you also have those who hold to the teaching of the Nicolaitans.*

The first condemnation referred to a similarity with the teachings of Balaam. Balaam had encouraged the eating of things sacrificed to idols; Romans had their false gods, and sacrificed to them. The meat was then taken and sold to the general public; Paul had addressed this problem in *I Corinthians 8* by saying if eating this meat offended fellow Christians, it should not be consumed. This practice was causing problems because some Christians were not sensitive to the needs and beliefs of others.

The second problem was similar in that many were accused of committing fornication. While this could be physical fornication which would certainly be ungodly, the most likely explanation would be spiritual fornication. Christians are married to Jesus; the church is the bride, and Jesus is the Bridegroom. These Christians had been unfaithful to their spiritual marriage vows. Earlier evidence indicated the church at Ephesus had rejected the teachings of the Nicolaitans, but some at Pergamum had followed along. The overall evaluation indicates this group was eager to follow any new teaching coming their way, regardless of the source; they were certainly vulnerable to the persecution that had begun and was sure to increase.

5 - Warnings, admonitions and advice

> *Revelation 2:16 Repent therefore! Otherwise, I will soon come to you and will fight against them with the sword of my mouth.*

Now it becomes clear why the imagery of the two-edged sword was given earlier; Jesus will war against those who oppose and abuse His kingdom. This type of conflict is often referred to as spiritual warfare or heavenly war. The word of God, the sword, will ultimately be used in judgment and punishment of wrongdoers.

6 - Command to listen

> *Revelation 2:17 He who has an ear, let him hear what the Spirit says to the churches ...*

7 - Rewards for those who overcome

> *Revelation 2:17 ... To him who overcomes, I will give some of the hidden manna. I will also give him a white stone with a new name written on it, known only to him who receives it.*

Three things are promised to the victorious: 1) hidden manna, 2) a white stone, and 3) a new name. Manna kept Israel alive in the wilderness; it was food sent from heaven. The manna reward would point to God's care for those who follow Jesus, the true Bread of Life. The whiteness of the stone indicates the purity of the recipient, and the stone would indicate permanence; overall, the idea is eternal life or salvation. One can speculate into eternity about the new name, but because the reader is told no one will know it except the one who receives it, all speculation is pointless. It is evident the new name is symbolic. **The meaning: God will eternally bless those who are victorious in the time of trial**.

| Jesus Christ [ ] |
| Through John |
| To the Angel |
| Church at Thyatira |
| Asia Minor |

1 - Salutation to Thyatira

Revelation 2:18   To the angel of the church in Thyatira write ...

Looking into *Peloubet's Bible Dictionary*, p. 698, one learns fabric dyeing was apparently the most important industry in Thyatira. Lydia came from Thyatira, and according to the book of *Acts*, she was a seller of purple. Apollo was the main god worshipped in Thyatira; however, Sambatha was also worshipped as the protector of all the varied religious beliefs in the city. The present name of the city is ak-Hissar, and scarlet cloth is still sold to this day.

2 - Jesus is the true author

Revelation 2:18 These are the words of the Son of God, whose eyes are like blazing fire and whose feet are like burnished bronze.

The true author of the letter is revealed as the "Son of God"; two qualities are symbolically given — 1) all knowing and 2) all powerful. The ability to know all things is indicated by the eyes like a flame of fire; another factor related to the "eyes like blazing fire" could be His displeasure over the conditions present in this congregation. Not only does Christ know these things, He has the ability to carry out judgment upon the wicked as shown through the feet like burnished bronze. Jesus has the ability to carry out what He sets out to do!

3 - Commendations and praise for strengths

Revelation 2:19 I know your deeds, your love and faith, your service and perseverance, and that you are now doing more than you did at first.

Revelation 2:24,25 Now I say to the rest of you in Thyatira, to you who do not hold to her teaching and have not learned Satan's so-called deep secrets (I will not impose any other burden on you). Only hold on to what you have until I come.

This congregation differs from the group in Ephesus in that they not only had performed Christian works, but they also did their work through love and faith. They ministered to those in need, had patience, and even more importantly, their dedication had grown as indicated through the fact that their last works were greater than the first. Despite their growth, this congregation had many problems to address before the great tribulation arrived. Despite the wickedness of the congregation as a whole, some had refrained from participating in the corruption. Praise God that salvation does not come through group insurance!

4 - Condemnation for faults

> *Revelation 2:20-23 Nevertheless, I have this against you: You tolerate that woman Jezebel, who calls herself a prophetess. By her teaching she misleads my servants into sexual immorality and the eating of food sacrificed to idols. I have given her time to repent of her immorality, but she is unwilling. So I will cast her on a bed of suffering, and I will make those who commit adultery with her suffer intensely, unless they repent of her ways. I will strike her children dead. Then all the churches will know that I am he who searches hearts and minds, and I will repay each of you according to your deeds.*

Jezebel was the wicked queen during the days of Elijah (*II Kings 9:22*); she symbolizes some person or power infecting Christians in Thyatira in a similar way the Jews were harmed under Jezebel's rule. The church seems to have been unfaithful to its marriage vows to Christ; its fornication with the world was going to come back upon it if changes were not made. Christ has the ability to see into the problems and to carry out justice upon the offenders. Persecution was at hand; something had to be done to get these weak Christians ready to overcome the temptation to serve the flesh.

5 - Warnings, admonitions, and advice

Revelation 2:24,25 Now I say to the rest of you in Thyatira, to you who do not hold to her teaching and have not learned Satan's so-called deep secrets (I will not impose any other burden on you). Only hold on to what you have until I come.

6 - Rewards for those who overcome

Revelation 2:26-28 To him who overcomes and does my will to the end, I will give authority over the nations — "He will rule them with an iron scepter; he will dash them to pieces like pottery" — just as I have received authority from my Father. I will also give him the morning star.

Earlier, those who had followed the teachings of Jezebel were told of their doom; the rest were told to refrain from this teaching and to maintain their spiritual status. Bad times were not far away, and the faithful were encouraged to remain so.

What about those who would be able to overcome? The authority over the nations to rule them with a rod of iron symbolizes the Christian's share in the triumph over evil; those who overcome live above the world. Later, John reveals that Christians will sit in judgment of the beast. *Revelation 22:16* says the morning star is Jesus; **the victorious Christian will receive Jesus as his reward**. All of this is once again symbolic of eternal life granted to those who overcome the temptation to vacate their position.

7 - Command to listen

Revelation 2:29 He who has an ear, let him hear what the Spirit says to the churches.

1 - Salutation to Sardis

Revelation 3:1
To the angel of the church in
Sardis write ...

Jesus Christ Through John	[ ]
	To the Angel Church at Sardis Asia Minor

Peloubet's Bible Dictionary, p. 698, gives some interesting information concerning the city of Sardis. Sardis was always an important city for commercial purposes. It is said that the art of dyeing wool originated in Sardis. False gods were worshipped there as is evidenced by the massive temple of Cybele. There are still considerable remains of the ancient city at Seri-Kalessi, now a tiny village.

2 - Jesus is the true author

Revelation 3:1 ... These are the words of him who holds the seven spirits of God and the seven stars. I know your deeds; you have a reputation of being alive, but you are dead.

The number 7 indicates perfection; God did not limit Christ in His power. The passage above and the one below reveal a major truth: Jesus possesses the entire Spirit of God.

John 3:34 For the one whom God has sent speaks the words of God, for God gives the Spirit without limit.

The power and authority of Jesus is highlighted as John sees Jesus holding the seven stars. Stars are angels; therefore, if Jesus held the stars, He is more powerful than angels and in control of them. This is the same message permeating the book of *Hebrews*.

3 - Condemnations for faults

The usual order of presentation has been to present the commendations before presenting negative areas; however, this letter gives criticism first. Perhaps this was done to show the seriousness of the problems present.

> *Revelation 3:1 To the angel of the church in Sardis write: These are the words of him who holds the seven spirits of God and the seven stars. I know your deeds; you have a reputation of being alive, but you are dead.*

The group wore the name of Jesus, but they were just going through the motions; their actions apparently were coming from dead hearts. With these condemnations present, the reader would next expect to hear warnings, and that is exactly what happens.

4 - Warnings, admonitions and advice

> *Revelation 3:2,3 Wake up! Strengthen what remains and is about to die, for I have not found your deeds complete in the sight of my God. Remember, therefore, what you have received and heard; obey it, and repent. But if you do not wake up, I will come like a thief, and you will not know at what time I will come to you.*

Actually, even more condemnation is leveled at the church when the warning is presented. Not only were some things dead already, many other good characteristics were dying at the time. Jesus warned them of their doom if they did not correct this digression. Death and sleep are often compared in the Bible; a church that is dead or asleep should certainly be challenged to "wake up." Jesus would come upon them without warning to bring justice upon the guilty.

5 - Commendations and praise for strengths

> *Revelation 3:4 Yet you have a few people in Sardis who have not soiled their clothes. They will walk with me, dressed in white, for they are worthy.*

The judgment of Jesus will certainly be on an individual basis; it is possible for a person to belong to a corrupt congregation, yet be saved by his own relationship in Christ. Remember: **Salvation does not come through group insurance!** A few members of God's kingdom in Sardis had kept the faith; at least this church had some who were prepared for victory in the face of the coming persecution.

6 - Rewards to those who overcome

Revelation 3:5 He who overcomes will, like them, be dressed in white. I will never blot out his name from the Book of Life, but will acknowledge his name before my Father and his angels.

Two truths can be learned from the statement "I will never blot out his name from the Book of Life." 1) To blot out a name from the Book of Life is equal to loss of soul, and 2) the failure to blot out the name indicates eternal life. Salvation was also indicated by the action of Christ's confessing the victors' names to the Father and His angels. The names Christ confesses are listed in the Book of Life. Being dressed in white is further indicative of salvation and purity that come through being in Jesus.

7 - Command to listen

Revelation 3:6 He who has an ear, let him hear what the Spirit says to the churches.

1 - Salutation to Philadelphia

Revelation 3:7 To the angel of the church in Philadelphia write ...

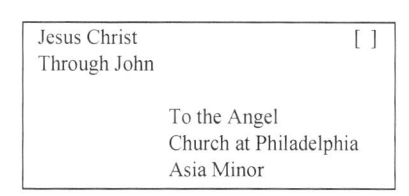

Jesus Christ	[ ]
Through John	
	To the Angel
	Church at Philadelphia
	Asia Minor

Peloubet's Bible Dictionary, p, 698, discloses some interesting facts about Philadelphia. Philadelphia is located in Turkey in what is known now as Ala-shehr, meaning the "reddish city." Records indicate the Jewish religion was popular in Philadelphia along with Christianity.

2 - Jesus is the true author

Revelation 3:7 ... These are the words of him who is holy and true, who holds the key of David. What he opens no one can shut, and what he shuts no one can open.

Three characteristics of Christ are revealed above — 1) His holiness, 2) His truthfulness, and 3) His Kingship, revealed through the key of David, king of Israel. The everlasting strength of Christ as King is evident because His decrees are irreversible — whatever is opened or shut is opened or shut forever.

3 - Commendations and praise for strengths

> *Revelation 3:8-10 I know your deeds. See, I have placed before you an open door that no one can shut. I know that you have little strength, yet you have kept my word and have not denied my name. I will make those who are of the synagogue of Satan, who claim to be Jews though they are not, but are liars — I will make them come and fall down at your feet and acknowledge that I have loved you. Since you have kept my command to endure patiently, I will also keep you from the hour of trial that is going to come upon the whole world to test those who live on the earth.*

Opportunities existed for this church (door was open), and they had capitalized upon them for the Master. They did this work despite false Jews (people claiming to be Christians who were not) working among them; because of their faithfulness, Jesus promised to keep them from the impending trial.

The coming persecution was clearly spelled out in this passage; it was to be a persecution affecting the entire known world. The persecution imposed by Rome certainly fit this picture since the Roman Empire possessed and controlled Asia, Europe, and Africa, the entire known world at that point in history. Another theme is advanced at this point — no matter how severe the trial becomes, God protects those who remain faithful to Him.

4 - Condemnations for faults

No criticism was found of this church — evidence of their strength and faithfulness in the Lord. But although no condemnation was found, warnings and advice were given to prepare them for whatever persecution would come their way.

5 - Warnings, admonitions and advice

Revelation 3:11 I am coming soon. Hold on to what you have, so that no one will take your crown.

No matter how strong this congregation was, members were warned they could lose their crowns by becoming lax in their service to the Master. Hard times were not far away; Domitian's reign of terror would begin shortly, and only the faithful would survive.

6 - Rewards to those who overcome

Revelation 3:12 Him who overcomes I will make a pillar in the temple of my God. Never again will he leave it. I will write on him the name of my God and the name of the city of my God, the new Jerusalem, which is coming down out of heaven from my God; and I will also write on him my new name.

Both the "temple of God" and "new Jerusalem" refer to the church as indicated earlier. These promises indicate eternal relationships with God because the victor would be a pillar in the temple; furthermore, the victor would be given a new name. God would also write His name on the one who is victorious.

7 - Command to listen

Revelation 3:13 He who has an ear, let him hear what the Spirit says to the churches.

1 - Salutation to Laodicea

Revelation 3:14 To the angel of the church in Laodicea write ...

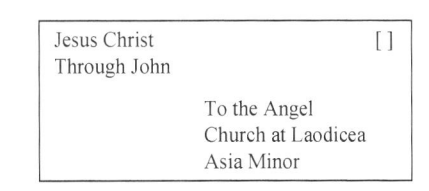

Jesus Christ Through John	[ ]
	To the Angel Church at Laodicea Asia Minor

According to *Peloubet's Bible Dictionary*, p. 698, Laodicea was named for the wife of Antiochus, one of the Seleucid emperors. Trade was major in this city of Asia. Just as *Revelation* predicted, the city was destroyed utterly.

2 - Jesus is the true author

Revelation 3:14 ... These are the words of the Amen, the faithful and true witness, the ruler of God's creation.

Three identifiers point clearly to Jesus as the author because He is 1) the Amen, 2) the faithful and true witness, and 3) the ruler of God's creation. The "Amen" indicates Jesus completes the goals and directions set by God. No other witness of God on earth was ever totally faithful and totally true. Jesus is ruler of God's creation and King over the kingdom of God. Some versions say "the beginning of God's creation" rather than ruler of God's creation. Both "beginning" and "ruler" would indicate His preeminence.

3 - Commendation and praise for strengths

When one looks for commendations and strengths, he finds a void in its place; none are mentioned! This church certainly was not ready for the coming trials.

4 - Condemnations for faults

Revelation 3:15-17 I know your deeds, that you are neither cold nor hot. I wish you were either one or the other! So, because you are lukewarm — neither hot nor cold — I am about to spit you out of my mouth. You say, `I am rich; I have acquired wealth and do not need a thing.' But you do not realize that you are wretched, pitiful, poor, blind and naked.

God would rather a person be committed to Satan than to ride the spiritual fence. Foods and drinks are desirable when hot or cold; how disgusting this must be for God to "vomit" lukewarm Christians from His system. This congregation had spent its time gathering worldly goods, but no eternal riches. They had nice clothing, but no white garments of the Spirit. They thought they could see plainly, but they needed God's anointment to see spiritually. They dabbled too much in the worldliness Rome could offer, but Rome could offer nothing in the way of eternal security.

5 - Warnings, admonitions and advice

Revelation 3:18-20 I counsel you to buy from me gold refined in the fire, so you can become rich; and white clothes to wear, so you can cover your shameful nakedness; and salve to put on your eyes, so you can see. Those whom I love I rebuke and discipline. So be earnest, and repent. Here I am! I stand at the door and knock. If anyone hears my voice and opens the door, I will come in and eat with him, and he with me.

The church was told to turn to the Spirit rather than to the world, the principle Christ established when he said man could not serve God and money. It was not too late for these people; Jesus was still at the door, but it was up to them to take the necessary steps to let the Savior into their lives. The author tells them to repent from their present position; if they were to be persecuted in this condition, it would be too easy to turn completely from serving Christ to follow the caesar.

6 - Rewards for those who overcome

Revelation 3:21 To him who overcomes, I will give the right to sit with me on my throne, just as I overcame and sat down with my Father on his throne.

Being home with Jesus is what eternal salvation is all about; Jesus had faced Rome and was home with God, and He promises Christians the same result if they overcome.

7 - Command to listen

Revelation 3:22 He who has an ear, let him hear what the Spirit says to the churches.

The graphic on the next page should help considerably in understanding the overall message of the seven letters. There were seven letters written to seven churches, and each letter was divided into seven sections. By studying each letter concerning Jesus as the author, the reader should have a stronger comprehension of the message and its significance as we proceed in our study of John's marvelous *Revelation*. Study the following chart carefully for the total impact.

7 Points in 7 Letters to 7 Churches

Church	Author	Praise	Faults	Advice	Rewards	Hear
Ephesus	Holds 7 stars; walks among 7 candlesticks	Hard workers; tested error; endured	Left first love	Repent and do first works	Victors receive tree of life	Whoever has ears let him hear
Smyrna	First and Last; Dead but now is alive	Your Spirits are alive	None are listed	Be faithful even in the face of death	Victors aren't hurt by second death	Whoever has ears let him hear
Pergamum	Has the two-edged sword	Faithful despite living in evil city	Followed Balaam & the Nicolaitans	Repent	Receive manna, white rock, new name	Whoever has ears let him hear
Thyatira	Eyes of flame; feet like bright bronze	Growing in love, faith & patience	Followed Balaam & Jezebel	The faithful should hold fast	Authority over nations; morning star	Whoever has ears let him hear
Sardis	Has 7 stars; Has 7 Spirits of God	There are a few who are worthy	Some are dead; many dying	Wake up!! Stir up what is not dead already	Dressed in white; name not blotted out	Whoever has ears let him hear
Philadelphia	Holy & True; has key of David	Little strength but kept name of Jesus	None are listed	Hold fast to crown & to God's name	Pillar in the temple of God	Whoever has ears let him hear
Laodicea	Faithful & True Witness; God's ruler	None are listed	Lukewarm poor, blind, & naked	Seek godly sight, riches, & clothing	Sit with Jesus on His throne	Whoever has ears let him hear
Overall Meaning	**Jesus is the true author**	**Mature: keep strong points**	**Correct weak areas**	**Be ready for trials**	**Eternal Life for Victors**	**Heed and Respond**

164

Chapter Ten

The Seven Seals

There is only one book in all of the Bible that God ever commanded to be sealed, the book of *Daniel*. Daniel wrote about a kingdom symbolized by a 10 horned beast; when Jesus removed the seven seals from the concealed book, the task of "revealing" what had been "sealed" about the 10 horned beast was complete. When Jesus removed the seventh seal in chapter 8 of *Revelation*, the once sealed book became an open book. Everything following the opening of the seventh seal concerns itself with the fall of the Roman Empire. Jesus revealed to John what Daniel had been ordered "to seal" over 600 years earlier.

By the time *Revelation* was written, tribulation had already begun; however, more severe times were rapidly approaching. Seutonius, in *Twelve Caesars*, states that Julius Caesar had been deified (made a Roman god after his death) although he predated the Roman Empire by a few years. Augustus and Claudius had been deified before the time *Revelation* was penned, and during the latter stages of the first century, Vespasian and Titus were also deified after their death. The government had already crucified the leader of the Christian movement, and now it was trying to force its subjects to worship caesars and Roman gods. The material in chapters 4 and 5 of *Revelation* was vital to those 1st century Christians because they needed assurance the Supreme Power of the Universe was God, not some caesar, dead or alive. Chapters 4 and 5 also serve in building the dramatic effect in preparation to the opening of the seals.

As *Revelation 4* begins, the author presents a powerful message about God as ruler of the universe. First, the door opening into heaven places emphasis on God; after all, heaven is His dwelling place; secondly, the voice like a trumpet gives even more impact that we are looking into heaven itself. The third indicator God is the central focus of the chapter is the heavenly throne. Look for these three factors in the following verses:

> *Revelation 4:1-2 After this I looked, and there before me was a door standing open in heaven. And the voice I had first heard speaking to me like a trumpet said, "Come up here, and I will show you what must take place after this." At once I was in the Spirit, and there before me was a throne in heaven with someone sitting on it.*

The open door, the powerful voice and the throne certainly give an imposing picture of **God, the one and only Ruler of the Universe**.

GOD IS THE CENTER OF THE UNIVERSE

The major theme of *Revelation 4* and *5* is that God is the center of the universe; this concept is developed in two ways. First, John sees seven circles around God. Since 7 is the perfect, total number, the symbolism indicates God is in control of all that exists. The second way God becomes the focal point of the two chapters is through hymns of praise sung by the various groups He oversees.

According to *Exodus 33:20*, one cannot see the face of God and live. John did not see the face of God when he looked into heaven; he saw brilliant colors of three stones forming the first three rings around God.

Revelation 4:3 And the one who sat there had the appearance of jasper and carnelian. A rainbow, resembling an emerald, encircled the throne.

God has the appearance of 3 stones radiating like a rainbow

Jasper has a transparent quality like quartz or diamonds; this stone, according to *Revelation 21:19*, was the first of the twelve stones in the foundation of the new Jerusalem. It was also used in the breastplate of the high priest in *Exodus 28:20*. The carnelian or sardius was the sixth stone in the foundation of new Jerusalem and was blood red in color. The rainbow around the throne was completed by an emerald, a bright green. The three stones, 3 being the number of the godhead, encircled God. The three colors appear symbolic: white or transparent being the purity of God; red indicating the blood of Jesus, and green pointing to eternal life. Humans can participate in eternal life through the blood of Jesus bringing forgiveness or purity.

After seeing three circles of brilliant color surrounding God, John saw the Almighty surrounded by 24 elders.

> *Revelation 4:4,5 Surrounding the throne were twenty-four other thrones, and seated on them were twenty-four elders. They were dressed in white and had crowns of gold on their heads. From the throne came flashes of lightning, rumblings and peals of thunder. Before the throne, seven lamps were blazing. These are the seven spirits of God.*

```
  12 Tribes
+ 12 Apostles
= 24 Elders
```

The twenty-four elders are a combination of two sets of twelve, the number of organized religion. God established twelve tribes under the law of Moses, and Jesus selected twelve apostles to carry out His will under the new covenant. Under the old law, the leaders of Israel were known as "elders," and under the new covenant, the leaders of the church were "elders." The twelve plus twelve combination of twenty-four elders surrounding God's throne signifies His followers from all ages.

*Exodus 4:29 Moses and Aaron brought together all the **elders of the Israelites** ...*

*I Timothy 5:17 The **elders** who direct the affairs of the **church** well ...*

The victory of the twenty-four elders is accented by additional parts of the vision. The garments of white indicate the purity of the elders; these were ones who had made it through the temptations of the world, both before and after Christ's resurrection. The victory theme is carried out by the crowns they were wearing; the Greek word is <u>stephanos,</u> a crown won in athletic contests. It is not the diadem crown of God indicating authority. One of the seven letters promised those who overcome would be dressed in white and that they would wear crowns; this is now presented as reality. Furthermore, they were sitting on thrones; *Romans 5:17* states that Christians "reign in life" through Jesus Christ. The power of God is underscored with the number 3 once more as lightnings, voices, and thunders were heard.

The Spirit of God was influential as symbolized through golden candlesticks of Old Testament time. The scene is one of reassurance that God takes care of those who choose to follow Him.

| Four Living Creatures are the Cherubim |

The fifth circle around God was composed of the four living creatures. Ezekiel wrote concerning the four living creatures, but he further identified them as cherubim in *Ezekiel 10:20*. Cherubim is the plural form of cherub, meaning angel. Because of their location and because other angels are found within the next circle around God, these seem to be a much higher rank of angels. As the description of the four living creatures is given, one notices a very definite link with the cherubim of *Ezekiel*.

1. Both sets of creatures were covered with eyes.

Revelation 4:6 Also before the throne there was what looked like a sea of glass, clear as crystal. In the center, around the throne, were four living creatures, and they were covered with eyes, in front and in back.

Ezekiel 10:12 Their entire bodies including their backs, their hands and their wings, were completely full of eyes, as were their four wheels.

Perhaps their being covered with eyes is indicative of a characteristic of God — omniscience; this also would seem to place them in a category higher than other angels.

2. Both sets of creatures had faces that were identical.

Revelation 4:7-8 The first living creature was like a lion, the second was like an ox, the third had a face like a man, the fourth was like a flying eagle.

Ezekiel 1:10 Their faces looked like this: Each of the four had the face of a man, and on the right side each had the face of a lion, and on the left the face of an ox; each also had the face of an eagle.

From where he stood, Ezekiel saw four faces on each of the living creatures as the cherubim were turning and moving back and forth. Since John saw the creatures in a fixed position around the throne; he would have seen only one face on each creature. If each creature were turned the same direction, each would present the same face to God, but John would see a different face of each. Assume for a moment the face of the man on each of the living creatures was the one turned toward God. Assume further as John's focus moved clockwise, he would see the face of the man at 12:00; the face of the eagle at 3:00; the face of the lion at 6:00; and the face of the ox at 9:00. Being on the outside of the circle looking at the four living creatures surrounding God, John would have seen the farthest creature from him having the face of a man.

The number 4 symbolizes the world; it would seem the four living creatures fulfilled a special role working between God and His creation. This is especially clear in Ezekiel's vision because of the appearance of the "war chariot." These beings are always close to God; in fact, some suggest the four symbols represent characteristics of God — strength of the lion, service of the ox, intellect of man, and speed of the eagle.

3. Both sets of creatures have wings.

| *Revelation 4:8 Each of the four living creatures had six wings and was covered with eyes all around, even under his wings. Day and night they never stop saying: "Holy, holy, holy is the Lord God Almighty, who was, and is, and is to come."* | *Ezekiel 1:6 But each of them had four faces and four wings.*
Ezekiel 1:8 Under their wings on their four sides they had the hands of a man. All four of them had faces and wings. |

Within this comparison, there is also an apparent difference — Ezekiel's creatures had four wings, two were spread to touch another living creature's wing, and two wings covered their bodies, with a man's hand under each. John saw each creature having six wings. A possible explanation can be applied from the different vantage point of each author. Ezekiel saw four wings and two hands; thus he saw six appendages also. John identified the appendages as wings. At least the reader knows that both authors saw multi-winged creatures with six appendages.

John saw the sea of glass, found also in two other sections of *Revelation*; the glassy sea can be seen before the throne of God. Later the redeemed are either near the sea or on the sea, depending on the translation. At the end of *Revelation*, the sea no longer exists to separate man from God because of salvation; the sea is finally removed when redemption and unity are complete. The sea of glass emphasizes the expanse of God's creation, His control, and the peace and calm of heaven.

> God is at the center of all His Angels

The sixth circle around God is composed of a host of angels so numerous they could not be counted. Angels are created beings who carry out the will of God. In fact, the word <u>angel</u> actually means "messenger." One cannot imagine the strength of the song sung by this multitude of angels.

Revelation 5:11 Then I looked and heard the voice of many angels, numbering thousands upon thousands, and ten thousand times ten thousand. They encircled the throne and the living creatures and the elders.

The seventh and last circle surrounding God was composed of every creature ever created. The 7 circles surrounding God indicate God is the center of all and regulates everything; furthermore the seventh ring itself is all inclusive. Nothing remains for an earthly ruler to control; **all of creation is under the rule of the Almighty**.

> God rules everything

Revelation 5:13 Then I heard every creature in heaven and on earth and under the earth and on the sea, and all that is in them ...

The majesty of God is magnified even more through the hymns of praise sung by the groups surrounding the throne.

GOD AND THE LAMB ARE PRAISED

♪ First Hymn Praises God ♪

The four living creatures sing the first song of praise to God. The song praises God for 1) His holiness, for 2) His being the Almighty, and 3) for His everlasting nature — 1) He was, 2) He is, and 3) He is to come.

Revelation 4:8 ... the four living creatures ... never stop saying: "Holy, holy, holy is the Lord God Almighty, who was, and is, and is to come."

The number 3 once again symbolizes the godhead since three "holies" are sung to God in praise of His existence in all three timeframes.

♪ Second Hymn Praises God ♪

Revelation 4:10,11 The twenty-four elders fall down before him who sits on the throne, and worship him who lives for ever and ever. They lay their crowns before the throne and say: "You are worthy, our Lord and God, to receive glory and honor and power, for you created all things, and by your will they were created and have their being."

The twenty-four elders did three things to praise God; 1) they fell before Him; 2) they removed their crowns; and 3) they sang praise. When they sang their hymn of praise, the song exalted God for three great attributes — 1) glory, 2) honor, and 3) power. The repetition of the number 3 when God is the focus should make the reader even more aware of its powerful symbolic message.

The focus in chapter 5 changes to the right hand of God, in which He holds a sealed scroll, most likely the book of *Daniel*. Earlier material proved beyond any question that there is a great connection between the material Daniel sealed and that which John revealed.

Revelation 5:1 Then I saw in the right hand of him who sat on the throne a scroll with writing on both sides and sealed with seven seals.

Daniel was ordered to "seal" his message until the "time of the end." Since John saw all seven seals removed, the time in which John lived must have been another "time of the end." Earlier material demonstrated that the phrase "time of the end" referred to the end of an era, not the end of all time. Since John was living in the days of Rome's power, the particular "time of the end" would refer to the end of Rome.

One cannot begin to imagine John's excitement when he saw the sealed book and wondered at its content. At the beginning of his work John learned a revelation was coming; he eagerly anticipated the disclosure as he viewed the sealed book in God's hand. The suspense is built even higher when it looks as if the sealed scroll might not be opened after all.

> *Revelation 5:2-4 And I saw a mighty angel proclaiming in a loud voice, "Who is worthy to break the seals and open the scroll?" But no one in heaven or on earth or under the earth could open the scroll or even look inside it. I wept and wept because no one was found who was worthy to open the scroll or look inside.*

No one in heaven, on earth, or beneath the earth was found worthy to remove the seals. However, the situation was not hopeless! John discovers one was found worthy to open the seals.

> *Revelation 5:5 Then one of the elders said to me, "Do not weep! See, the Lion of the tribe of Judah, the Root of David, has triumphed. He is able to open the scroll and its seven seals."*

John was told earlier he was to receive a revelation from Jesus; Jesus is the Lion of the tribe of Judah; He is the Root of David, and He triumphed by His resurrection from the dead. John turns expecting to see the Lion of Judah, but what he sees is a Lamb!

> *Revelation 5:6,7 Then I saw a Lamb, looking as if it had been slain, standing in the center of the throne, encircled by the four living creatures and the elders. He had seven horns and seven eyes, which are the seven spirits of God sent out into all the earth. He came and took the scroll from the right hand of him who sat on the throne.*

The Lamb appeared as though it had been slain; Jesus became worthy to open the seals due to His sacrifice. The Lamb is standing in the middle of the throne where God was sitting. What a unique way of saying Jesus and God were One! The Lamb was characterized as having seven horns and seven eyes; the seven eyes were symbolic of the seven spirits of God. John saw Jesus in the middle of the throne, filled with the complete (seven spirits) spirit of God.

Jesus took the scroll from God; He was to open the seals Daniel had placed upon his prophecy over 600 years earlier. The spotlight was first upon God; then it turned upon the scroll in the right hand of God. The focal point finally shifts to Jesus as He holds the scroll.

♪ First Hymn Sung to Jesus ♪

Revelation 5:8-10   And when he had taken it, the four living creatures and the twenty-four elders fell down before the Lamb. Each one had a harp and they were holding golden bowls full of incense, which are the prayers of the saints. And they sang a new song: "You are worthy to take the scroll and to open its seals, because you were slain, and with your blood you purchased men for God from every tribe and language and people and nation. You have made them to be a kingdom and priests to serve our God, and they will reign on the earth."

Two groups sang the song of praise to Jesus — the twenty-four elders and the four living creatures. Each of these groups had earlier sung a hymn of praise to God before the appearance of the Lamb. The significant number 3 appears again as Jesus is praised for three acts — 1) He was slain; 2) He purchased men with His blood; and 3) He made people kings and priests. Peter wrote to Christians reminding them that they were priests and kings.

1 Peter 2:9   But you are a chosen people, a royal priesthood, a holy nation, a people belonging to God, that you may declare the praises of him who called you out of darkness into his wonderful light.

When the text of the hymn mentions mankind, humanity is divided into four categories — every tribe, and tongue, and people, and nation; the number 4 refers to the world.

♪ Second Hymn Sung to Jesus ♪

The fourth song of praise in this sequence was sung by angels surrounding the throne of God; it was the second song of praise for Jesus Christ.

Revelation 5:12 In a loud voice they sang: "Worthy is the Lamb, who was slain, to receive power and wealth and wisdom and strength and honor and glory and praise!"

The reason for praise is that **the Lamb is worthy** because He had been slain. Through His death, Jesus became victorious, and the hymn praises His worthiness by dying to receive seven accolades for His — 1) power, 2) wealth, 3) wisdom, 4) strength, 5) honor, 6) glory, and 7) praise. Seven symbolizes the **perfection** of Jesus and the **perfection** Jesus offers to mankind.

♪ One Hymn Praises both God and the Lamb ♪

Revelation 5:13 ... To him who sits on the throne and to the Lamb be praise and honor and glory and power, for ever and ever!

This last hymn of praise was sung by the seventh and last ring around God: every creature in heaven, on earth, and under the earth. It was the fifth song to be sung, and it was the third song of praise to God and the third song of praise to the Lamb. Both are praised for three attributes — 1) honor, 2) glory and 3) power. The number 3 symbolizes the godhead. Five is the number symbolizing grace, and it is the fifth song that unites God and Jesus in celebration.

I Corinthians 1:4 I always thank God for you because of his grace given you in Christ Jesus.

Titus 2:11 For the grace of God that brings salvation has appeared to all men.

The sealed book was now in the hands of the Son of God; the praises to God and to the Lamb have built the drama to its zenith.

JESUS OPENS THE SEALS

The imagery of *Revelation 6* comes from *Zechariah 6:5-8*, where the prophet saw four colors of horses — black, red, white, and grizzled. John saw horses that were white, red, black, and livid. Zechariah's horses were God's vehicles to patrol the earth; John's four horses brought a message concerning the fate of the earth.

The first four seals have several things in common. First, they were each introduced by one of the four living creatures; the command "Come" apparently was made to each rider rather than to John since it was the rider who came after the issuing of the command. Second, the first four seals all reveal riders on horses; the colors are highly symbolic. Third, the first four seals all reveal a relationship between man and his choice of serving God or worldliness. Fourth, the four present a picture that appears very bleak at first because they show those who follow the rider on the white horse will suffer extensive persecution.

1st Seal

Revelation 6:1,2 I watched as the Lamb opened the first of the seven seals. Then I heard one of the four living creatures say in a voice like thunder, "Come!" I looked, and there before me was a white horse! Its rider held a bow, and he was given a crown, and he rode out as a conqueror bent on conquest.

The most logical explanation for the rider on the white horse is Jesus Christ. Daniel had prophesied the coming of the King of kings would set up conflict on earth between the kingdom of God and the fourth great empire on earth, Rome. Now it is seen as reality; already the Romans had crucified the King of God's kingdom, but God would ultimately destroy Rome. Four characteristics of the rider on the white horse all point to Jesus Christ. First, white symbolizes purity; Jesus came into the world in all purity; He lived in all purity; He died in all purity. He appears on a white horse in *Revelation 19:6*, but in that appearance His clothing is stained with blood to take away the sins of the world. Because of His sacrifice, His followers can be clothed in pure white. Second, the rider on the white horse is carrying a bow; this is consistent with the messianic prophecy of David. The arrows are perfect symbols since Christ came into the world to conquer souls and gain converts. The piercing of the heart would be indicative of this act.

> *Psalms 45:4,5 In your majesty ride forth victoriously in behalf of truth, humility and righteousness; let your right hand display awesome deeds. Let your sharp arrows pierce the hearts of the king's enemies; let the nations fall beneath your feet.*

The arrows are perfect symbols since Christ came into the world to conquer souls and gain converts. The piercing of the heart would be indicative of this act.

Third, the rider is wearing the victor's crown. Jesus came in conflict with the Roman Empire, competing for the souls of men. To highlight His quest for victory over the lives of humanity, the rider of this horse is wearing a victor's crown, the stephanos.

Fourth, the rider came to conquer; when John used the word conquer in other places, the word referred to Christ and His believers; this is true in *John 16:33, Revelation 3:21* and *Revelation 5:5*. When Jesus came into this world and specifically into the Roman Empire, a great conflict was set in motion.

2nd Seal

> *Revelation 6:3,4 When the Lamb opened the second seal, I heard the second living creature say, "Come!" Then another horse came out, a fiery red one. Its rider was given power to take peace from the earth and to make men slay each other. To him was given a large sword.*

What was the next spiritual event after the arrival of the rider on the white horse? The event was the crucifixion of the rider and the persecution of His followers. Two keys are found in this passage; first, the horse is red, signifying bloodshed that had taken place and was to continue. Rome had tried Jesus Christ and sanctioned His death upon the cross. Rome had persecuted several Christian leaders and would kill many more who professed the name of Jesus.

The next key is the type of sword being carried; the Greek word for this sword is machaira, a knife used in sacrifices. It is not the Greek word rhomphaia, the sword used in war. War comes with the opening of the fourth seal and is not the subject of this seal. The revealing of this seal highlights the sacrifice Jesus and His followers had made and would make in serving God. This seal will become even clearer when Jesus opens the fifth seal to show slain saints beneath the altar of God.

3rd Seal

> *Revelation 6:5,6 When the Lamb opened the third seal, I heard the third living creature say, "Come!" I looked, and there before me was a black horse! Its rider was holding a pair of scales in his hand. Then I heard what sounded like a voice among the four living creatures, saying, "A quart of wheat for a day's wages, and three quarts of barley for a day's wages, and do not damage the oil and the wine!"*

Besides martyrdom, another consequence of the arrival of the rider on the white horse was economic persecution. The price of wheat and barley was so prohibitive that the goods bought on a full day's wages could feed only a small family for one day. If the entire day's wages would pay only for the food for one day, what could be done to furnish the other necessities of life? The oil and wine would not be harmed; these items could be purchased by the rich, but they were also significant in worship — perhaps indicating God would see His people through. Most Christians, being economically poor, would suffer hard times. If they had bowed down and worshipped caesars, access to the system was theirs, but this would have jeopardized their souls; thus, many simply went without. The thirteenth chapter of *Revelation* develops the concept even further.

> *Revelation 13:16,17 He also forced everyone, small and great, rich and poor, free and slave, to receive a*

mark on his right hand or on his forehead, so that no one could buy or sell unless he had the mark, which is the name of the beast or the number of his name.

The second and third horses are similar in that both revealed persecutions coming to those who had been converted to the cause of Jesus. Some try to make the third seal refer to famine, but that is a part of the fourth seal.

4th Seal

Revelation 6:7,8   When the Lamb opened the fourth seal, I heard the voice of the fourth living creature say, "Come!" I looked, and there before me was a pale horse! Its rider was named Death, and Hades was following close behind him. They were given power over a fourth of the earth to kill by sword, famine and plague, and by the wild beasts of the earth.

The use of the number 4 is significant in the above verses. It is the fourth seal that has been opened; it is the fourth creature who ushers in the vision; it is the fourth rider who appears; it symbolizes death that can occur in four ways. Four is the number of the world, and every human is subject to trial, tribulations, and death. Being a citizen under Roman rule, Christians were not exempt from these circumstances.

Physical death was not a concern to most followers of God; the Christian feared only spiritual death, also called the second death. The first type of death came from the Greek word rhomphaia, the large sword used in warfare. The Roman Empire was soon to become embroiled in many wars, and many Christians would die as a result of the events. The second threat listed is famine; the third is plague or disease. Fourth, many would die from wild beasts of the earth; many Christians were thrown to the beasts because of their beliefs.

When all four horses are considered, the following scenario occurs: 1) Christ came into the world conquering the souls of men; 2) the Roman Empire crucified Jesus and sacrificed His followers. 3) The empire also used economic sanctions to punish those who chose to serve Christ rather than the caesar. 4) Christians would also die in other ways simply because they lived in the Roman Empire during an era of turmoil. Things certainly looked bleak for the followers of Christ after the opening of the first four seals, and when the fifth seal is opened, the resulting vision brings no surprise at all.

5th Seal

> *Revelation 6:9 When he opened the fifth seal, I saw under the altar the souls of those who had been slain because of the word of God and the testimony they had maintained. They called out in a loud voice, "How long, Sovereign Lord, holy and true, until you judge the inhabitants of the earth and avenge our blood?" Then each of them was given a white robe, and they were told to wait a little longer, until the number of their fellow servants and brothers who were to be killed as they had been was completed.*

It is logical that slain saints should be seen after witnessing the revelations of the first four seals, and it is only logical they should be beneath the altar since they had been sacrificed for God. Daniel had prophesied these martyrs would be avenged, and they cried for God to bring His vengeance on the persecutor. Although they had died physically, the slain saints were victorious in eternal glory. They were pure and dressed in white because of their allegiance to the rider on the white horse; He had washed them in His blood. The promise was made to Sardis in *Revelation 3:4* that those who overcame would be dressed in white.

The opening of this seal not only tells about the ones who had already died for the cause of Christ, it also reveals that others would be killed for the cause. This is as true today as it was when Rome was sacrificing Christians. The specific message may have referred to those who were about to go through the terrible persecutions of Rome, but the secondary application has replayed the scene countless times and will continue as long as the earth lasts. It logically follows that if seal five revealed slain saints beneath the altar asking for vengeance, vengeance would not be far away.

6th Seal

> *Revelation 6:12-17 I watched as he opened the sixth seal. There was a great earthquake. The sun turned black like sackcloth made of goat hair, the whole moon turned blood red, and the stars in the sky fell to earth, as late figs drop from a fig tree when shaken by a strong wind. The sky receded like a scroll, rolling up, and every mountain and island was removed from its place. Then the kings of the earth, the princes, the generals, the rich, the mighty, and every slave and every free man hid in caves and among the rocks of the mountains. They called to the mountains and the rocks, "Fall on us and hide us from the face of him who sits on the throne and from the wrath of the Lamb! For the great day of their wrath has come, and who can stand?"*

The prophets in referring to various collapses of Jerusalem portrayed the "time of their end" in ways sounding very similar to the material above.

> *Isaiah 60:20 Your sun will never set again, and your moon will wane no more; the LORD will be your everlasting light, and your days of sorrow will end.*

> *Joel 3:15 The sun and moon will be darkened, and the stars no longer shine.*

> *Amos 8:9 "In that day," declares the Sovereign LORD, "I will make the sun go down at noon and darken the earth in broad daylight."*

Often when God was victorious in the Old Testament, calamities such as these were mentioned as indications of heavenly intervention and changes on earth. It sounds like the end of all earth time, but **John was envisioning the end of the Roman Empire**. The calamity was so great that seven types of destruction are shown to indicate God's total power in His wrath: 1) the earth would quake, 2) the sun would turn black, 3) the moon would turn to blood, 4) stars would fall, 5) the heavens would be destroyed, 6) mountains would collapse, and 7) islands would disappear. Also, seven types of earth dwellers were affected, once again indicating completeness: 1) kings, 2) princes, 3) chief captains, 4) rich, 5) strong, 6) bondmen, and 7) freemen. Vindication was what the slain had requested, and vindication was the result; the chapter ends with a great question: **"Who is able to stand?"** This question is answered in *Revelation* 7 before the opening of the 7th seal.

Before Armageddon arrives, John reveals who will be victorious.

Only one seal remained to be opened, and with the revelations brought by the opening of the first six seals, the reader might be filled with despair. The message changes in tone as *Revelation* 7 opens. Those sealed by the blood of the Lamb will be victorious. Furthermore, God knows every person who receives His seal; not one of the redeemed will be lost when He rewards the faithful. John next saw four angels holding back the winds of destruction until all the redeemed are marked for protection.

> *Revelation 7:1 After this I saw four angels standing at the four corners of the earth, holding back the four winds of the earth to prevent any wind from blowing on the land or on the sea or on any tree. Then I saw another angel coming up from the east, having the seal of the living God. He called out in a loud voice to the four angels who had been given power to harm the land and the sea: "Do not harm the land or the sea or the trees until we put a seal on the foreheads of the servants of our God."*

The number 4 is significant again in relating to the world, the four corners representing east, west, north, and south. Christians in the first century should have taken great comfort in realizing God would not allow harm to fall upon the earth without having a plan to protect the faithful. Before the flood, God had Noah prepare an ark; Lot's family was ushered from Sodom and Gomorrah before fire and brimstone destroyed the place. Before God passed over Egypt to bring death of the first born, He had Israel mark their doorposts with blood. God has always had a plan to protect the faithful when destruction is brought upon the earth. The protection arrived when the fifth angel came from the east (sunrise) carrying the seal of God. Ezekiel saw a marking of God's faithful before destruction came upon Israel; they were marked on their foreheads just as the faithful were in this scene. The seal of God is the Spirit He places within our hearts. This is a basic truth; **God has always known His followers, and he does today!**

> *II Corinthians 1:22 Set his seal of ownership on us, and put his Spirit in our hearts as a deposit, guaranteeing what is to come.*
>
> *Ephesians 1:13 And you also were included in Christ when you heard the word of truth, the gospel of your salvation. Having believed, you were marked in him with a seal, the promised Holy Spirit.*

It is significant that the sealing was to take place upon the forehead since thoughts come from the mind. Ezekiel also envisioned a "sealing" or "marking" of the faithful; the purpose in both instances was for the identification of God's people and protection of the chosen when disaster was brought upon the world. After seeing the angel with the seal, John next heard the number of those who were sealed.

> *Revelation 7:4-8 Then I heard the number of those who were sealed: 144,000 from all the tribes of Israel. From the tribe of Judah 12,000 were sealed, from the tribe of Reuben 12,000, from the tribe of Gad 12,000, from the tribe of Asher 12,000, from the tribe of Naphtali 12,000, from the tribe of Manasseh 12,000, from the tribe of Simeon 12,000, from the tribe of Levi 12,000, from the tribe of Issachar 12,000, from the tribe of Zebulun 12,000, from the tribe of Joseph 12,000, from the tribe of Benjamin 12,000.*

Much speculation has occurred as to the identity of the 144,000 who were sealed. This throng is obviously symbolic for several reasons. First, the number 144,000 is formed by multiplying 12 times 12 to arrive at 144. The number <u>144</u> is then multiplied by 1,000 to create 144,000. The number <u>1,000</u> is powerful; it is the total number ten cubed, 10 X 10 X 10. Remember, one thousand is the strongest method of saying **ALL, EVERY, TOTAL, FOREVER**. When one multiplies 1,000 times 144, the product is 144,000; the symbolic meaning is that God knows every person ever sealed with His Spirit, from both the Old Law and from the New Law, from the beginning of time until today.

Second, the symbolism is evident because the listing of the tribes is unique. In Old Testament listings the tribe of Joseph is sometimes mentioned, but when the tribes of Ephraim and Manasseh are recorded, Joseph and Levi are left out. When land possessions are enumerated, Levi is left out; therefore Ephraim and Manasseh are counted to bring the number to 12. Whenever Levi is involved in the listing, Ephraim and Manasseh are not mentioned; rather, Joseph is listed as a tribe. In this listing, Levi is included; one would expect Joseph to be listed, but not Ephraim and Manasseh. Read the list carefully, and note: **Dan and Ephraim are left out; Joseph and Manasseh are named.** This is not like any other list found in the entirety of the Old Testament! Ephraim and Dan were most likely omitted because of their evil nature as apostate tribes; whatever the reason, this list is obviously symbolic.

Third, it is interesting that the listing begins with Judah, because Judah was not the oldest brother. Judah, however, was the tribe through which Jesus would come to bless the entire world, not just the nation of Israel. Does the list just include Israel? Remember that **Israel is symbolic of the church**. Paul said Jews today are not physical Jews, but those who form spiritual Jerusalem. Chapter 7 of this volume explains the shift in emphasis of Jerusalem and Israel under the Old Covenant to new Jerusalem and spiritual Israel under the New Covenant.

> *Galatians 3:26-29 You are all sons of God through faith in Christ Jesus, for all of you who were baptized into Christ have clothed yourselves with Christ. There is neither Jew nor Greek, slave nor free, male nor female, for you are all one in Christ Jesus. If you belong to Christ, then you are Abraham's seed, and heirs according to the promise.*

Fourth, when the 144,000 are seen in *Revelation 14*, they are on Mount Zion. The writer of *Hebrews* makes it perfectly clear Mount

Zion is symbolic of the church. The sealing of the 144,000 in *Revelation 7* identified those who were entering the church; seeing the 144,000 on Mount Zion in *Revelation 14* should come as no surprise — it verified that the sealing was successful. The 144,000 are located right where God planned for them to be — **in His Church!**

> *Hebrews 12:22-24 But you have come to Mount Zion...* ***to the church of the firstborn****, whose names are written in heaven ...*

Furthermore, it is obvious the number 144,000 John saw on Mount Zion is not the exact total of the redeemed in heaven because John saw a much larger number than this in heaven who had already come through persecution. Ironically, the redeemed in heaven would seem to picture those redeemed under the first covenant, and the listing of tribes would symbolize spiritual Jews under the new covenant.

> *Revelation 7:9,10 After this I looked and there before me was a great multitude that no one could count, from every nation, tribe, people and language, standing before the throne and in front of the Lamb. They were wearing white robes and were holding palm branches in their hands. And they cried out in a loud voice: "Salvation belongs to our God, who sits on the throne, and to the Lamb."*

The four-fold listing of "nation, tongue, tribe and people" highlights their earthly existence. Their victory is evident in three ways: 1) they were wearing white; 2) they held palm branches in their hands; 3) they praised God and the Lamb for their salvation. As the section continues, the ring of angels in heaven praised God with seven words characteristic of the Almighty: 1) blessing, 2) glory, 3) wisdom, 4) thanksgiving, 5) honor, 6) power, and 7) might.

The ones who were seen were so numerous they could not be counted. The next part of the section described who they were and in what ways they were blessed.

> *Revelation 7:13-17 Then one of the elders asked me, "These in white robes — who are they, and where did they come from?" I answered, "Sir, you know." And he*

> *said, "These are they who have come out of the great tribulation; they have washed their robes and made them white in the blood of the Lamb. Therefore, "they are before the throne of God and serve him day and night in his temple; and he who sits on the throne will spread his tent over them. Never again will they hunger; never again will they thirst. The sun will not beat upon them, nor any scorching heat. For the Lamb at the center of the throne will be their shepherd; he will lead them to springs of living water. And God will wipe away every tear from their eyes."*

Comfort must have prevailed when John saw this scene; it is clear the faithful would come through all persecution because God knows their identity. If God knows who they are and if God has the power to reward, nothing can stop the faithful from being victorious. Not only does John see the protected on the earth, but also he sees the previously victorious in heaven. If either group pictured Israel, it would be the latter group that had already come through tribulations of the past. Someone might ask, "How could this be Israel if they were washed in the blood of the Lamb?" This is explained in the following scripture:

> *Hebrews 9:15 For this reason Christ is the mediator of a new covenant, that those who are called may receive the promised eternal inheritance — now that* **he has died as a ransom to set them free from the sins committed under the first covenant.**

The writer of *Hebrews* clarifies even further:

> *Hebrews 9:26 Then Christ would have had to suffer many times since the creation of the world. But now he has appeared once for all at the end of the ages to do away with sin by the sacrifice of himself.*

Since Jesus appeared once for all, His death benefitted those who sacrificed the blood of animals in preparation of His coming as much as those who were to wash their robes in His blood after His arrival on earth.

It is because Jesus cleansed them that they are in heaven; it was certainly worth it for the early Christians to reject the temptations of Rome in remaining faithful to God with all these benefits awaiting them. Now that the reader has been assured of victory, it is time for the Lamb to remove the final seal from the scroll.

7th Seal

Revelation 8:1 When he opened the seventh seal, there was silence in heaven for about half an hour.

When the seventh seal was removed, there were no more seals to conceal the works of God. One of the purposes for Jesus' coming to earth was to end the sealing of prophecy. The events in His life fulfilled the prophets of old, and now Jesus has completed the removal of all seven seals. The remainder of the book of *Revelation* was revealed when Jesus removed that last seal. **No wonder there was silence for thirty minutes**!

Jesus did not leave any seals for future prophets to reveal; Jesus revealed all to John who, in turn, revealed the message to his readers in the first century. With the removal of the seals, all the preparations have been made. It is now time for John to explain to his readers the exciting things that had been sealed for over 600 years; these events were to happen shortly after the book was penned in the first century.

Once the seals are removed to reveal what is coming, trumpets will sound next to give ample warning for men to turn to God.

Chapter Eleven

The Seven Trumpets

Jesus' opening of the seventh seal brought the half hour of silence; afterwards, John saw seven angels with trumpets.

> *Revelation 8:2 And I saw the seven angels who stand before God, and to them were given seven trumpets.*

The opening of the seven seals lets readers know God was about to bring an end to the Roman Empire; the trumpets sounded a warning of imminent collapse. The warning of trumpets was done more to prepare Christians than it was to warn Rome.

After seeing the seven angels, John saw another angel taking incense from the altar.

> *Revelation 8:3-5 Another angel, who had a golden censer, came and stood at the altar. He was given much incense to offer, with the prayers of all the saints, on the golden altar before the throne. The smoke of the incense, together with the prayers of the saints, went up before God from the angel's hand. Then the angel took the censer, filled it with fire from the altar, and hurled it on the earth; and there came peals of thunder, rumblings, flashes of lightning and an earthquake.*

The altar was last seen when the fifth seal was opened to reveal slain saints praying beneath the altar for God's vengeance. When the angel mixed the incense with the prayers of the saints, this strengthened the message sent to God. It is rather apparent that God's vengeance is approaching when the angel took fire from the altar and threw it upon the earth. The action of the angel brought four reactions — thunder, rumblings, lightning, and earthquake. The number 4 adds strength to the message because it is the number of the world.

Dramatic buildups are effective in *Revelation* to heighten anticipation of coming events. The chapter begins with seven angels being given trumpets. Excitement builds as John sees the prayers for vengeance gaining more strength with the efforts of an angel. As the buildup continues, John sees the angels with the trumpets making preparations to sound their warnings.

First Trumpet Sounds

Revelation 8:7 The first angel sounded his trumpet, and there came hail and fire mixed with blood, and it was hurled down upon the earth. A third of the earth was burned up, a third of the trees were burned up, and all the green grass was burned up.

The first trumpet warned of disaster striking the earth. To show this was merely a warning rather than a picture of final destruction, one-third of all vegetation was destroyed. Some point to the last part of the verse that says "all the green grass was burned up" and claim this is a departure from the one-third theme; however, if taken in context, all of the green grass in the one-third of the world affected was burned; there is no contradiction.

Concerning the devastation that nature would bring upon Rome, it might be interesting to the reader to read an article in the May 1984, *National Geographic Magazine* about the eruption of Mt. Vesuvius. *Revelation* was written during the time of Vespasian between 69 and 79 AD. Vespasian died in July of 79 AD, just two months before Mt. Vesuvius destroyed Pompeii and Herculaneum as effectively as any nuclear device could have done the job. Disasters such as this, coupled with other problems of the empire, helped hasten its fall.

Second Trumpet Sounds

Revelation 8:8,9   The second angel sounded his trumpet, and something like a huge mountain, all ablaze, was thrown into the sea. A third of the sea turned into blood, a third of the living creatures in the sea died, and a third of the ships were destroyed.

When the third part of the sea became blood, one is reminded of the plague over Egypt when the Nile turned to blood. Just as the earth had only one-third destroyed, only one-third of the sea was affected by the trumpet.

Third Trumpet Sounds

Revelation 8:10,11   The third angel sounded his trumpet, and a great star, blazing like a torch, fell from the sky on a third of the rivers and on the springs of water — the name of the star is Wormwood. A third of the waters turned bitter, and many people died from the waters that had become bitter.

To understand "wormwood," one needs to turn to the prophet Jeremiah.

Jeremiah 9:15   Therefore, this is what the LORD Almighty, the God of Israel, says: "See, I will make this people eat bitter food and drink poisoned water."

Some versions use the word <u>wormwood</u> in *Jeremiah*. The NIV uses more modern language in explaining that the water was poisoned. Jeremiah uses this as a symbol for suffering because of evil. The significance of the star's turning the water to wormwood is that God brings about the destruction; it is not mere happenstance. It is a warning once again, because only one-third of the fresh water is polluted by the trumpet. At this point the earth, the seas, and the fresh water have all been affected; John next foresees the universe afflicted by plague.

Fourth Trumpet Sounds

Revelation 8:12 The fourth angel sounded his trumpet, and a third of the sun was struck, a third of the moon, and a third of the stars, so that a third of them turned dark. A third of the day was without light, and also a third of the night.

This reminds one of the plague of darkness brought against Egypt; however, in this instance it was used as a warning since total darkness did not occur. The overall effect of the four trumpets is similar to the disastrous plagues brought upon Egypt when God brought the nation down for abusing His people. All four trumpets point to natural disasters serving as warnings; 1) land, 2) sea, 3) rivers, and 4) universe are all affected.

Each occurrence of natural disaster should remind us that God is in control of the universe. A day is coming in which the earth and all its elements will be destroyed, but in this particular case the warning was sounded that Rome was about to suffer the wrath of God. The number 4 underscores the common feature of this group of trumpets; the elements of the earth and its surroundings played big in the fall of this evil nation. Just as God protected His people in the fall of Egypt, He promised once more to protect His own when Rome began to crumble. God has protected His people throughout the history of the world, and in this post-modern era, God still stands ready to protect His followers when earthly nations fall.

Before the fifth trumpet sounds, another dramatic delay occurs to emphasize the severity of coming disaster.

Revelation 8:13 As I watched, I heard an eagle that was flying in midair call out in a loud voice: "Woe! Woe! Woe to the inhabitants of the earth, because of the trumpet blasts about to be sounded by the other three angels!"

The eagle was seen in mid-heaven, screaming "Woe" three times; these factors, along with the three remaining trumpets, accentuate the divine nature of the destruction about to come upon Rome. The three "woes" refer to the last three warnings about to be sounded. Once these three trumpets have sent their warnings, the plagues on Rome will begin. The destruction was to come upon "the inhabitants of the earth," a phrase that refers to those not sealed of God — worldly people.

Fifth Trumpet Sounds

Revelation 9:1 The fifth angel sounded his trumpet, and I saw a star that had fallen from the sky to the earth. The star was given the key to the shaft of the Abyss.

To fully understand the vision, it is important to examine the fifth bowl to be poured upon the earth. The trumpets and bowls parallel each other with the trumpets sounding warnings and the bowls inflicting the plagues of finality. The fifth vial brings total darkness upon the earth, darkness being the symbol of sin and evil. The image of the fifth trumpet is also one of evil; God oftentimes permits evil to run its course to destroy the perpetrators. Gibbon wrote that one of the reasons for the collapse of Rome was internal corruption, and the evil abyss certainly paints the picture. It is easy to get "hung up" on the individual components of the vision without looking to the total picture and the relationship of the image to the overall message.

The first part of the vision deals with the falling of the star from heaven, the giving of the key, and the opening of the evil abyss. In chapter 1 of *Revelation* a star was used to represent each angel for the separate churches in Asia. Several indicators point to this angel as a fallen, evil angel; perhaps it is one of the angels to which Peter referred.

> *II Peter 2:4 For if God did not spare angels when they sinned, but sent them to hell, putting them into gloomy dungeons to be held for judgment ...*

Three clues suggesting the angel is evil are as follows: 1) the angel **had fallen**, 2) the angel did not do these things by his own power; he was given the key or the power to unleash evil. God can bring an end to evil and this sinful world any time He so wills. 3) When the key was used, it brought forth evil; the abyss is the place where Satan abides. Darkness is a biblical characteristic of evil. Evil is always lurking and waiting for someone to join the dark life of sin; the angel brings this about. All one has to do is read about Roman corruption to know one of the reasons for its downfall was its evil ways that went uncontrolled. As the vision continues, the picture is clearly one of sin and the effects it generates.

> *Revelation 9:2 When he opened the Abyss, smoke rose from it like the smoke from a gigantic furnace. The sun and sky were darkened by the smoke from the Abyss.*

Darkness is the enemy of light. The fifth trumpet sounds the warning of what darkness will bring; the total darkness brought by the pouring of the fifth bowl indicates the end result of sin.

> *II Corinthians 4:4 The god of this age has blinded the minds of unbelievers, so that they cannot see the light of the gospel of the glory of Christ, who is the image of God.*

> *James 1:14-15 Each one is tempted when, by his own evil desire, he is dragged away and enticed. Then, after desire has conceived, it gives birth to sin; and sin, when it is full-grown, gives birth to death.*

> *Revelation 9:3 And out of the smoke locusts came down upon the earth and were given power like that of scorpions of the earth. They were told not to harm the grass of the earth or any plant or tree, but only those people who did not have the seal of God on their foreheads. They were not given power to kill them, but*

> *only to torture them for five months. And the agony they suffered was like that of the sting of a scorpion when it strikes a man. During those days men will seek death, but will not find it; they will long to die, but death will elude them.*

The passages above explain the mission and nature of the locusts coming from the smoke of the abyss. It is obvious these locusts are symbolic because they did not harm vegetation as normal locusts do. Their purpose was to harm men, those who had not been sealed. The image of locusts was used because of their power to destroy. It's obviously a warning because the locusts were not given the power to kill, only to torture for five months. The description of the locusts creates a scene of horror.

> *Revelation 9:7-11 The locusts looked like horses prepared for battle. On their heads they wore something like crowns of gold, and their faces resembled human faces. Their hair was like women's hair, and their teeth were like lions' teeth. They had breastplates like breastplates of iron, and the sound of their wings was like the thundering of many horses and chariots rushing into battle. They had tails and stings like scorpions, and in their tails they had power to torment people for five months. They had as king over them the angel of the Abyss, whose name in Hebrew is Abaddon, and in Greek, Apollyon.*

The locusts are compared to horses; locusts' heads look much like the heads of horses, and the name for locust in German even comes from their word for horse. These locusts had on their heads the appearance of a crown of gold; they were striving to be victorious over men, to gain the souls of those not sealed of God. The face of man, hair of woman, and teeth of the lion all give a picture of terror hard to equal. The locusts had breastplates that looked like iron; this gave evil the appearance of power — they were "as" of iron. Satan's strength can be overcome by God's power; Satan's power is temporary and limited. The sound of the wings was tremendously loud, compared to the sound of many chariots rushing to war. The loudness of their wings underscores the destructive power of evil.

The actual power of the locusts was in their tails, a tail compared to that of a scorpion. The sting of the locust was to last for five months; this is the actual life span of a locust, but the symbol goes much deeper than this. Five is one-half of the total number ten; the number 5 is symbolic of grace that is always present, even when evil prevails. It is through God's grace and His light that man can be protected from the evil of the world. **When one does not accept grace, he faces the sting of sin!** Man has a choice of reaching for grace to rise above evil, or he can choose to pursue evil. When the latter choice is made, and when evil has run its course, there is a point of no return regardless of the desire to repent. To choose evil is to invite disaster; Rome learned the lesson, and every evil civilization since that time has experienced this principle.

To wrap up the picture of evil, John reveals the name of the locusts' leader — the name in Hebrew is Abaddon; the name in Greek is Apollyon; the name in English is **Destroyer.** The picture is a frightening one of Satan's leading his forces against humanity.

It is significant to learn the ones harmed by the locusts had not been sealed. Before the trumpets were ever sounded, God had sealed His followers and knew who belonged to Him; those harmed had chosen to follow the ways of the world. The message to understand at this time is that those who seek evil are in the end consumed and destroyed by the very goal they sought. The end of evil is destruction, and there is no way out, not even death itself. One of the chief reasons for the collapse of the Roman Empire was its excesses in sin — internal corruption.

Another dramatic effect occurs when the reader is reminded only one of the three woes was finished; two more were coming.

Revelation 9:12 The first woe is past; two other woes are yet to come.

Sixth Trumpet Sounds

Revelation 9:13-16 The sixth angel sounded his trumpet, and I heard a voice coming from the horns of the golden altar that is before God. It said to the sixth angel who had the trumpet, "Release the four angels who are bound at the great river Euphrates." And the four angels who had been kept ready for this very hour and day and month and year were released to kill a third of mankind. The number of the mounted troops was two hundred million. I heard their number.

All one has to do to discover the general message of the trumpet is to read about the sixth bowl because it parallels the sixth trumpet. The message is clearly one of war; God used war as one of the means to bring an end to the Roman Empire. The trumpet only sounded a warning of the ultimate fall because one-third of mankind was killed in the confrontation. Pierre Grimal, in *The Civilization of Rome*, said the relation between Rome and the Parthians was ruptured as early as 112 AD, and invasions on the part of both powers occurred frequently. Even though other countries later overthrew Rome, war and the fall happened because of God's will.

God's will is further evidenced because of three factors—1) the voice releasing the angels was the voice of God. 2) God had earlier restrained these angels until His purposes had been accomplished; the time had arrived. 3) The specific time was determined by God down to the hour, day, month, and year; this makes the fall more than mere happenstance. This should remind the reader of Daniel's prophecy about God's determining when Babylon would fall, when Medo-Persia would rise and collapse, when Greece would become a power, and when it would fold. This merely carries through with the theme of evil's bringing its own destruction. God also planned for the demise of the Roman Empire with His decree for its fall. Rome reached its highest level of power around the year 116 under Trajan; after that point, Rome was on the way downhill. Its destruction was already set in motion.

Some versions give the number of the army as double ten thousand X ten thousand. The 200 million troops would be overwhelming if the number were literal; however, one must remember this is a symbolic book, and number symbols help to clarify the message. The number 10 symbolizes completeness, totality. The number 1,000 is the cube of the number 10; ten thousand X ten thousand gives the impression of a no win situation, and then this number is doubled. ROME WOULD SURELY FALL! The appearance of the horses and the horsemen present a picture of absolute power.

> *Revelation 9:17-19 The horses and riders I saw in my vision looked like this: Their breastplates were fiery red, dark blue, and yellow as sulfur. The heads of the horses resembled the heads of lions, and out of their mouths came fire, smoke and sulfur. A third of mankind was killed by the three plagues of fire, smoke and sulfur that came out of their mouths. The power of the horses was in their mouths and in their tails; for their tails were like snakes, having heads with which they inflict injury.*

The repetition of the phrase "fire, smoke, and sulfur," plus the tails like serpents certainly punctuate the satanic theme. God, once again, used earthly forces to accomplish His will. The purpose of the trumpet was to warn those willing to listen. The warning was earlier seen when verse 15 stated the war would kill one-third of humanity; it was not the final destruction that would come with the pouring of the vials. Verse 18 repeats the point that one-third of mankind was killed. God constantly sends warnings to those willing to listen, but people respond in one of two ways. Some are searching for God and His will; these will find God's will and react accordingly. Others hear the warnings God sends but do not heed because they are not searching for God nor for His will. How did the wicked react when the warnings were sounded?

> *Revelation 9:20,21 The rest of mankind that were not killed by these plagues still did not repent of the work of their hands; they did not stop worshiping demons, and idols of gold, silver, bronze, stone and wood —*

idols that cannot see or hear or walk. Nor did they repent of their murders, their magic arts, their sexual immorality or their thefts.

The number symbols are powerful in these two verses; those who did not respond to God worshipped 6 ungodly items: 1) demons, 2) gold idols, 3) silver idols, 4) bronze idols, 5) stone idols, and 6) wood idols. The idols were substitutions for the real God, but they did not possess the quality of 3; they could not 1) see, 2) hear, or 3) walk. The number 3 is usually reserved for the godhead; the absence of three qualities within these false gods indicates they are pseudo-gods. The worldly remained in their wicked condition symbolized by 4 evils: 1) murders, 2) magic arts, 3) sexual immorality, and 4) thefts. The number symbols in *Revelation* are quite amazing!

THREE ADDITIONAL VISIONS AFTER TRUMPET SIX

After the sounding of trumpet six to warn of warfare, John saw three visions foretelling what would happen to the people of God during the persecution of the beast. The first vision was the angel with a little scroll; "little" would be another way of indicating the short time until fulfillment of the prophecy. Another clue the events were to come quickly is seen as the angel holds an open scroll. All seven seals had been removed from the "sealed" scroll; no wonder the angel now held an "open" scroll!

Revelation 10:1-3 Then I saw another mighty angel coming down from heaven. He was robed in a cloud, with a rainbow above his head; his face was like the sun, and his legs were like fiery pillars. He was holding a little scroll, which lay open in his hand. He planted his right foot on the sea and his left foot on the land, and he gave a loud shout like the roar of a lion. When he shouted, the voices of the seven thunders spoke.

In reality, the angel appears to be Jesus Christ. In other places Jesus is symbolized by a Lion, a Lamb, and a rider on a horse; there should be no difficulty in an angel's being used to symbolize Jesus. The following characteristics of the angel indicate it is actually Jesus who is being pictured by the vision: 1) He is arrayed with a cloud;

Jesus was last seen by earth dwellers as He ascended through the clouds to heaven. 2) A rainbow is on His head; the rainbow was a characteristic of God in *Revelation 4*. 3) His face was as the sun; the sun is a symbol of God.

Another strong clue to the identity is the legs like fiery pillars; this is very similar to the description of Jesus in *Revelation 1*. In *Revelation* 8:1, Jesus removed the seventh and last seal from the once sealed scroll; all the seals were removed, leaving Jesus holding an open scroll. This angel is holding an open scroll in His hand. **Who else could it be but Jesus?** Even the angel's having one foot on the earth and one on the land point to Jesus; He is the Lord of the earth and the Lord of the sea. His strong voice "like a lion" would be another symbol of Jesus; He was earlier called the "Lion of the tribe of Judah."

During this scene, the seven thunders speak. The message of the seven thunders signifies the will of God is imminent; there is no time for John to record the message of the seven thunders.

> *Revelation 10:3-7 And he gave a loud shout like the roar of a lion. When he shouted, the voices of the seven thunders spoke. And when the seven thunders spoke, I was about to write; but I heard a voice from heaven say, "Seal up what the seven thunders have said and do not write it down." Then the angel I had seen standing on the sea and on the land raised his right hand to heaven. And he swore by him who lives for ever and ever, who created the heavens and all that is in them, the earth and all that is in it, and the sea and all that is in it, and said, "There will be no more delay! But in the days when the seventh angel is about to sound his trumpet, the mystery of God will be accomplished, just as he announced to his servants the prophets."*

No one in this life will ever know what the seven thunders uttered since God forbade John's passing it on to his readers. Apparently it is not important to know what the seven thunders said. Since seven thunders are used, it appears the message from the thunders is straight from God and meant only for the ears of John. When John was ordered not to take the time to write the message, it magnifies the urgency and immediacy of the events about to occur.

The next part of the message is very similar to a vision seen in *Ezekiel 3:3*. Ezekiel was shown an open scroll, was told to eat it, was told it would be sweet to his mouth, and was told to take the message to the world. These are the same circumstances surrounding John's vision of the angel with the open scroll.

> *Revelation 10:8 Then the voice that I had heard from heaven spoke to me once more: "Go, take the scroll that lies open in the hand of the angel who is standing on the sea and on the land." So I went to the angel and asked him to give me the little scroll. He said to me, "Take it and eat it. It will turn your stomach sour, but in your mouth it will be as sweet as honey." I took the little scroll from the angel's hand and ate it. It tasted as sweet as honey in my mouth, but when I had eaten it, my stomach turned sour. Then I was told, "You must prophesy again about many peoples, nations, languages and kings."*

John was first told to take the scroll from the angel; then the angel commanded him to consume the scroll. The actual Greek idiom is "eat it down"; John was to internalize the message of God before teaching it to others. It was essential for John to have complete understanding. It seems clear from earlier material that John fully comprehended what Daniel the prophet wrote some seven centuries earlier. The scroll was both bitter and sweet indicating good was to be mingled with bad in the coming events. It was sweet news that God would bring vengeance upon the Roman Empire, and it was sweet that the purposes of God would be fulfilled in the victory of the church. It was bitter because many would be destroyed eternally!

John was to continue prophesying to four groups — peoples, nations, tongues, and kings. The number 4 indicates his message was for the entire world. Although it was a letter to the seven churches and dealt with problems about to confront Christians in the Roman Empire, these great truths have been repeated over the last twenty centuries. This part of the vision merely re-commissions John to do what God had earlier told him to accomplish. Most likely, the scroll was the book of *Daniel*; with the seals removed, it was an open scroll.

The second event within the interim was the measuring of the temple, altar, and worshippers.

> *Revelation 11:1   I was given a reed like a measuring rod and was told, "Go and measure the temple of God and the altar, and count the worshipers there. But exclude the outer court; do not measure it, because it has been given to the Gentiles. They will trample on the holy city for 42 months."*

In *Ezekiel 40:3* a man appeared with a reed to measure the temple. In chapters 40 and 41, all details within the temple are measured, each item and each part of the structure. The measuring in *Revelation* is symbolic; the actual temple was not to be measured, but rather the people of God. Since Jerusalem fell in 70 AD under the siege of Titus, it is possible the temple did not even exist at the time of the writing of *Revelation*.

Paul tells us those who have the indwelling of the Spirit of God within them are "God's temple."

> *I Corinthians 3:16,17   Don't you know that you yourselves are God's temple and that God's Spirit lives in you? If anyone destroys God's temple, God will destroy him; for God's temple is sacred, and you are that temple.*

The measuring of the three items — temple, altar, and worship — identify and confirm God's people; this action is very similar to the sealing of the 144,000. God knows those who belong to Him!

John was told not to measure the outer court. There was no reason to measure the outer court because those in the outer court had clearly made their choice for the world. The ones in the outer court were to tread the holy city for forty-two months; as noted earlier, the holy city is spiritual Jerusalem or the church. The time itself, forty-two months, is the same as three and one-half years, 1260 days, and "time, times and half a time." *Revelation* tells of two events that would occur during the forty-two month timeframe — 1) The beast would persecute Christianity and 2) God would protect His people.

The third event in the vision can actually be included with the second, but because of its uniqueness, it will be treated separately. During the 1260 days that the church, symbolized as the "holy city," was being trampled, God's witnesses would continue their work of preaching to the world.

> *Revelation 11:3-5 And I will give power to my two witnesses, and they will prophesy for 1,260 days, clothed in sackcloth. These are the two olive trees and the two lampstands that stand before the Lord of the earth.*

Zechariah saw two olive trees, one on each side of a lampstand; the two who were anointed to serve the Lord at that time were Zerubbabel, governor of Judah, and Joshua, the high priest.

> *Zechariah 4:11 Then I asked the angel, "What are these two olive trees on the right and the left of the lampstand?" 4:14 So he said, "These are the two who are anointed to serve the Lord of all the earth."*

To understand the meaning of the two witnesses, notice what the two were able to do.

> *Revelation 11:6 These men have power to shut up the sky so that it will not rain during the time they are prophesying; and they have power to turn the waters into blood and to strike the earth with every kind of plague as often as they want.*

The above scripture clearly identifies Moses and Elijah; Moses struck the Nile, and the water turned to blood (*Exodus 7:20*). Elijah had power to stop rain for several years.

> *James 5:17 Elijah was a man just like us. He prayed earnestly that it would not rain, and it did not rain on the land for three and a half years.*

Moses and Elijah are the two who met with Jesus and three apostles on the Mount of Transfiguration, but how does this tie to the vision seen by John? Moses and Elijah represent the Law and the Prophets; Jesus had said, if people do not believe Moses and the prophets, they will not believe one coming back from the dead (*Luke 16:31*). The Bible for the early church was the Law and the Prophets; Rome not only crucified Jesus, they also tried to kill those who witnessed for the cause of Christ. Anytime Christians are shut down from teaching about Jesus, the Law and the Prophets are shut down. However, the Law and the Prophets would not be destroyed.

> *Revelation 11:5 If anyone tries to harm them, fire comes from their mouths and devours their enemies. This is how anyone who wants to harm them must die.*

When God's witnesses professed the great truths about Jesus, it was the Word of God that proceeded from their mouth. The Word of God has power to destroy the enemy. Those who teach the Word of God utilize the Law and the Prophets to witness the Gospel of Jesus Christ.

1. Their purpose was to prophesy or teach.
2. They were called candlesticks just as the churches were called candlesticks in *Revelation 1 - 3*.
3. They were protected for the same length of time the beast was to war with the saints.

> *Revelation 11:7-10 Now when they have finished their testimony, the beast that comes up from the Abyss will attack them, and overpower and kill them.*

Daniel had foretold coming persecution to the kingdom of God, and *Revelation* is filled with warnings of the coming tribulation. The killing of the witnesses symbolizes the conflict between the two kingdoms. Christians were never told they would face no problems living on this planet. The opening of the fifth seal revealed slain saints beneath the altar. Before the opening of the seventh seal, the chosen people of God were marked to protect them from the destruction of the four winds. Even when it appeared the church had been eradicated, God was still with the witnesses and brought about their resurrection.

Verse 8 says this will take place in the "great city"; this is a reference to Rome, but the Scripture refers to its "figurative" nature.

> *Revelation 11:8 Their bodies will lie in the street of the great city, which is figuratively called Sodom and Egypt, where also their Lord was crucified.*

We are told the place where the two witnesses were slain is symbolic; it is given three titles — Sodom, Egypt, and the place where Jesus was crucified. All three merely intensify the wickedness of Rome; each city had been used by Satan at one time or another to accomplish evil purposes.

Revelation 11:9 For three and a half days men from every people, tribe, language and nation will gaze on their bodies and refuse them burial.

The phrase "men from every people, tribe, language, and nation" uses the number 4 to signify worldly people who have not accepted God. During this period of history, the refusal of burial was a statement of total renunciation. It appears the beast had been victorious, and worldly people rejoiced. The timeframe is interesting because the beast was to hold sway over the earth for 42 months, and God's people would be protected during the same period. The witnesses lie in the street a day for each year they were testifying. A similar situation is found when Ezekiel was ordered to lie in the street of Jerusalem one day for each year of apostasy of God's people — 390 days for northern Israel and 40 days for Judah *(Ezekiel 4:4-6).*

Revelation 11:10 The inhabitants of the earth will gloat over them and will celebrate by sending each other gifts, because these two prophets had tormented those who live on the earth.

The testimony of the witnesses, the people of God, had "tormented" worldly people because it condemned them for their sins. The three and one-half day period of death is a day for each of the three and one-half years of testifying (1260 days). Jesus' personal ministry was three and one-half years, and the beast was to persecute for three and one-half years. There is certainly a symbolic link between the witnesses and Jesus Christ. The witnesses were not to remain dead because God protects His own.

Revelation 11:11,12 But after the three and a half days a breath of life from God entered them, and they stood on their feet, and terror struck those who saw them. Then they heard a loud voice from heaven saying to them, "Come up here." And they went up to heaven in a cloud, while their enemies looked on.

The resurrection of the two prophets parallels the resurrection of Jesus Christ. Jesus was killed by Rome just as they were; an earthquake accompanied the resurrection; His resurrection astounded those who witnessed the occasion. The witnesses, just as Jesus, ascended into the heavens by a cloud. The resurrection of Jesus proved Christians who die in the Lord will be resurrected to a better life.

> *I Corinthians 15:16-20 For if the dead are not raised, then Christ has not been raised either. And if Christ has not been raised, your faith is futile; you are still in your sins ... But Christ has indeed been raised from the dead, the firstfruits of those who have fallen asleep.*

The resurrection of the two witnesses is significant because it indicates the conflict appeared to be going in evil's favor for awhile, but God protected the church and brought it through the tribulation. In an earlier time of history, it looked as if it were over for Israel before they crossed the Red Sea. The friends of Daniel walked out of the fire unharmed. It looked like doom for awhile, but the lions' mouths were shut against Daniel so no harm came to him. The tomb of Jesus was empty after it appeared all was desolate. All of these examples and many more prove God will triumph, and **we can overcome through Him.**

> *Revelation 11:13 At that very hour there was a severe earthquake and a tenth of the city collapsed. Seven thousand people were killed in the earthquake, and the survivors were terrified and gave glory to the God of heaven.*

The effect of the resurrection of the witnesses was great when 1/10 of the city fell and 7,000 died. These are the effects of the warning of the sixth trumpet; the 1/10 figure signifies this is not the final destruction to come upon the beast or the earth. The number 7,000 is also symbolic; the number 7 is a complete number, and the 1,000 figure is the number ten cubed. The seven times 1,000 would add power showing God will destroy all of those who fail to follow His will.

Another dramatic moment occurs to signal the end of the sixth trumpet and to build the effects of the sounding of the seventh trumpet.

> *Revelation 11:14 The second woe has passed; the third woe is coming soon.*

Seventh Trumpet Sounds

Revelation 11:15 The seventh angel sounded his trumpet, and there were loud voices in heaven, which said: "The kingdom of the world has become the kingdom of our Lord and of his Christ, and he will reign for ever and ever."

Once the seventh trumpet sounded, there were no more warnings to be given. There is a fine line between the sounding of the last warning and the beginning of the first plague. Daniel had foretold victory of God's kingdom over the four kingdoms of the earth. It was true in Daniel's day; it was true when Rome fell, and it is true today. The number 4 is symbolic of the world; no worldly nation was ever meant to last forever, but the kingdom of God is eternal. The preceding passage also states that Jesus will reign "for ever and ever."

The sounding of the seventh trumpet brought many visions relating to the kingdom of God; the next chapter will explore these visions.

Chapter Twelve

Visions From the 7th Trumpet

The visions following the seventh trumpet reveal information about four different participants involved in conflict: 1) Jesus Christ, 2) Satan, 3) the followers of God, and 4) the Roman Empire and followers of Satan. Some of the visions will give new information about one or more of the participants, while other visions will repeat earlier concepts with new imagery.

God has always been the absolute ruler of the universe; however, God created a spiritual kingdom on the earth by sending the King of kings and Lord of lords to establish and oversee His work. The kingdom had been promised in the writings of Daniel. It was to be created in the days of the kings of the fourth empire, Rome, and the arrival of God's kingdom brought rejoicing in heaven.

> *Revelation 11:15 The seventh angel sounded his trumpet, and there were loud voices in heaven, which said: "The kingdom of the world has become the kingdom of our Lord and of his Christ, and he will reign for ever and ever." And the twenty-four elders, who were seated on their thrones before God, fell on their faces and worshiped God, saying: "We give thanks to you, Lord God Almighty, the One who is and who was, because you have taken your great power and have begun to reign. The nations were angry; and your wrath has come. The time has come for judging the dead, and for rewarding your servants the prophets and your saints and those who reverence your name, both small and great — and for destroying those who destroy the earth."*

When the twenty-four elders fell on their faces and worshipped the Almighty, God reacted to the praise with a show of power.

> *Revelation 11:19   Then God's temple in heaven was opened, and within his temple was seen the ark of his covenant. And there came flashes of lightning, rumblings, peals of thunder, an earthquake and a great hailstorm.*

HEAVENLY CONFLICT

The next vision after the final trumpet's warning and in preparation to the pouring of the bowls involves a dragon, a woman, a male child, and the other offspring of the woman. The dragon symbolizes Satan. The woman represents Israel (the nation that gave birth to Jesus). The male child is Jesus Christ. The other offspring are the followers of Jesus Christ. The conflict describes the victory Jesus won through coming to earth and dying on the cross.

> *Revelation 12:1-6   A great and wondrous sign appeared in heaven: a woman clothed with the sun, with the moon under her feet and a crown of twelve stars on her head. She was pregnant and cried out in pain as she was about to give birth. Then another sign appeared in heaven: an enormous red dragon with seven heads and ten horns and seven crowns on his heads. His tail swept a third of the stars out of the sky and flung them to the earth. The dragon stood in front of the woman who was about to give birth, so that he might devour her child the moment it was born. She gave birth to a son, a male child, who will rule all the nations with an iron scepter. And her child was snatched up to God and to his throne. The woman fled into the desert to a place prepared for her by God, where she might be taken care of for 1,260 days.*

The Woman Is Israel

Three of the characters are described in the previous scripture — the child, the woman, and the dragon. At first glance, the woman might appear to be Mary; however, the entire section seems to point to Israel, the nation chosen through which to bring Jesus to earth. She is radiant as she stands on the moon and is clothed by the sun. The crown with twelve stars on her head points clearly to Israel. About two thousand years before Christ was born, God promised Abraham his offspring would bless the entire earth. Abraham's grandson **Jacob became Israel**, and his sons formed twelve tribes. There is no problem symbolizing the woman as God's chosen people; Jesus called His followers His mother.

> *Mark 3:32-35 A crowd was sitting around him, and they told him, "Your mother and brothers are outside looking for you." "Who are my mother and my brothers?" he asked. Then he looked at those seated in a circle around him and said, "Here are my mother and my brothers! Whoever does God's will is my brother and sister and mother."*

Another great clue points to the woman's being the nation of Israel; the woman fled to the wilderness where she was protected for 1260 days. God led Israel out of Egypt into a wilderness where their only means of survival was God. The 1260 days is another way of saying forty-two months, "time, times and half-a time," and three and one-half years. In *Daniel* Israel was nearly destroyed during a three and one-half year persecution by Antiochus *Epiphanes*. In *Revelation* this timeframe was used by the beast to persecute the woman and trample the holy city. This imagery actually draws a link between physical Israel and spiritual Israel, the church. Jesus came through Israel, but He came to bless all who serve Him, regardless of national birth. The complete link will be made when John writes concerning the other offspring of the woman.

The Child Is Jesus

Several reasons point to the symbolism of the child's representing Jesus Christ: **1)** the dragon, which will be shown to be Satan, opposed His birth on earth. **2)** He was to rule all the nations with an iron scepter; Jesus rules with an iron scepter.

Revelation 19:15 ... He will rule them with an iron scepter.

3) In *Revelation 12:5*, the child ascends to God and to His throne. There is none other that could fit this symbol than Jesus Christ.

The Dragon Is Satan

The next symbol is rather clear also; the dragon is Satan, and the dragon's red color symbolizes evil. The dragon did everything within his power to keep Jesus from being born on earth. The dragon has diadems upon his seven heads indicating the purpose of Satan to rule over the souls of men; Satan has a kingdom, but it is the kingdom of darkness.

Luke 11:18   If Satan is divided against himself, how can his kingdom stand?

The dragon was seen sweeping stars from the sky; stars were symbolized in *Revelation 1:20* as angels. These could refer to angels with evil intent who followed Satan in his evil pursuits. *Revelation 9:1* pictured an angel who had fallen from heaven being given the key to the abyss. When the third trumpet was sounded, an angel fell from heaven to poison the waters. The Bible often alludes to fallen angels.

II Peter 2:4 ... God did not spare angels when they sinned, but sent them to hell ...

Jude 1:6 And the angels who did not keep their positions of authority but abandoned their own home — these he has kept in darkness, bound with everlasting chains for judgment on the great Day.

The War Between the Dragon and the Child

The first six verses of the passage introduce three of the participants; 1) the woman, 2) the child, and 3) the dragon; next, a flashback occurs to describe the conflict between the dragon and the male child. The struggle surrounding the dragon and Jesus Christ is called "war in Heaven"; the forces of God were led by Michael.

Revelation 12:7-9 And there was war in heaven. Michael and his angels fought against the dragon, and the dragon and his angels fought back. But he was not strong enough, and they lost their place in heaven. The great dragon was hurled down — that ancient serpent called the devil, or Satan, who leads the whole world astray. He was hurled to the earth, and his angels with him.

The *American Standard*, *Revised Version*, and *World English Bible* give this participant six names or titles — 1) dragon, 2) Satan, 3) serpent, 4) devil, 5) deceiver, and 6) accuser; the number 6 denotes mortality, and Satan does his work through worldly men. At times it may appear struggles on earth deal only with the physical realm, but Paul explains there is a heavenly battle at the same time.

Ephesians 6:12 For our struggle is not against flesh and blood, but against the rulers, against the authorities, against the powers of this dark world and against the spiritual forces of evil in the heavenly realms.

This "war in heaven" began when Jesus Christ came to earth. War was earlier pictured when the rider on the livid horse was followed by warfare. There have been many "wars in heaven," but none have had such tremendous effects as the one described below:

> *Revelation 12:10-12 Then I heard a loud voice in heaven say: "Now have come the salvation and the power and the kingdom of our God, and the authority of his Christ. For the accuser of our brothers, who accuses them before our God day and night, has been hurled down. They overcame him by the blood of the Lamb and by the word of their testimony; they did not love their lives so much as to shrink from death.*

The war was won because of two factors — the shedding of the blood of Christ and the testimony of saints. God did His part by "giving His one and only son"; Jesus did His part by dying of the cross for the redemption of His followers. Christians must do their part in this "war in heaven" by their testimony.

The winning of the war in heaven accomplished four significant things for the cause of God: salvation, power, kingdom, and the authority of Christ. After His death and resurrection, Christ said in *Matthew 28:18, "All authority in heaven and on earth has been given to me..."* The victory against sin was won when Jesus died and was resurrected to life.

The People of God

Ironically, Satan lost the battle when Rome killed Jesus Christ; Jesus ascended into the heavens to return to God. So what could Satan do to continue the conflict?

> *Revelation 12:13 When the dragon saw that he had been hurled to the earth, he pursued the woman who had given birth to the male child.*

Earlier it was observed that the woman referred to Israel, the nation God chose through which to bring the Redeemer. Throughout history when Satan tried to destroy "the woman," God protected her. John sees the protection of God covering the woman as Satan tried to destroy her.

> *Revelation 12:14-16 The woman was given the two wings of a great eagle, so that she might fly to the place prepared for her in the desert, where she would be taken care of for a time, times and half a time, out of the serpent's reach. Then from his mouth the serpent spewed water like a river, to overtake the woman and sweep her away with the torrent. But the earth helped the woman by opening its mouth and swallowing the river that the dragon had spewed out of his mouth.*

Three critical times in the history of Israel are covered by the previous citing: 1) The forty years in the wilderness could have thwarted God's plan to bring the Redeemer through Israel, but God saw to Israel's every need and led them across Jordan into Canaan. 2) Satan could have destroyed Israel at the Red Sea when the Egyptians were in hot pursuit, but God separated the waters to spare them. This concept is symbolized when the dragon tried to destroy the woman with water spewing from his mouth; God dried the waters. 3) Antiochus *Epiphanes* could have destroyed God's plan to bring the Savior through Israel when he persecuted Israel three and one-half years; however, while the beast was persecuting for "time, times and half a time," God protected Israel (the woman) for "time, times and half a time." Satan did all within his power to destroy Israel to stop the coming of the Messiah, but God was there at all times. The woman was protected.

> *Revelation 12:17 Then the dragon was enraged at the woman and went off to make war against the rest of her offspring — those who obey God's commandments and hold to the testimony of Jesus.*

The imagery clearly changes to encompass all of God's people, both Israel and the church. The dragon could not harm Jesus any further; he had crucified Him, but God raised Jesus from the dead and returned Him to heaven. He was unable to stop the people of God from delivering Jesus to earth because God protected "mother" Israel. To continue his opposition against God, the dragon (Satan) began persecuting the woman's offspring, all those who were obedient to God's commands and those who held to the teachings of Jesus. Who are these people? They are Christians; they are the church throughout time; they are new Jerusalem or spiritual Israel as detailed in chapter 7 of this volume.

> *Galatians 3:29 If you belong to Christ, then you are Abraham's seed, and heirs according to the promise.*

According to John, the "offspring" of the woman were to be persecuted. In the previous verse, Paul claimed those who belong to Jesus Christ are the offspring of Abraham; they are his "seed." What will happen to the offspring, those who choose to serve Jesus? As John's visions continue, the consequences of serving Jesus will be revealed. One immediate result of being a Christian was the persecution that came from the Roman Empire. For the first time, John describes the tool of Satan as a beast that came up from the sea.

The Beast Is Rome

> *Revelation 13:1,2 And the dragon stood on the shore of the sea. And I saw a beast coming out of the sea. He had ten horns and seven heads, with ten crowns on his horns, and on each head a blasphemous name. The beast I saw resembled a leopard, but had feet like those of a bear and a mouth like that of a lion. The dragon gave the beast his power and his throne and great authority.*

Chapter one of this volume detailed a ten point comparison of this beast with the one in *Daniel* to show they were the same. I will simply list the points at this time, but the reader may wish to return to that part of this text to refresh his memory.

1. Both beasts had ten horns.
2. Both originated from the sea.
3. Daniel's beast was preceded by a lion, bear, and leopard, while John's beast looked like a leopard, bear, and lion.
4. Both beasts controlled the known world.
5. Both beasts said great things.
6. Both beasts would war with the saints.
7. Both would persecute for three and one-half years.
8. Both would be judged by the saints.
9. Both would be destroyed.
10. The kingdom of God would overcome both.

The beast of *Revelation* looked like a leopard, had the feet of a bear, and the mouth of a lion because it had consumed the three kingdoms preceding it. This was in the exact reverse order Daniel had seen of the four beasts in his vision. Daniel was looking forward in time to Rome, and John was looking backward in time from Rome to Babylon. Both were pointing to the Roman Empire, the very time in which the original readers of *Revelation* were living.

The words "Anti-Christ" are never used in *Revelation*, but an Anti-Christ is described in chapter 13. Some Egyptian pharaohs deified themselves, and Antiochus IV named himself *Epiphanes*, meaning "god with us." Mark Galli wrote in *Christian History*, July 1, 1990, issue 27:

> Domitian was the first emperor to have himself officially titled in Rome as "God the Lord." He insisted that other people hail his greatness with acclamations like "Lord of the earth," "Invincible," "Glory," "Holy," and "Thou Alone."

Other emperors followed Domitian's example, claiming to be God. Anyone who defies God and calls for others to follow him is an "Anti-Christ." The Bible does not refer to only one "Anti-Christ." Clearly, John envisions Roman caesars and their attempt to persuade citizens to worship caesars rather than Jesus Christ.

Revelation 13 makes a strong statement concerning "Anti-Christ" by giving him counterfeit characteristics, cheap imitations of the Son of God.

1. The appearance of the beast

> *Revelation 13:1 ... He had ten horns and seven heads, with ten crowns on his horns, and on each head a blasphemous name.*

The beast had the appearance of Satan; it had seven heads and ten horns just like those of the dragon.

> *Revelation 12:3 ... an enormous red dragon with seven heads and ten horns and seven crowns on his heads.*

How does this imitate Jesus Christ? Just as Jesus had the appearance of God, the beast had the appearance of his superior.

> *John 14:9 ... Anyone who has seen me has seen the Father. How can you say, "Show us the Father"?*

2. The beast had a kingdom

> *Revelation 13:2 ... The dragon gave the beast his power and his throne and great authority.*

This mimics Jesus Christ because *Revelation 12:10* says Jesus Christ had power, a kingdom, and authority. What is the difference between the two if both possessed the same things? The difference stems from the origin of the kingdoms. Jesus was given His authority from God; the beast was granted his power from the dragon, Satan. Before deciding to worship the caesar rather than Jesus Christ, one would be wise to determine the root of the power.

3. The beast and the death wound

> *Revelation 13:3 One of the heads of the beast seemed to have had a fatal wound, but the fatal wound had been healed. The whole world was astonished and followed the beast.*

The beast even mocked the death and resurrection of Jesus Christ. Jesus' death wound was healed by His resurrection from the dead. It is obvious the beast is exhibiting a counterfeit because it "seemed to have a fatal wound." This does not mean Rome literally had an apparent death wound healed; this is only showing the caesars were mimicking Jesus Christ. One might remember the prophetic statement in *Genesis 3:15, "He shall bruise thy head."* This is exactly where the wound was. Some folks in Rome seemed to believe Domitian was the return of Nero. Tertullian, writing in the late second or early third century wrote:

> "Domitian, too, a man of Nero's type in cruelty, tried his hand at persecution."

Citizens of Rome during the first century would certainly understand the imagery found in the statement, "appear to be a death wound healed." Rumors were being circulated that Domitian was Nero reincarnated. Clement, a contemporary of Domitian, wrote in *First Epistle to the Corinthians,* comparing their present circumstances with the time of Nero. (*I Clement 7:1*)

> These things we enjoin you, beloved, not only by way of admonition to you, but as putting ourselves also in mind. For we are in the same arena, and the same contest is imposed upon us.

According to tradition, Clement was drowned at sea by having an anchor tied to him. There is no question Domitian carried a huge resemblance to Nero when it came to persecution. Those to whom the letter was written would understand the message.

4. Worship of the beast glorified a higher authority

> *Revelation 13:4 Men worshiped the dragon because he had given authority to the beast, and they also worshiped the beast and asked, "Who is like the beast? Who can make war against him?"*

The apparent death and healing of the beast caused worship to be offered to the dragon. By worshipping the beast, one was actually giving praise to the dragon, Satan. One is able to come to God by worshipping Jesus Christ. Before choosing whether to worship the beast or Jesus, one should be aware of where the decision leads.

> *John 14:6 Jesus answered, "I am the way and the truth and the life. No one comes to the Father except through me."*

5. The beast warred against his enemies

> *Revelation 13:4 ... "Who is like the beast? Who can make war against him?"*

> *Revelation 13:7 He was given power to make war against the saints and to conquer them...*

The beast wars against saints to counter Jesus' war against His enemies. John earlier saw a sword coming from Jesus' mouth, and he learned the sword would be used to fight against those who opposed Him. Some modern writers have tried to make a case claiming there is evidence Domitian persecuted and executed Jews; however, they claim there is no concrete evidence of Domitian's persecution of Christians. Remember that Domitian had deified himself to be called Lord and Master; Jews were not the only ones who would reject his "lordship"! Do we think Domitian persecuted Jews but found Christians who refused to recognize his title and shook their hands? *Revelation 17:11* calls the eighth king "the beast"; and evidence given above in point 3 furnishes proof that Christians were persecuted and died under his rule.

> *Revelation 2:16 Repent therefore! Otherwise, I will soon come to you and will fight against them with the sword of my mouth.*

Toward the end of *Revelation*, Jesus emerges to war against the beast. The beast was destroyed by the sword coming from the mouth of Jesus; thus the question was answered — **"Who can make war against the beast?" JESUS CHRIST!**

> *Revelation 19:11 I saw heaven standing open and there before me was a white horse, whose rider is called Faithful and True. With justice he judges and makes war.*

> *Revelation 19:19,20 Then I saw the beast and the kings of the earth and their armies gathered together to make war against the rider on the horse and his army. But the beast was captured, and with him the false prophet who had performed the miraculous signs on his behalf. ... The two of them were thrown alive into the fiery lake of burning sulfur.*

Both Jesus Christ and the beast war against their enemies. Who are their enemies? The enemies of the beast are the followers of Jesus; the enemies of Jesus are the followers of the beast. The results are already in — **Jesus is victorious!**

6. The beast said great things

> *Revelation 13:5 The beast was given a mouth to utter proud words and blasphemies ...*

To oppose Jesus Christ, the beast had to counter the teachings of Jesus. Jesus spoke the beatitudes; He uttered parables to teach men the way to live. When He spoke, He spoke the awesome words of God that could lead men to eternal life. The beast also uttered powerful words, but they were nothing more than boastfulness and blasphemy; the beast's words lead to death.

> *Revelation 13:6 He opened his mouth to blaspheme God, and to slander his name and his dwelling place and those who live in heaven.*

7. The beast had his power for three and one-half years

> *Revelation 13:5 ... and to exercise his authority for forty-two months.*

The time for the earthly work of each is also used as an antithesis. The Quadri-paschal theory contends Jesus' public life covered four Passovers, **three and one-half years.** The information about the length of the ministry came from A.T. Robertson's *A Harmony of the Gospels*, p. 270.

> This theory follows from making *John 5:1* a Passover or Purim before or Pentecost or Tabernacles after an

unnamed Passover. This seems to be the more probable length of the Savior's public work on earth. How short a space was even this to compass such a marvelous work. The ministry of Jesus seems crowded beyond our comprehension. It would be certain that the Savior's public life lasted about three years and a half, if it was admitted that *John 5:1* referred to a Passover.

8. The beast controlled the world

Revelation 13:7,8 ... And he was given authority over every tribe, people, language and nation. All inhabitants of the earth will worship the beast — all whose names have not been written in the Book of Life belonging to the Lamb that was slain from the creation of the world.

As a result of the heavenly conflict between the beast and Jesus, both would gain followers. The beast's followers are identified in two ways in the preceding quotation. 1) The followers are from every tribe, people, language and nation. The four-fold listing highlights the worldly nature of the beast's disciples. 2) Their names are not written in the Book of Life.

On the other hand, the followers of Jesus are called out of the world, and their names are written in the Book of Life. Once again it becomes very clear the beast is the antithesis of Jesus; he is an "Anti-Christ."

Revelation 21:27 Nothing impure will ever enter it, nor will anyone who does what is shameful or deceitful, but only those whose names are written in the Lamb's Book of Life.

Revelation 20:15 If anyone's name was not found written in the Book of Life, he was thrown into the lake of fire.

All humans have the choice of whether to follow Christ or the ways of the world; however, every choice has its own set of consequences. All of us ultimately get what we seek; we reap what we sow. John warns his readers about these consequences as the text continues.

Revelation 13:9,10 He who has an ear, let him hear. If anyone is to go into captivity, into captivity he will go. If anyone is to be killed with the sword, with the sword he will be killed. This calls for patient endurance and faithfulness on the part of the saints.

9. The sea beast had ministers

John next saw a land beast, the minister of Satan; this land beast was the antithesis of the ministers of Christ.

Revelation 13:11 Then I saw another beast, coming out of the earth. He had two horns like a lamb, but he spoke like a dragon.

The land beast looked good; it looked like a lamb. If Satan's ministers looked evil, people would know to flee. However, Satan's ministers present evil in dim light to entice the world.

II Corinthians 11:14 And no wonder, for Satan himself masquerades as an angel of light.

Take another look; the beast may have looked like a lamb, but it spoke like a dragon. The beast had the appearances of good, but its inner being was pure dragon. The land beast would do the will of the sea beast, just as Jesus' followers would serve Him and sound godlike. The land beast had several functions in doing the will of the sea beast.

10. The land beast sought worshippers for the sea beast

Revelation 13:12 He exercised all the authority of the first beast on his behalf, and made the earth and its inhabitants worship the first beast, whose fatal wound had been healed.

Jesus' followers also had a mission; they were to find disciples for Jesus by preaching to the world.

Matthew 28:19,20 Therefore go and make disciples of all nations, baptizing them in the name of the Father and of the Son and of the Holy Spirit, and teaching them to obey everything I have commanded you. And surely I am with you always, to the very end of the age.

11. The disciples of the beast did great things

The followers of the sea beast were empowered to do great things in carrying out the edicts of the emperor. John said these followers of the beast had the ability to "perform great and miraculous signs." Everything the ministers did elevated the sea beast and brought power to his name. The world was influenced to follow the beast because of the amazing things they saw. Those who did not worship the sea beast were persecuted and killed.

> *Revelation 13:13-15 And he performed great and miraculous signs, even causing fire to come down from heaven to earth in full view of men. Because of the signs he was given power to do on behalf of the first beast, he deceived the inhabitants of the earth. He ordered them to set up an image in honor of the beast who was wounded by the sword and yet lived. He was given power to give breath to the image of the first beast, so that it could speak and cause all who refused to worship the image to be killed.*

The followers of Jesus were able to perform miracles to make disciples for Jesus Christ. Those who do not follow Jesus will suffer eternal separation from God. The theme of "consequences for choices" is carried even further with this message.

12. The beast sealed his followers

> *Revelation 13:16 He also forced everyone, small and great, rich and poor, free and slave, to receive a mark on his right hand or on his forehead, so that no one could buy or sell unless he had the mark, which is the name of the beast or the number of his name.*

Jesus had sealed the faithful in the seventh chapter of *Revelation*; the sealing took place to identify God's followers. To ape the work of God, Satan seals his supporters to be able to give them benefits. The bad news: these benefits are temporary! This is not a literal marking of Satan's followers; it is another antithesis to underscore the "nature of the beast." The beast is an "Anti-Christ," so he retaliates with his own sealing and persecutes those not marked by the beast. The coins of Rome were stamped with the image of Domitian, bearing the inscription "Lord and Master." No one could purchase goods in Rome without using these cursed coins. There were benefits in serving the state and worshiping the caesars, but all benefits were temporary. Many Christians could have eased their lives and stopped individual persecution had they merely rejected Jesus Christ; however, they were promised eternal salvation if they remained faithful to Jesus.

13. The number of the beast was 666

> *Revelation 13:18   This calls for wisdom. If anyone has insight, let him calculate the number of the beast, for it is man's number. His number is 666.*

One of the most abused passages now appears. Keep in mind the context of a human being trying to appear like Jesus. Roman leaders tried to force worship of the caesars; in context, the number 666 is not that puzzling! To understand the message in the number 666, it is important to explain how names and numbers can be associated in using Greek symbols. Every Greek letter was also a number; thus a sequence of symbols could be read as a word or as a numerical statement. From the discovery around 500 BC by Pythagoras until around 500 AD, "Gematria" was a popular recreation in which names were hidden in numbers. Techniques and strategies were developed in attempts to decode the hidden messages often presented in the form of numbers. Gematria certainly added to the intrigue of *Revelation* when the message was received in the first century. The following chart explains the numerical value of each of the Greek letters.

Numerical Values of the Greek Alphabet

Alpha	α	1
Beta	β	2
Gamma	γ	3
Delta	δ	4
Epsilon	ε	5
Zeta	ζ	7
Eta	η	8
Theta	θ	9
Iota	ι	10
Kappa	κ	20
Lambda	λ	30
Mu	μ	40
Nu	ν	50
Xi	ξ	60
Omicron	ο	70
Pi	π	80
Rho	ρ	100
Sigma	σ, ς	200
Tau	τ	300
Upsilon	υ	400
Phi	φ	500
Chi	χ	600
Psi	ψ	700
Omega	ω	800

There were twenty-four Greek letters; Jesus called Himself the Alpha and the Omega, the first and the last. This would also make Jesus number <u>1</u> and number <u>800</u>, the numbers symbolizing creation and resurrection. Three other symbols were created by the Greeks to total twenty-seven numbers: the Stigma = 6, Koppa = 90, and Sampsi = 900. The Greek symbols will make it possible for the reader to understand more clearly the significance of 666.

The entirety of *Revelation* 13 has been presenting the beast as "Anti-Christ;" it is only logical to follow the same concept in determining the counterpart to the number 666. Tertullian (160-220 AD) stated in *Against Heresy III*, that the number of the name Jesus is 888. Ethelbert Bullinger in his book *Number in Scripture, p. 203*, details how this number is derived.

> Eight is the Dominical Number, for everywhere it has to do with the Lord. It is the number of His name, ΙΗΣΟΥΣ
>
> $$\begin{aligned} I &= 10 \\ H &= 8 \\ \Sigma &= 200 \\ O &= 70 \\ Y &= 400 \\ \Sigma &= \underline{200} \\ & \textbf{888} \end{aligned}$$

The third and last letters of Jesus' name are a Sigma; in lower case, the Sigma has different forms because the Greek spelling used a different form to end a word when the letter Sigma was a repeat. Anyone can take the table of letter and number values and check the name of Jesus.

$$\begin{aligned} \text{Iota} \quad I &= 10 \\ \text{Eta} \quad \eta &= 8 \\ \text{Sigma} \quad \sigma &= 200 \\ \text{Omicron} \quad o &= 70 \\ \text{Upsilon} \quad \upsilon &= 400 \\ \text{Sigma} \quad \varsigma &= \underline{200} \\ & \textbf{888} \end{aligned}$$

According to *Luke 2:21*, Jesus was circumcised and named on the eighth day after His birth. On the eighth day he was named Jesus; His number was 888. Chapter eight of this volume demonstrated that the number 8 is symbolic of resurrection, endlessness, eternity, and immortality.

The number 6 is the number of mortality since man was created on the sixth day; this would symbolize humanity. Logical opposites are created through the number 6 and the number 8 in representing mortality versus immortality. Since the name of Jesus is 888, the logical counterpart is 666. Throughout this volume, Rome has been portrayed as the beast, and certainly the Roman numeral system yields the clearest 666 one can imagine when totaling the first six digits.

$$\begin{aligned} I &= 1 \\ V &= 5 \\ X &= 10 \\ L &= 50 \\ C &= 100 \\ D &= \underline{500} \\ & \mathbf{666} \end{aligned}$$

There are only seven Roman numerals, and even if the seventh Roman numeral were added, the M would bring the grand total to 1,666; anyone could still see the picture. It is more logical, however, that one would look at the first 6 numbers since 6's are highlighted by the number of the name. What is the message? **Do not worship caesars!** They say they are gods; **NO!!! They are mere mortals.** Jesus is the object of worship!!! The passage said the same thing when it stated that the number **666 is the number of a MAN!!!** The caesars are human; the number 666 refers to the folly of following humans in general, with the Roman government the specific target.

> Followers of Christ
> are Redeemed

Another beautiful contrast is found at the beginning of *Revelation 14*; the previous chapter pictured an imposter land beast looking like a lamb and sounding like a dragon. In this vision, John sees the true Lamb and the 144,000 who were sealed.

> *Revelation 14:1-5 Then I looked, and there before me was the Lamb, standing on Mount Zion, and with him*

144,000 who had his name and his Father's name written on their foreheads. And I heard a sound from heaven like the roar of rushing waters and like a loud peal of thunder. The sound I heard was like that of harpists playing their harps. And they sang a new song before the throne and before the four living creatures and the elders. No one could learn the song except the 144,000 who had been redeemed from the earth. These are those who did not defile themselves with women, for they kept themselves pure. They follow the Lamb wherever he goes. They were purchased from among men and offered as firstfruits to God and the Lamb. No lie was found in their mouths; they are blameless.

Earlier in chapter 7 of *Revelation* the 144,000 were on earth awaiting the great persecution. It was clear they would be protected because there was another group in heaven who had already come through persecution; the number was so large it could not be counted. In this scene the 144,000 who were on earth had reached their spiritual goal. The action of "sealing" the followers of God was successful. What a comfort this must have been to Christians about to undergo persecution for the cause of Christ. **The battle was won before it even started.** The 144,000 redeemed were on Mount Zion. In the Old Testament Mount Zion was the citadel of David; it was symbolic of God's faithful people. In the New Testament it is referred to only in *Revelation* and *Hebrews*; it signifies new Jerusalem, the church.

Hebrews 12:22 But you have come to Mount Zion, to the heavenly Jerusalem, ... to the church of the firstborn, whose names are written in heaven ...

Rejoicing was heard in heaven as a new song was sung no one could learn except the redeemed; salvation is the theme of the vision. Some believe the many waters symbolize the rhythm of the music, that the sound of thunder indicates the loudness of the song, and that the sound of harps symbolizes the beauty of the song. Whatever the case, the significance of redemption should not be overlooked.

Seven characteristics indicating perfection were given for the 144,000. 1) They were not defiled by women, suggesting spiritual purity. 2) They followed the Lamb. 3) They were purchased from among men with His blood. 4) They were the firstfruits unto God. 5) They were the firstfruits unto Christ. 6) They were not guilty of lies. 7) They were blameless. These were ones who did not relent to the temptations offered by the Roman Empire; they had remained faithful to God through it all. They were given a choice in *Revelation 13* of following the real Christ or His counterpart the beast; they had wisely and correctly chosen to follow the Lamb.

John next envisioned three angels with special messages. The first of these angels had glad tidings to deliver concerning coming judgment and redemption for those who feared God and gave Him glory.

> *Revelation 14:6,7 Then I saw another angel flying in midair, and he had the eternal gospel to proclaim to those who live on the earth — to every nation, tribe, language and people. He said in a loud voice, "Fear God and give him glory, because the hour of his judgment has come. Worship him who made the heavens, the earth, the sea and the springs of water."*

This angel gave hope to those who "live on the earth," symbolizing the worldly with a fourfold listing: nation, tribe, language, and people. It was not too late to turn; ultimate victory was so certain for the faithful it could be proclaimed before it actually happened. God could save those who turned, and this concept is also confirmed with the number 4 — God made 1) the heavens, 2) the earth, 3) the sea, and 4) the springs of water. It was time for citizens to turn to God and for Christians to keep their commitment to Jesus.

Followers of the beast are doomed

> *Revelation 14:8 A second angel followed and said, "Fallen! Fallen is Babylon the Great, which made all the nations drink the maddening wine of her adulteries."*

The second angel proclaims doom to the wicked city and its inhabitants. The beast is synonymous with Babylon; *Revelation 13* referred to the beast in this way, and chapters 17 and 18 will do more of the same. Babylon was the wicked kingdom in which Daniel lived; this certainly creates an even stronger tie to the book of *Daniel*. Daniel told exactly when ancient Babylon would fall, and it did. Readers in the first century could be certain that its "twin" Rome would fall as well; this is so certain the announcement of its fall was made before the actual event occurred.

The third angel proclaims judgment on those who wore the mark of the beast.

> *Revelation 14:9-12   A third angel followed them and said in a loud voice: "If anyone worships the beast and his image and receives his mark on the forehead or on the hand, he, too, will drink of the wine of God's fury, which has been poured full strength into the cup of his wrath. He will be tormented with burning sulfur in the presence of the holy angels and of the Lamb. And the smoke of their torment rises for ever and ever. There is no rest day or night for those who worship the beast and his image, or for anyone who receives the mark of his name." This calls for patient endurance on the part of the saints who obey God's commandments and remain faithful to Jesus.*

Revelation 13 gave all people on earth a choice of whom to follow — Jesus or the beast; those who followed the beast were benefitted with economic favors from the government. The time had come to pay the price; remember the principle in chapter 13 — you get what you seek. They drank with Babylon; consequently, they must drink the wrath of God. The extent of their torment was great, coming with fire and brimstone in the presence of angels and the Lamb. The torment was to last forever — quite a price to pay for the temporary enjoyment they had on earth. Notice the composite impact of all three angels — the first told of hope for those who accepted Jesus; the second told of the fall of "Babylon," and the third told of eternal doom for those selecting the worldliness of "Babylon."

> The Followers of
> God are protected

Revelation 14:13 Then I heard a voice from heaven say, "Write: Blessed are the dead who die in the Lord from now on." "Yes," says the Spirit, "they will rest from their labor, for their deeds will follow them."

This is quite a contrast from the doom painted in the previous scene. For those who have been faithful, death is a closed door for Satan; he can do no more harm. Because of this, the faithful are able to rest from their labors. The theme of what happens to those who follow the Lamb and what happens to those who follow the beast really develops rapidly at this point in *Revelation*. Two reapers appear, and the faithful are gathered by the first reaper — the imagery points to Jesus Christ.

Revelation 14:14 I looked, and there before me was a white cloud, and seated on the cloud was one "like a son of man" with a crown of gold on his head and a sharp sickle in his hand.

The reaper is identified as "like unto a son of man," a familiar descriptor of Jesus. He was sitting on a white cloud to emphasize His position; furthermore, He has the golden crown of victory, stephanos, and He has the sickle of judgment. All indications point to Jesus as the first reaper.

Revelation 14:15,16 Then another angel came out of the temple and called in a loud voice to him who was sitting on the cloud, "Take your sickle and reap, because the time to reap has come, for the harvest of the earth is ripe." So he who was seated on the cloud swung his sickle over the earth, and the earth was harvested.

Some find difficulty in an ordinary angel telling Christ what to do; however, the angel appears to merely relate the command of God to send forth the sickle.

> The followers of the beast gathered by the second reaper

Revelation 14:17 Another angel came out of the temple in heaven, and he too had a sharp sickle. Still another angel, who had charge of the fire, came from the altar and called in a loud voice to him who had the sharp sickle, "Take your sharp sickle and gather the clusters of grapes from the earth's vine, because its grapes are ripe."

VISIONS OF THE ALTAR

When seal five was opened, John saw slain saints beneath the altar praying for vengeance upon the great persecutor. John later saw an angel adding incense to the altar to assist the prayers of saints. As the theme advances, the angel over fire comes from the altar to give the command for destruction; the prayers of the saints will be answered.

Revelation 14:19,20 The angel swung his sickle on the earth, gathered its grapes and threw them into the great winepress of God's wrath. They were trampled in the winepress outside the city, and blood flowed out of the press, rising as high as the horses' bridles for a distance of 1,600 stadia.

Once again truth is presented that one reaps what he sows. Evil doers were responsible for the blood of slain saints; now it was time for them to be reaped in the harvest of the lost. The two-fold reaping should remind the reader of the wheat and the tares parable Jesus Christ had presented. Earlier in the book, John saw those outside the city trampling new Jerusalem; now he sees the picture turned as those outside the city were trodden. The blood from the treading was over 200 miles long and as deep as a horse's bridle. One author suggested that all the blood in the world would not fill a river this size. Perhaps true, but one certainly cannot miss a scene that should paint the horror of God's wrath in vivid colors.

Keep in mind that all visions covered in this chapter are part of the seventh trumpet, which is part of the seventh seal. The time for warning is past; it is now time for the seven vials to be poured to culminate in the demise of the Roman Empire. The secondary meaning warns that there comes a time in the life of a nation when evil results in the ultimate collapse. The stage has now been set to examine the pouring of the vials of God's wrath!

Chapter Thirteen

The Seven Bowls of God's Wrath

The opening of the seals revealed the coming of Rome's collapse; the sounding of the trumpets warned of the doom; the pouring of the bowls of wrath completes the vengeance of God.

> *Revelation 15:1 I saw in heaven another great and marvelous sign: seven angels with the seven last plagues — last, because with them God's wrath is completed.*

Earlier visions pointed to the vengeance of God; when the fifth seal was opened, the reader sees slain saints beneath the altar asking how long it would be before God retaliates against their tormentor. Prior to trumpet warnings, an angel offered incense on a golden altar; the smoke combined with the prayers of the saints to strengthen the call for action, and fire from the altar was hurled to the earth. The time of waiting was over; the Day of the Lord had arrived. John saw the victorious standing by the sea of glass.

> *Revelation 15:2-4 And I saw what looked like a sea of glass mixed with fire and, standing beside the sea, those who had been victorious over the beast and his image and over the number of his name. They held harps given them by God and sang the song of Moses the servant of God and the song of the Lamb: "Great and marvelous are your deeds, Lord God Almighty. Just and true are your ways, King of the ages. Who will not fear you, O Lord, and bring glory to your name? For you alone are holy. All nations will come and worship before you, for your righteous acts have been revealed."*

Three symbolic events occur within the book of *Revelation* to send the message that God has taken steps to identify His followers:

1) They were sealed in the 7th chapter.

2) They were measured in chapter 11.

3) Their names were in the Lamb's Book of Life in chapter 13.

These steps were essential for assurance; in chapters 2 and 3 God had promised eternal salvation to those who overcome. The three events above reassure the reader that God knows the names of the victorious. The reality of the theme is fulfilled in chapter 7 when John tells of a numberless band of sealed victors who had made it through the tribulation; it is also fulfilled in chapter 14 when he saw the 144,000 who had been sealed on earth standing on mount Zion because they were triumphant.

The sea of glass appears first in chapter 4; it was "before the throne" along with the four living creatures and twenty-four elders. In the current scene the redeemed from the earth were standing either "by" or "upon" the sea, depending on which translation is being used. The victors, John is told, have overcome three things — 1) the beast, 2) his image, and 3) the number of his name; the use of the number 3 emphasizes their heavenly conquest. The victorious were holding harps and singing the song of Moses and the song of the Lamb. When the Israelites were delivered from Egypt in the 15th chapter of *Exodus*, they sang a song of deliverance, the song of Moses. The combining of this song with "the song of the Lamb" indicates deliverance has brought all of the redeemed before the living God. The song itself praised God for 1) His works, 2) His ways, 3) His name, and 4) His acts. Ironically, the redeemed were recognized by the number 3, and God was praised by using the number 4; this is a departure from the usual 3 for God and 4 for the world. **This should not seem too strange because Jesus became man (4) so man might become like God (3).**

> *Ephesians 4:22-24 You were taught, with regard to your former way of life ... To be made new in the attitude of your minds; and to put on the new self,* **created to be like God** *...*

Egypt was hit with ten plagues, the divine number of totality to indicate God's involvement in the fall; Rome was to be destroyed by seven plagues, also a divine number. It is clear the plagues on both Egypt and Rome were sent from God.

> *Revelation 15:5-7 After this I looked and in heaven the temple, that is, the tabernacle of the Testimony, was opened. Out of the temple came the seven angels with the seven plagues. They were dressed in clean, shining linen and wore golden sashes around their chests. Then one of the four living creatures gave to the seven angels seven golden bowls filled with the wrath of God, who lives for ever and ever.*

Notice that the angels came from the temple of God. In the Old Testament, the temple was the place where Israel could meet with God; it contained the cherubim and the mercy seat, along with the Ten Commandments located in the Ark of the Covenant. The seven angels were dressed in pure white linen covered with precious stones; the reader is reminded of the priests in the ancient tabernacle. The attire is also similar to the vision of Christ in chapter 1 of *Revelation*.

One of the four living creatures gave the bowls of wrath to the angels. The four living creatures were cherubim or angels who were extremely close to God in dealing with the world. The living creatures were present when Ezekiel saw God in chapters 1 and 10 of *Ezekiel*. John saw the four living creatures in *Revelation*, chapters 4 and 5, when he was privileged to see God on His throne. The living creatures ushered in the first four visions presented with the opening of the seven seals in chapter 6. The living creatures were there when the faithful of God were sealed in chapter 7, and they were there when the 144,000 were victorious on mount Zion. Now the living creatures give instructions to the angels with the bowls of wrath. When the angels left the temple, no one was able to enter until God's purpose was fulfilled.

> *Revelation 15:8 And the temple was filled with smoke from the glory of God and from his power, and no one could enter the temple until the seven plagues of the seven angels were completed.*

To accomplish the purpose of God, the order was given to pour the bowls. Because the order comes from the loud voice inside the temple, it is clear that God's will is about to unfold.

> *Revelation 16:1 Then I heard a loud voice from the temple saying to the seven angels, "Go, pour out the seven bowls of God's wrath on the earth."*

First Bowl of Wrath

> *Revelation 16:2 The first angel went and poured out his bowl on the land, and ugly and painful sores broke out on the people who had the mark of the beast and worshiped his image.*

The first plague was similar to the boils God sent on Egypt when He was delivering Israel. This plague parallels the first trumpet of warning that sent partial destruction to the earth, harming those who had chosen not to follow God; it did not harm the faithful. How amazing! How divine! The ones hurt by the plague had marked themselves so God would know whom to strike; **they had the mark of the beast!**

Second Bowl of Wrath

Revelation 16:3 The second angel poured out his bowl on the sea, and it turned into blood like that of a dead man, and every living thing in the sea died.

The second plague parallels the second trumpet. The second trumpet warned of harm to the sea by portraying destruction to one-third of the sea life and ships; the second plague turned all of the sea to blood, and everything within it died. This is reminiscent of the water's turning to blood when God brought the ten plagues upon Egypt.

Third Bowl of Wrath

Revelation 16:4 The third angel poured out his bowl on the rivers and springs of water, and they became blood.

Revelation 16:5-7 Then I heard the angel in charge of the waters say: "You are just in these judgments, you who are and who were, the Holy One, because you have so judged; for they have shed the blood of your saints and prophets, and you have given them blood to drink as they deserve." And I heard the altar respond: "Yes, Lord God Almighty, true and just are your judgments."

We've heard the theme before: what one sows, he also reaps! Because Rome had poured out the blood of Christians, the guilty were forced to drink blood because all their fresh water became gore. This plague parallels the third trumpet in affecting the fresh water, but the trumpet only warned by affecting one third of the rivers; the pouring of the bowl turned all of the fresh water into blood. The angel of waters praised God for His judgment. Earlier in *Revelation 7*, John had introduced the angel over wind who commanded four angels to hold back the four winds to permit the sealing of God's people. The angel over fire made an appearance in the reaping of the earth in *Revelation 14*; in this sequence we learn about the angel of waters. John also heard the altar praising God. The altar has played a significant role throughout the book in anticipating and praising God's vindication.

Fourth Bowl of Wrath

Revelation 16:8,9 The fourth angel poured out his bowl on the sun, and the sun was given power to scorch people with fire. They were seared by the intense heat and they cursed the name of God, who had control over these plagues, but they refused to repent and glorify him.

Many Christians were burned at the stake as martyrs for the cause of Jesus Christ; God destroys their tormentors with fire from the sun. This plague is similar to the fourth trumpet which gave warnings about the universe; both brought destruction from the heavens. The major difference in the trumpet and the bowl is that the fourth trumpet was a warning, and the fourth bowl was reality of finality. God's justice is made plain because these men were so perverse their plight led them to blaspheme the name of God. They deserved what they received!

These first four bowls are all used as a unit to tell of one of the major reasons for the fall of Rome — natural disasters striking the empire. Remember that Mount Vesuvius erupted in 79 AD with unimaginable destruction, but other cataclysmic events would follow. Every nation has natural disasters; however, the number of disasters and their magnitude, coupled with the corruption of the country and the foreign invasions were more than any nation could withstand.

Fifth Bowl of Wrath

Revelation 16:10,11 The fifth angel poured out his bowl on the throne of the beast, and his kingdom was plunged into darkness. Men gnawed their tongues in agony and cursed the God of heaven because of their pains and their sores, but they refused to repent of what they had done.

The fifth trumpet warned about the ultimate effect of evil as horrible locusts came from the abyss where Satan dwells. Smoke from the abyss darkened the light of the sun. While the smoke created from the warning of the fifth trumpet only darkened the sky, darkness was total with the pouring of the fifth bowl. Darkness, the opposite of God's light, came upon those who had chosen darkness in life. This darkness came because the evil ones did not repent of their deeds when warnings were issued; furthermore, they did not change when total darkness came upon them. This plague also parallels the darkness that came upon Egypt. The message: Evil is destructive; evil cannot continue into infinity because of its very nature of upheaval.

Sixth Bowl of Wrath

Revelation 16:12-16 The sixth angel poured out his bowl on the great river Euphrates, and its water was dried up to prepare the way for the kings from the East. Then I saw three evil spirits that looked like frogs; they came out of the mouth of the dragon, out of the mouth of the beast and out of the mouth of the false prophet. They are spirits of demons performing miraculous signs, and they go out to the kings of the whole world, to gather them for the battle on the great day of God Almighty. "Behold, I come like a thief! Blessed is he who stays awake and keeps his clothes with him, so that he may not go naked and be shamefully exposed." Then they gathered the kings together to the place that in Hebrew is called Armageddon.

    The name <u>Armageddon</u> has generated much fear and misunderstanding through the years. Many are still waiting today for the original Armageddon to come; the specific Armageddon John spoke of came with the fall of the Roman Empire. Other "Armageddons" have occurred in the same sense that many "Waterloos" have transpired; however the original Armageddon refers to the fall of Rome. When the sixth trumpet warned of war coming to the Roman Empire, the river Euphrates separated two hundred million troops from the four angels of God, indicating Armageddon was "WAR IN HEAVEN." The river Euphrates is once again used to tie the trumpet and bowl together; war is the theme, but this time instead of partial destruction for a warning, the Roman Empire would be devastated by war.

The river Euphrates was dried up to prepare for the coming of the kings from the east. The reader might remember that Babylon fell because the drying up of the river permitted the invading armies to enter the city under the wall. This also indicates God's providence in bringing the events about; although Rome controlled most of the civilized world around the Mediterranean Sea, they could never conquer Parthia, a continuing thorn in their side. The collapse took place over a number of years, but warfare contributed heavily to the nation's demise. The drying up of waters is a frequent theme in God's word — the drying of the waters after the flood, the drying of the Red Sea to permit Israel to leave Egypt, the drying of the Jordan to allow the crossing of Israel into Canaan, and even the drying of the water when the dragon pursued God's people in *Revelation 12*.

The forces of evil were led by three frogs coming from the mouth of the dragon, sea beast, and land beast; the frogs represent the evil nature of the enemy of God. The existence of frogs with the number *3* makes the opposition against God even more pronounced. Frogs at one time had plagued Egypt, and now "symbolic frogs" were coming from evil forces; evil will not prevail. Those who try to literalize the battle of Armageddon need to consider these symbols. The battle of Armageddon would not be led by three literal frogs!

Jesus warned that Rome's collapse would occur when He came as a "thief in the night"; this is similar to the warning He gave concerning the fall of Jerusalem in *Matthew 24, Mark 13, and Luke 21.* Christians had been warned throughout the book not to become involved with the evils of Rome and its caesars, but rather to put God first. Those who were ready when the Lord came in judgment of Rome would be protected. Jesus' judgment has come "like a thief" many times throughout history when evil nations were destroyed because of their godlessness. God's people must always be ready!

The place where the battle was to occur was called "Har-Mageddon" in Hebrew and "Armageddon" in Greek. It is most likely a play on the word Megiddo, a place where many of God's battles were fought in Old Testament times. Megiddo was the sight of Gideon's victory, and it was the place where Saul defeated the Philistines. It was Megiddo where Barak and Deborah overthrew Jabin, the Canaanite King. To the early Christian, even the site of the battle would prove God would be victorious. The name Armageddon also sounds very similar to the location of the aftermath of a battle described by Ezekiel called Hamon Gog in *Ezekiel 39:15*. The pouring of the seventh bowl would bring the plague of war on the Roman Empire; war, coupled with natural disasters and evil, would end one of the most powerful earthly nations ever known.

Seventh Bowl of Wrath

Revelation 16:17-21 The seventh angel poured out his bowl into the air, and out of the temple came a loud voice from the throne, saying, "It is done!" Then there came flashes of lightning, rumblings, peals of thunder and a severe earthquake. No earthquake like it has ever occurred since man has been on earth, so tremendous was the quake. The great city split into three parts, and the cities of the nations collapsed. God remembered Babylon the Great and gave her the cup filled with the wine of the fury of his wrath. Every island fled away and the mountains could not be found. From the sky huge hailstones of about a hundred pounds each fell upon men. And they cursed God on account of the plague of hail, because the plague was so terrible.

God is the One Who said, "It is done." This time has been anticipated throughout the book of *Revelation*, and now the "time of the end" of the evil nation is so certain it was announced even before the actual fall. The events of the fall are very similar to those mentioned when the sixth seal was opened; it is symbolic of the end of Rome, but certainly parallels "the time of the end" of every evil nation existing before and after the beast. It also parallels the end of time. Three natural disasters fall upon the city — 1) a lightning storm, 2) an earthquake, and 3) a hail storm. The city was divided into three parts by the earthquake, once again showing divine purpose fulfilled. The destruction of the earthquake reveals the fierceness of God's wrath coming upon the city because of her wickedness. The hail stones would literally have been 108 to 130 pounds each, the weight of a talent. All of this signals the tremendous vindication God was to bring upon the Roman Empire. The total fall of Rome is pictured; however, John will give additional visions and information concerning the wicked empire and its collapse in the concluding chapters of *Revelation*. Along with this John sees glorious pictures for those who are redeemed through their acceptance of Jesus Christ as Lord.

Chapter Fourteen

The Destruction of the Beast

The 17th chapter of *Revelation* speaks of the harlot, Babylon, and the sea beast; John makes links tying all three to different facets of Rome. The first six verses relate the vision of the beast that would be destroyed in Armageddon.

> *Revelation 17:1-6 One of the seven angels who had the seven bowls came and said to me, "Come, I will show you the punishment of the great prostitute, who sits on many waters. With her the kings of the earth committed adultery and the inhabitants of the earth were intoxicated with the wine of her adulteries." Then the angel carried me away in the Spirit into a desert. There I saw a woman sitting on a scarlet beast that was covered with blasphemous names and had seven heads and ten horns. The woman was dressed in purple and scarlet, and was glittering with gold, precious stones and pearls. She held a golden cup in her hand, filled with abominable things and the filth of her adulteries. This title was written on her forehead:*
>
> MYSTERY
> BABYLON THE GREAT
> THE MOTHER OF PROSTITUTES
> AND OF THE ABOMINATIONS OF THE EARTH.
>
> *I saw that the woman was drunk with the blood of the saints, the blood of those who bore testimony to Jesus. When I saw her, I was greatly astonished.*

John was amazed by the vision, but an angel explained the meaning to him in the remaining verses of the chapter.

> *Revelation 17:7-11 Then the angel said to me: "Why are you astonished? I will explain to you the mystery of the woman and of the beast she rides, which has the seven heads and ten horns. The beast, which you saw, once was, now is not, and will come up out of the Abyss and go to his destruction. The inhabitants of the earth whose names have not been written in the Book of Life from the creation of the world will be astonished when they see the beast, because he once was, now is not, and yet will come. This calls for a mind with wisdom. The seven heads are seven hills on which the woman sits. They are also seven kings. Five have fallen, one is, the other has not yet come; but when he does come, he must remain for a little while. The beast who once was, and now is not, is an eighth king. He belongs to the seven and is going to his destruction.*

> Understanding the mystery of Babylon, the beast, and the prostitute: **all 3 refer to Rome!**

The beast clearly refers to some nation or empire; the prostitute is interrelated with the beast in two ways: 1) she rides with the beast, and 2) she has the name Babylon written on her forehead. Babylon was destroyed about six hundred years before John's visions were recorded. The name Babylon obviously is used as a symbol referring to another wicked empire. In what way is the harlot the wicked city? Many people have prostituted themselves spiritually to gain the benefits offered by a wicked government. The prostitute symbolizes citizens riding the system that entices the populace to evil.

The heads of the beast symbolize two facets of the nation in which the prostitute resides. We are told the seven heads are the seven hills on which the woman sits. The woman sits on a beast, but she also sits on "seven hills," this clearly pictures Rome as the beast; from ancient times Rome has been called the "city on 7 hills"!

The seven heads also describe the government of the empire by detailing its kings from 27 BC through 95 AD. A figure of speech called synecdoche is used by identifying the 8th king as the beast, but we learn that the 8th king belongs to the seven. Domitian, the 8th caesar, represented the government of this evil empire. With this overview in mind, a verse-by-verse analysis is possible.

> *Revelation 17:1 One of the seven angels who had the seven bowls came and said to me, "Come, I will show you the punishment of the great prostitute, who sits on many waters."*

Rome controlled the entire known world at the time of John's writing. The "many waters" represent the nations dominated by Roman rule.

> *Revelation 17:2   "With her the kings of the earth committed adultery and the inhabitants of the earth were intoxicated with the wine of her adulteries."*

When an empire falls, all nations closely linked to it suffer in the fall. The passage above alludes to this situation by indicating other city-states took part in the evils practiced by the caesars. The reference to adultery points to the spiritual corruption permeating the nation. Worldliness is evident in the phrase "the inhabitants of the earth"; these would be victimized along with the harlot for their part in sinning against God.

> *Revelation 17:3 Then the angel carried me away in the Spirit into a desert. There I saw a woman sitting on a scarlet beast that was covered with blasphemous names and had seven heads and ten horns.*

The prostitute was seen in a wilderness, but this is in contrast with the radiant woman God protected from the beast in the wilderness. Some claim the radiant woman became the prostitute because of transgressions. If this were true, the woman would be an adulteress; however, the word prostitute comes from the Greek word porne, meaning whore. **This prostitute had never been the bride of Christ.** This is another instance of antithesis in *Revelation* — there is a righteous woman in the wilderness, and there is an ungodly woman in the wilderness.

> *Revelation 17:4 The woman was dressed in purple and scarlet, and was glittering with gold, precious stones and pearls. She held a golden cup in her hand, filled with abominable things and the filth of her adulteries.*

The description of the prostitute underscores the wickedness of the empire. Purple indicates royalty, and scarlet represents sin; the stones and gold speak of the quest Rome had for worldly possessions. Earlier scripture said those who were sealed with the mark of the beast would have the power to buy and to sell. The harlot had thoroughly involved herself with caesar worship and had reaped the worldly benefits from the alliance.

> *Revelation 17:5 This title was written on her forehead:*
>
> MYSTERY
> BABYLON THE GREAT
> THE MOTHER OF PROSTITUTES
> AND OF THE ABOMINATIONS OF THE EARTH.

Babylon's being the symbol of Rome is a logical link because of the wickedness of Babylon in the days of Daniel. Daniel is the one who first prophesied Rome would fall, and now the two cities are brought together by the name of Babylon written on the forehead of the prostitute who sits on the beast. In the Old Testament, wicked cities were called harlots or prostitutes. *Nahum 3:4* called Ninevah a harlot; *Isaiah 23:17* called Tyre a prostitute.

> *Revelation 17:6 I saw that the woman was drunk with the blood of the saints, the blood of those who bore testimony to Jesus. When I saw her, I was greatly astonished.*

It is no secret that Rome was vile. Neither is it a secret that Rome put to death Jesus Christ and many of His followers. Generally one views just a little evil at a time; the astonishment of John appears to be over the magnitude of seeing all of the corruption at one time.

> *Revelation 17:7 Then the angel said to me: "Why are you astonished? I will explain to you the mystery of the woman and of the beast she rides, which has the seven heads and ten horns."*

The following explanation is not conjecture; the symbols are explained by an angel.

> *Revelation 17:9 "This calls for a mind with wisdom. The seven heads are seven hills on which the woman sits."*

Earlier in this chapter we learned that Rome's nickname from antiquity has been "the city on 7 hills," and the revealing of this information would unquestionably link the prostitute with the Roman Empire. The names of the seven hills of Rome are as follows: Aventine, Capitoline, Palatine, Caelian, Esquiline, Viminal, and Quirinal.

> Rome's history of caesars exactly fits the kings of John's *Revelation*!

> *Revelation 17:10 "They are also seven kings. Five have fallen, one is, the other has not yet come; but when he does come, he must remain for a little while."*

This passage should command attention because of the phrase "one is." The seven heads of the beast represent the kings of the evil empire being revealed. If five kings have fallen and one is, this means the sixth king of the kingdom is on the throne at the very time John was penning the letter. **It can be no nation other than Rome**! The five who had fallen refer to Augustus, Tiberius, Gaius, Claudius, and Nero. **The one on the throne at the time would be Vespasian,** and this would date the writing somewhere between 69 and 79 AD, the period covered by the rule of Vespasian. The seventh king who is to come for a "little while" refers to Titus, seventh of the legitimate caesars. Titus had the shortest reign of any of the true caesars — two years. The reader is encouraged to study the diagrams and discussion in chapter one of this volume to get a better comprehension of this passage.

> *Revelation 17:11 "The beast who once was, and now is not, is an eighth king. He belongs to the seven and is going to his destruction."*

After giving details concerning the first seven kings, the author adds an eighth king. Domitian would be number eight in both Daniel's explanation and in John's. Daniel began with ten kings and added an eleventh who overcame three kings within the same kingdom. When three are removed from eleven, the resulting number is 8. John left out the three pretenders to the throne. He began with seven kings and then added another to arrive at the number 8. It is interesting to look at the divine number 8 and learn that Domitian called himself Lord and God and was deified during his lifetime. **Domitian literally put himself in the place of God.**

Yes, Domitian was the 8th, but he became an 8 by removing 3, the number of the godhead. Any time an Anti-Christ arises, it happens by setting the Trinity aside! The beast tried to present the appearance of God in a three-fold description: the beast "was, and now is not and is going to his destruction." **God Was** (the beast was). **God Is** (the beast is not — Domitian had not yet come to the throne). **God Is to Come;** the beast is going to his destruction. These details further the Anti-Christ theme presented in chapter 12 of this volume. The statement that the beast is going to his destruction could refer specifically to Domitian, but it could also refer to Rome in general; furthermore, it refers philosophically to every evil person claiming to have Christ-like authority and power. Those who try to take the place of God have only one destiny — eternal destruction!

While the heads of the beast symbolize the first eight Roman caesars, what about the 10 horns of the beast? John was told the 10 horns were symbolic of kings, but to which kings does he refer?

> *Revelation 17:12-14 "The ten horns you saw are ten kings who have not yet received a kingdom, but who for one hour will receive authority as kings along with the beast." "They have one purpose and will give their power and authority to the beast. They will make war against the Lamb, but the Lamb will overcome them because he is Lord of lords and King of kings — and with him will be his called, chosen and faithful followers."*

Although Daniel's beast had an eleventh horn arise to break off three of the beast's horns, leaving eight, John saw the fourth kingdom as a beast with ten horns rather than eight. The theme of ten horns was carried forward so there would be no question that the beast of *Daniel* was the same beast of *Revelation*. The ten horns were used in *Daniel* to symbolize the caesars of Rome; since John used the seven heads to represent caesars who attained the crown through rightful means, the horns of the beast had to take on new symbolic meaning. Three explanations are offered.

Traditionally, horns represent kings, and this is true in this instance but kings in what respect? One key to meaning is found first with the statement that they "are kings who have not yet received a kingdom." These kings would have to come after the time of Domitian, since the emperors of Rome from Augustus through Domitian are symbolized by the seven heads. After the despotic rule of Domitian, the following emperors ruled Rome:

1.	Nerva	96— 98 AD
2.	Trajan	98—116 AD
3.	Hadrian	117—138 AD
4.	Antoninus Pius	138—161 AD
5.	Marcus Aurelius	161—180 AD
6.	Commodus	180—192 AD
7.	Septimius Severus	193—211 AD
8.	Caracalla	211—217 AD
9.	Heliogabalus	218—222 AD
10.	Alexander Severus	222—235 AD

The average length of rule of the ten caesars who reigned after Domitian was nearly fourteen years. After these ten caesars, everything in Rome seemed to turn upside down. Maximinus ruled from 235-238, but he was assassinated, and instability became the rule of the day. From 238 to 244 AD, seven emperors sat on the throne. During the forty-five years after Severus' reign, fifteen rulers claimed power, one every three years. The problem with this scenario, however, is that the ten kings were to turn on the beast; this explanation doesn't fit.

A more likely scenario would be that the ten kings who "will receive authority," are kings of weaker nations who would give their allegiance to Domitian and suffer along with him when he was deposed. After all, in *Revelation 17:11* the beast is referred to as the eighth king; this would be Domitian. Receiving "their authority as kings along with the beast" could refer to rulers of surrounding city-states loyal to Domitian, the emperor of Rome. This would be a reasonable explanation since Domitian's overthrow would have brought an end to the satellite rulers who participated in his evil. The overthrow of Domitian and his power structure brought a period of peace to the world. Gibbon on page 11 of *Decline and Fall of the Roman Empire*, described the world after Domitian's death.

> In the second century of the Christian era, the Empire of Rome comprehended the fairest part of the earth, and the most civilized portion of mankind ... During a happy period (AD 98-180), the public administration was conducted by the virtue and abilities of Nerva, Trajan, Hadrian, and the two Antonines.

Some have suggested that these are ten kings who persecuted Christians. In various articles and books dealing with persecutions, I found names of several caesars who are listed as persecutors. Most came from *Ecclesiastical History*, written by Eusebius in the middle of the fourth century. Problems exist: 1) Nero was already dead, and Domitian is included in the group, and 2) there is no evidence of any of these rulers turning on the beast. The list of the top 10 persecutors is found below:

> Nero, Domitian, Trajan, Marcus Aurelius, Severus, Maximinus, Maxentius, Decius, Valerian, Diocletian, and Galerius

The phrase, "for one hour," simply indicates these are humans who will have a limited reign. Contrast the "one hour" rule with the eternal authority of God. We know these also "shall war against the Lamb." The ten kings all oppose Jesus Christ, and all are destroyed because they cannot conquer the Lord of lords and King of kings.

> *Revelation 17:15 Then the angel said to me, "The waters you saw, where the prostitute sits, are peoples, multitudes, nations and languages."*

At one time Rome controlled the entire known world. The waters symbolized the people who came under Roman influence and were controlled by her power. Notice the multiple of four — 1) peoples,

2) multitudes, 3) nations, and 4) languages. The number 4 sends the message that the "prostitute" controlled the world since 4 is the number that represents the world and worldliness.

> *Revelation 17:16 "The beast and the ten horns you saw will hate the prostitute. They will bring her to ruin and leave her naked; they will eat her flesh and burn her with fire."*

If the beast and the prostitute both relate to Rome, how is it possible for the beast to turn on the prostitute? Remember, the beast represented rule, and the prostitute symbolized the general population. We have all witnessed situations in which a nation's leaders padded their own pockets and saw to their own welfare while forgetting the people whom they supposedly serve. The idea is one of internal turmoil; this kind of destruction is probably the most devastating of all — an empire or nation crumbling from within. The citizens would suffer because of their own government.

> *Revelation 17:17 "For God has put it into their hearts to accomplish his purpose by agreeing to give the beast their power to rule, until God's words are fulfilled."*

The decay and destruction of the beast was to come about in what is called "Armageddon" because of God's purposes. Satan can have no power other than that which God allows him to have. The reason internal chaos was to occur was God's determination to accomplish His goal in this way.

> *Revelation 17:18 "The woman you saw is the great city that rules over the kings of the earth."*

This verse cements the idea that the woman is the city, but we also learned that Babylon is the city and the beast is the city. The entire chapter simply speaks to the point that Rome is going to fall because God is going to bring internal instability resulting in absolute chaos. Other nations who follow the Roman path are doomed to the same consequences.

The Fall of Babylon

The 17th chapter of *Revelation* identified the beast as Rome and said the beast would fall. Chapter 18 expands the fall in Armageddon and shows the absolute devastation to befall Rome. After being astonished at the extensive wickedness of the beast, John must have been thrilled to learn God would completely destroy the wicked empire. This revelation came through three angelic proclamations.

> The Proclamation of the
> First Angel

Revelation 18:1-3   After this I saw another angel coming down from heaven. He had great authority, and the earth was illuminated by his splendor. With a mighty voice he shouted: "Fallen! Fallen is Babylon the Great! She has become a home for demons and a haunt for every evil spirit, a haunt for every unclean and detestable bird. For all the nations have drunk the maddening wine of her adulteries. The kings of the earth committed adultery with her, and the merchants of the earth grew rich from her excessive luxuries."

The caesars had chosen to deify themselves and push for worldly gain; this pursuit of satanic goals turned the entire nation over to demons. These people had also been given a choice of serving God or worldliness, but they had chosen to seek worldliness. After this, Rome was only fit for vultures and birds of prey. Any nation that becomes godless has but one common destiny — destruction!!! To protect the faithful, God called his people out of the city.

> The Proclamation of the
> Second Angel

> *Revelation 18:4 Then I heard another voice from heaven say: "Come out of her, my people, so that you will not share in her sins, so that you will not receive any of her plagues."*

It is possible for God's people to live within a nation without taking part in her excesses. Too many times Christians are affected by the world rather than affecting the world for Christ. Those who participate in the sins of the nation will also have to accept the plagues; this is the purpose for God's requesting that His people "Come out of her." The reason God's people cannot participate in the sins of the empire is given in the next verse.

> *Revelation 18:5 "For her sins are piled up to heaven, and God has remembered her crimes."*

When the fifth seal was opened in *Revelation 6*, saints were praying for the vengeance of God to come upon their persecutors. Many other scenes have indicated vengeance would come when God was ready for the event to occur! The call for vindication is repeated once more by the second angel's proclamation.

> *Revelation 18:6-8 "Give back to her as she has given; pay her back double for what she has done. Mix her a double portion from her own cup. Give her as much torture and grief as the glory and luxury she gave herself. In her heart she boasts, `I sit as queen; I am not a widow, and I will never mourn.' Therefore in one day her plagues will overtake her: death, mourning and famine. She will be consumed by fire, for mighty is the Lord God who judges her.*

The theme of "What one sows is what he reaps" is seen once more in the cry for vindication. Strength was added to the punishment as she was to receive **double** what she had mingled for others. According to this passage, Rome felt nothing could ever happen to her — "I sit as a queen... I will never mourn." Because of Rome's evil and godless pride, God would bring it to an end with seven plagues; divine control is evidenced in three dooms — 1) death, 2) mourning and 3) famine. God was stronger than Rome, and He would burn her with fire — the very end Daniel had predicted for the fourth kingdom upon earth.

Wicked Mourn the Fall of the Evil Empire in Armageddon

There would be many who would mourn over the fall of Rome because of alliances and ties with the government. Three groups are identified; first, the kings of the earth mourned the fall.

> *Revelation 18:9,10 "When the kings of the earth who committed adultery with her and shared her luxury see the smoke of her burning, they will weep and mourn over her. Terrified at her torment, they will stand far off and cry: "'Woe! Woe, O great city, O Babylon, city of power! In one hour your doom has come!' ... "*

Those who depended upon her for trade and protection would suffer when she fell; Rome controlled much of the known world in the first century, so many would suffer the consequences. The kings stood at a distance and wept because Babylon was in flames, but they did nothing attempting to reverse the event. This furthers the idea found in *Revelation 17* that the kings would turn on the city. They mourned and tried to separate themselves after the fall was reality.

A second group of mourners also stood aside and watched the destruction as they mourned over their own losses.

> *Revelation 18:11-13* "The merchants of the earth will weep and mourn over her because no one buys their cargoes any more — cargoes of gold, silver, precious stones and pearls; fine linen, purple, silk and scarlet cloth; every sort of citron wood, and articles of every kind made of ivory, costly wood, bronze, iron and marble; cargoes of cinnamon and spice, of incense, myrrh and frankincense, of wine and olive oil, of fine flour and wheat; cattle and sheep; horses and carriages; and bodies and souls of men."

Any nation as powerful as Rome creates trade alliances so strong that other nations suffer when the center falls. God gave mankind a choice; one can participate in the glory of the empire, or one can choose to serve Jesus Christ. Jesus said people cannot do both; they must make a choice. The weeping of the merchants was not for Rome's demise; it was for their own loss.

Most of the twenty-nine items in the list that were lost are luxuries; it might be remembered that Jesus warned not to lay up treasures on earth. The last item on the list is the most important — **souls of men**. Jesus died so these souls could be free from sin, but the Roman Empire had lured them away with things of the world; even more so, they sold souls into Satan's commission. The overall picture presented was of Rome's being the leading market of the world; when she fell, the merchants of the world suffered with her. To put trust in worldly goods is to put trust in the perishable. The prostitute of *Revelation 17* was dressed in fine linen, purple and scarlet, and decked with jewels; these all perished at the time designated by God. In looking into the individual items of the list, one becomes aware these are given in several categories. These items are not listed randomly; notice how clearly the divisions occur within the list:

Category 1

Four precious metals and jewels are listed — 1) gold, 2) silver, 3) precious stones, and 4) pearl. Four is the number of the world; these are items that will be found in chapter 21 telling of the heavenly city, but here they were used to lure men into worldliness.

Category 2

There are four kinds of cloth — 1) fine linen, 2) purple, 3) silk, and 4) scarlet. These clearly differ from the metals and jewels above to form a new category.

Category 3

The number <u>6</u>, the number for mortality, was used in listing items carved and worked with the hands — 1) citron wood, 2) ivory, 3) costly wood, 4) bronze, 5) iron, and 6) marble. These all seem rather permanent to man, but the number <u>6</u> indicates their perishable nature because of being formed by the hands of man. These were items used in creating false gods to worship. This grouping is also an obvious break from types of cloth.

Category 4

There are five aromatic items used for the body, for food enhancement, and for air freshening — 1) cinnamon, 2) spice, 3) incense, 4) myrrh, and 5) frankincense. The number 5 represents grace, but the herbs once used for serving God had become perverted in trade. All of these items were mere dressing that made the imperfect look, smell, and taste better for the moment.

Category 5

There were four food items that can be grown in the garden; four is the symbol of the world — 1) wine, 2) oil, 3) flour, and 4) wheat.

Category 6

There were three types of livestock — 2) cattle, 2) sheep, and 3) horses.

Category 7

Two items relate to the abuse of men through Roman exhibitions — 1) chariots and 2) slaves. Notice the balance began with two sets of four, increased to a set of six and then began decreasing in number, 6, 5, 4, 3, 2, **and now the 1 becomes the focal point of the entire list** because this is what is sold out when the other 28 items are all important.

Category 8

THE SOULS OF MEN!!!

Twenty eight would be the number of the world, 4, times 7, a complete number. These 28 items plus the souls of men complete the list of 29 in this sequence. Armageddon was heavenly warfare; the biggest losses are not territory and physical lives; the biggest loss of all is the loss of souls!

The scriptures next describe the mourning of the merchants over their loss when the great empire collapsed.

> *Revelation 18:14-17 "They will say, `The fruit you longed for is gone from you. All your riches and splendor have vanished, never to be recovered.' The merchants who sold these things and gained their wealth from her will stand far off, terrified at her torment. They will weep and mourn and cry out: `Woe! Woe, O great city, dressed in fine linen, purple and scarlet, and glittering with gold, precious stones and pearls! In one hour such great wealth has been brought to ruin!' ..."*

By standing far off, the merchants were trying to separate themselves from disaster after the affliction had begun. People like to ride in the ocean liner, but nobody wants to be there when the ship is sinking. This third group to be affected by the collapse of the great empire is mentioned in the following verse:

> *Revelation 18:17 ... "Every sea captain, and all who travel by ship, the sailors, and all who earn their living from the sea, will stand far off. When they see the smoke of her burning, they will exclaim, `Was there ever a city like this great city?' They will throw dust on their heads, and with weeping and mourning cry out: `Woe! Woe, O great city, where all who had ships on the sea became rich through her wealth! In one hour she has been brought to ruin!' ... "*

The cry came when they saw the destructive signs of smoke in the city. They mourned because their method of livelihood had been taken away. Reference was made once more to the rapid fall; it would take place in one hour. This is symbolic of the coming divine destruction. Notice that all three groups mourned, but all stood far off, and none did anything. Human effort would have been futile anyway; **when God's hour for destruction arrives, nothing can prevent the event from taking place.**

The Righteous Rejoice over the Fall

Revelation 18:20 "Rejoice over her, O heaven! Rejoice, saints and apostles and prophets! God has judged her for the way she treated you."

Daniel and John had both seen visions of the beast's falling because of the judgment of saints; the idea was repeated at this point as fulfillment.

The Proclamation of the Third Angel

Revelation 18:21-24 Then a mighty angel picked up a boulder the size of a large millstone and threw it into the sea, and said: "With such violence the great city of Babylon will be thrown down, never to be found again. The music of harpists and musicians, flute players and trumpeters, will never be heard in you again. No workman of any trade will ever be found in you again. The sound of a millstone will never be heard in you again. The light of a lamp will never shine in you again. The voice of bridegroom and bride will never be heard in you again. Your merchants were the world's great men. By your magic spell all the nations were led astray. In her was found the blood of prophets and of the saints, and of all who have been killed on the earth."

The rejoicing occurred because the prayers of the saints had been answered; the promise of the fall of Rome was so inescapable it could be announced before the fact. When the angel took a large stone like a millstone and threw it into the sea, it disappeared just as "Babylon," symbolic of Rome, was to disappear. In *Jeremiah 52:60-64*, the prophet was told to write down on a scroll the calamities that would come upon Babylon; he was then to tie a stone to the scroll and throw it into the Euphrates. The sinking of the stone was symbolic of the sinking of Old Babylonia. Notice that all amusement would cease — no harpers, no minstrels, no flute players, and no trumpeters. The number 4 revealed that worldly pleasure would be ended in Rome. All business would cease — no craftsmen to work, no noise of the mill, and no light of the lamp within the city. The existence of light was once present in the city, but the city had chosen darkness. Since they had chosen darkness; darkness is given them. God's removal of light from the city signifies the fall. The lack of voices of the bridegroom and bride seems to refer to a total spiritual void. Jesus is the bridegroom, and the church is the bride; all semblance of spirituality would disappear to make the collapse of the city complete. **No wonder God's people were called out!**

Three reasons were given for the fall of the empire — 1) the merchants had chosen the pursuit of worldliness; 2) Rome had tried to achieve religious status by means other than God (they had used magic spells); and 3) Rome had shed the blood of prophets, saints, and all that had been slain on earth. The wickedness of Rome was emphasized once more as being the reason for the fall. The reader should remember the message of the fifth trumpet and fifth bowl that God allows wickedness to run its course to destruction.

In chapter 19 of *Revelation,* John heard four hymns celebrating the fall of Babylon. The hymns came from the multitudes in heaven shouting, "Hallelujah"; this is the only place in the New Testament where the word "hallelujah" is found. The first "hallelujah" hymn praises God for His magnificence and for His condemnation of the prostitute.

> *Revelation 19:1,2 After this I heard what sounded like the roar of a great multitude in heaven shouting: "Hallelujah! Salvation and glory and power belong to our God, for true and just are his judgments. He has condemned the great prostitute who corrupted the earth by her adulteries. He has avenged on her the blood of his servants."*

The emphasis of this song of praise is on God's judgment of the prostitute. The saints had prayed for vengeance, and it had come. However, salvation was delivered to the saints; this song was sung by the great multitude in heaven. Chapters 4 and 5 of *Revelation* established seven rings around God, the last being "every living thing ever created." Notice the words roar and shouting; the sound of this hallelujah song must have been deafening!

This same multitude again shouted, "Hallelujah"; this hymn rejoices over the collapse of the beast.

> *Revelation 19:3 And again they shouted: "Hallelujah! The smoke from her goes up for ever and ever."*

While the first two "hallelujahs" came from all living creatures ever created, the next was sung by the twenty-four elders and the four living creatures. The hymns were moving toward the throne as first the outer ring composed of all created beings sing, and then the inner circles composed of elders and living creatures follow in praise. The hymns of *Revelation 4* and *5* moved from the center outward to indicate God's control. These hymns move inward to build God's praise to the highest level.

> *Revelation 19:4 The twenty-four elders and the four living creatures fell down and worshiped God, who was seated on the throne. And they cried: "Amen, Hallelujah!"*

The movement toward the throne continues with the next statement coming from the throne. The voice commanded praise from four groups — 1) God's servants, 2) those who fear God, 3) the small, and 4) the great.

> *Revelation 19:5 Then a voice came from the throne, saying: "Praise our God, all you his servants, you who fear him, both small and great!"*

The magnitude of an event should determine the level of praise; God has answered the prayers of the saints and has fulfilled His own promise to destroy the beast. This action is met with perhaps the loudest possible praise to God. Read the descriptive phrases carefully that portray the power of the "hallelujah" chorus.

> *Revelation 19:6-8 Then I heard what sounded like a great multitude, like the roar of rushing waters and like loud peals of thunder, shouting: "Hallelujah! For our Lord God Almighty reigns. Let us rejoice and be glad and give him glory! For the wedding of the Lamb has come, and his bride has made herself ready. Fine linen, bright and clean, was given her to wear." (Fine linen stands for the righteous acts of the saints.)*

The marriage relationship with Christ is significant throughout the Bible. *Jeremiah 31:32, "... they broke my covenant, though I was a husband to them," Matthew 25* tells the story of the 10 virgins and their preparations for the wedding feast. Paul stresses this relationship in *2 Corinthians 11:2 — "I promised you to one husband."* The bride of Christ refers to the church, those who have chosen to serve Him. The wedding garments are alluded to in *Matthew 22* as being necessary; according to John's vision, the wedding clothes are symbolic of spirituality — "the righteous acts of the saints."

TWO BANQUETS

1. Wedding feast for victors
2. Vulture feast for losers

Banquet Feast for the Redeemed

Revelation 19:9 Then the angel said to me, "Write: 'Blessed are those who are invited to the wedding supper of the Lamb!'" And he added, 'These are the true words of God.'"

The wedding supper of the Lamb is another way of indicating the victory in Armageddon for those who remained faithful to Jesus Christ, the bridegroom. Subsequent passages explain the counterpart to this vision when birds of prey feast on those sealed by the beast. When John saw these things, his feelings overwhelmed him. These truths have been valid throughout history and remain valid in the post-modern generation as "secondary Armageddons" take place.

Revelation 19:10 At this I fell at his feet to worship him. But he said to me, "Do not do it! I am a fellow servant with you and with your brothers who hold to the testimony of Jesus. Worship God! For the testimony of Jesus is the spirit of prophecy."

Colossians 2:18 proclaims that angel worship is not to occur!

> *"Do not let anyone who delights in false humility and the worship of angels disqualify you for the prize."*

Because of this principle, John was forbidden to worship the angel. The angel explains that he is merely a fellow servant of Jesus. John was also told to worship God because the testimony of Jesus was the spirit of prophecy. Jesus came to fulfill the prophets. Because He fulfilled the spirit of prophecy, one should heed Jesus and not an angel.

The wedding feast of the Lamb was followed by Christ's waging war against the wicked. The church at Pergamum in chapter 2 of *Revelation* was told Christ would come with the sword in His mouth to war against the unfaithful. This becomes reality as the vision of Armageddon continues:

> *Revelation 19:11-16 I saw heaven standing open and there before me was a white horse, whose rider is called Faithful and True. With justice he judges and makes war. His eyes are like blazing fire, and on his head are many crowns. He has a name written on him that no one knows but he himself. He is dressed in a robe dipped in blood, and his name is the Word of God. The armies of heaven were following him, riding on white horses and dressed in fine linen, white and clean. Out of his mouth comes a sharp sword with which to strike down the nations. "He will rule them with an iron scepter." He treads the winepress of the fury of the wrath of God Almighty. On his robe and on his thigh he has this name written: KING OF KINGS AND LORD OF LORDS.*

This is clearly Jesus Christ because of earlier imagery:

1. He was seen in heaven.
2. He was called the Faithful and True.
3. His eyes were a flame of fire.
4. He wore the kingly diadem or crown.
5. His blood sprinkled garments leave no question at all.

6. His name was the "Word of God"; see *John 1:1*.
7. He led the armies in heaven.
8. He had a sharp sword proceeding from His mouth.
9. He was to rule with a rod of iron.
10. His treading the winepress shows His judgment role.
11. He is KING OF KINGS AND LORD OF LORDS.
12. His horse is white.

Jesus rules with an iron scepter, and he treads the winepress of God's wrath; this war will have losers. The losers are pictured in another feast, the counterpart of the wedding supper of the Lamb; this is the supper of vultures preying upon those who lost. Armageddon symbolizes spiritual warfare that has victors who receive eternal blessings and losers who are spiritually destroyed.

Vulture Feast for the Lost

Revelation 19:17,18   And I saw an angel standing in the sun, who cried in a loud voice to all the birds flying in midair, "Come, gather together for the great supper of God, so that you may eat the flesh of kings, generals, and mighty men, of horses and their riders, and the flesh of all people, free and slave, small and great."

This banquet was the feast of wrath, contrasting greatly with the love feast of the Lamb. The menu list to be consumed by the birds flying in mid-air included the following: 1) kings, 2) generals, 3) mighty men, 4) horses, 5) riders of horses, 6) free, 7) bond, 8) small, and 9) great. Nine is the number for judgment and finality; what a fitting picture for the termination of evil! In summation, it includes all worldly men; vultures were to consume them — when evil continues, the end result is programmed for destruction.

When the sixth trumpet was sounded, John saw the coming of spiritual war; when the 6th bowl was poured, Armageddon became reality. In *Revelation 16*, the great city was split into three parts and was destroyed as a result of Armageddon. A study of *Revelation* 17, revealed the beast, Babylon, and the prostitute were all symbols of the Roman Empire, loser in Armageddon. This vision gives more insight into the same event. In the following verses, it will be seen that the beast was destroyed; this beast refers to the same city split into three parts when Armageddon was first mentioned. The feast of vultures and the following information simply develop the events of Armageddon.

> *Revelation 19:19 Then I saw the beast and the kings of the earth and their armies gathered together to make war against the rider on the horse and his army. But the beast was captured, and with him the false prophet who had performed the miraculous signs on his behalf. With these signs he had deluded those who had received the mark of the beast and worshiped his image. The two of them were thrown alive into the fiery lake of burning sulfur. The rest of them were killed with the sword that came out of the mouth of the rider on the horse, and all the birds gorged themselves on their flesh.*

The strength of the order of events is strong; John envisions the feast of vultures before the collapse of Rome because the result is known and certain before it ever occurred. Evidence clearly indicates this was Jesus going to war against three groups — 1) the beast, 2) the false prophet, and 3) all those who followed the beast. While the primary message concerning Armageddon relates to the collapse of Rome, the principle has proven true with all nations before and after the first century. Any that follow the way of wickedness will be destroyed.

The specific battle is not some final battle to be fought in the future. Rome did not fall because Parthians and barbaric tribes invaded the country; the empire fell because God and His heavenly army had determined its collapse. The book of *Revelation* is not only a book about the fall of Rome; **it is also a book explaining that all empires have a birth, a life, and a death.** Nations opposing God have a common destiny — destruction! The more wicked a nation becomes, the more **imperative it becomes for Christians to distance themselves from its excesses**.

The next chapter continues with this theme of winners and losers in spiritual warfare in what has become one of the most controversial sections in the book of *Revelation*.

Chapter Fifteen

Consequences for Winners & Losers in "1,000 Year" Theme

The original Armageddon referred to the collapse of Rome; however, "Armageddon" becomes a symbol for the destiny of all nations destroyed because of evil. Chapter 20 of *Revelation* uses a 1,000 year theme to symbolize more blessings for the spiritual victors and more losses due the wicked.

Meaning of 1,OOO Years

Forty-four verses proclaim God's love will last FOREVER; twenty-six of these verses are found in *Psalms 136*. On the other hand, *Exodus 20:6, Deuteronomy 5:10,* and *Deuteronomy 7:9* all proclaim that God will keep his faithful covenant of love to "a thousand generations." If God's love is forever, and if God's covenant of love is extended to a thousand generations, the two phrases have the same meaning – ETERNAL! Two identical scriptures present this truth in the clearest of language:

1 Chronicles 16:15 and Psalms 105:8

He remembers his covenant forever, the word he commanded, for a thousand generations.

Chapter 8 of this volume has already covered the method of determining meaning of large numbers; they must be reduced to the base. One thousand is one of the most powerful numbers symbolizing "totality, all, everything, forever" because it is the perfect number 10 cubed. This section of the book will explain the significance of 1,000 years as it is 1) applied to the redeemed; 2) as it relates to those who choose to remain dead in sin; and 3) it will explain the time of Satan's being chained. These three applications will all be harmonized when viewing the 1,000 years as "the entire lifespan for each and every person."

Satan Chained 1,000 Years

The chaining of Satan has two applications, physical and Spiritual; each of these interpretations have great truths for us to examine.

> *Revelation 20:1-3 And I saw an angel coming down out of heaven, having the key to the Abyss and holding in his hand a great chain. He seized the dragon, that ancient serpent, who is the devil, or Satan, and bound him for a thousand years. He threw him into the Abyss, and locked and sealed it over him, to keep him from deceiving the nations anymore until the thousand years were ended ...*

Satan's Being Chained for 1,000 Years Explained with World-View Implications

Satan's chaining has both physical and Spiritual applications. On one hand it can be applied as a world view; Satan lost quite a world power when the Roman Empire fell because the beast had furthered worldliness through international trade. The fall of the Roman Empire shook the entire known world, and many national economies were destroyed. What effect would the fall of the beast have upon the dragon Satan? An appropriate vision indicates the effect by picturing Satan as being "bound" for 1,000 years. When Satan lost the ally, who did his bidding, what better symbol could be used than to chain the dragon?

With this world view of the chaining, the symbol of 1,000 indicates the complete loss of the evil empire. Satan's power through Rome was destroyed completely, but Christians living within the evil empire survived to carry God's kingdom forward. Viewed in this way, the binding of Satan for 1,000 years is a symbolic way of saying Satan's loss completely limited his power regarding the "beast" Rome. Remember the mourning of the kings of the world, the merchants, and the mariners who transported goods. Satan was to be unchained for a short time; this could refer to his finding a new "beast" to further his cause. When that beast falls, Satan is chained again. Does Satan have another beast ally in the works? The United States of America is certainly not exempt! I believe great truths are found in the above analysis of Satan's 1,000 year chaining on the physical level of nations and those who live within them. This was the focal part of earlier books I wrote; however, currently I am seeing a deeper, spiritual application.

Spiritual Implications of Satan's Being Chained for 1,000 Years

While the world-view is important in one respect, the most important message found in the "thousand year" theme deals with the spiritual side of things. With this view, we all face the consequences of our own spiritual Armageddon. The prelude to Armageddon actually begins in *Revelation 12:7* when John saw war in heaven with Michael and his angels fighting the dragon. Notice how the war was won.

> *Revelation 12:11 They overcame him by the blood of the Lamb and by the word of their testimony; they did not love their lives so much as to shrink from death.*

If Satan is chained by the blood of the Lamb, why have many nations and citizens succumbed to evil and traveled the path to destruction?

When a ferocious lion is chained, it is powerless to those who stay outside the reach of the chain; however, all who willfully go within the chain's limits are subject to whatever the lion does to them.

> *1 Peter 5:8-9 Be self-controlled and alert. Your enemy the devil prowls around like a roaring lion looking for someone to devour. Resist him, standing firm in the faith, because you know that your brothers throughout the world are undergoing the same kind of sufferings.*

Satan has demonic, destructive powers and can roar and devour within the limits God permits; however Paul's explanation of temptation gives a good description of Satan's limits on the chain:

> *1 Corinthians 10:13 No temptation has seized you except what is common to man. And God is faithful; he will not let you be tempted beyond what you can bear. But when you are tempted, he will also provide a way out so that you can stand up under it.*

Satan is totally chained and totally powerless over Christians for the entirety of every person's lifetime, but anyone, including Christians, may choose to walk inside the chains' reach.

When the sixth trumpet sounded, 200 million troops were lined up at the Euphrates River, and across the river John saw four angels chained to a tree to be released for spiritual warfare. In chapter 19 of *Revelation* the "war in heaven" that destroyed the beast was won by the blood of the Lamb and the testimony of saints. Satan is chained because Jesus shed His blood to atone for the sins of the world. One who has not made a total commitment to the Lord is inside the chained area, but the blood of the Lamb continues to protect those who walk in the light.

> *1 John 1:7 But if we walk in the light, as he is in the light, we have fellowship with one another, and the blood of Jesus, his Son, purifies us from all sin.*

Whether a nation lives or dies is irrelevant when it comes to one's relationship with the Lord. Satan roars at the end of the chain, but Christians must walk in the light outside of Satan's reach. The following scriptures say Satan will be released at some point; the purpose will be explained when John writes about Gog and Magog and Satan's release.

> *Revelation 20:3 ... After that he must be set free for a short time.*

Revelation 20:7 When the thousand years are over, Satan will be released from his prison.

1,000 Years Applied to the Living and the Dead

The "thousand year" theme is carried out further. John sees victors as those who came to life and reigned for a thousand years, and he sees losers as those who chose to remain dead a thousand years, their entire lifetime. Their being alive or being dead came because of how they chose to spend their time on earth.

God Gives People the Opportunity to Choose Life or Death

Deuteronomy 30:19 This day I call heaven and earth as witnesses against you that I have set before you life and death, blessings and curses. Now choose life, so that you and your children may live.

Ecclesiasticus 15:13-17 The Lord hates all that is foul, and no one who fears him will love it either. He himself made human beings in the beginning, and then left them free to make their own decisions. If you choose, you will keep the commandments and so be faithful to his will. He has set fire and water before you; put out your hand to whichever you prefer. A human being has life and death before him; whichever he prefers will be given him. (New Jerusalem Bible)

At first glance, one would think choosing life would be an easy choice, but the choice for life means giving up worldly ways to follow Jesus Christ. Worldly ways can be temporarily fulfilling to the flesh. Jesus said the vast majority of the world would choose the ways of wickedness leading to death, but the choice can still be made to enter the road leading to life — not a particularly popular choice for the majority.

Matthew 7:13-14 "Enter through the narrow gate. For wide is the gate and broad is the road that leads to destruction, and many enter through it. But small is the gate and narrow the road that leads to life, and only a few find it."

Who Are the Dead?

Because of sin and its destructive power, everyone is spiritually dead until the choice is made to live.

Romans 5:12 Just as sin entered the world through one man, and death through sin, and in this way death came to all men, because all sinned.

Ephesians 2:1 As for you, you were in your transgressions and sins.

Ephesians 4:18-19 They are darkened in their understanding and separated from the life of God because of the ignorance that is in them due to the hardening of their hearts.

1 Timothy 5:6 The widow who lives for pleasure is dead even while she lives.

One of the cities that received a letter from Jesus was physically alive, but they were spiritually dead.

Revelation 3:1 "To the angel of the church in Sardis write: These are the words of him who holds the seven spirits of God and the seven stars. I know your deeds; you have a reputation of being alive, but you are dead.

The preceding scriptures all point to a basic truth: those who have chosen a lifestyle of sin are "dead" in their sins. They could have chosen life, but some choose to remain dead in sin throughout their entire lives

Who Are the Living?

The living are those who have chosen to be resurrected to new life. They were physically alive before, but they were dead spiritually; the new life is spiritual life, and it is eternal.

> *Ephesians 2:4-6 But because of his great love for us, God, who is rich in mercy, made us alive with Christ even when we were dead in transgressions — it is by grace you have been saved. And God raised us up with Christ and seated us with him in the heavenly realms in Christ Jesus.*

When one is dead and brought to life, a resurrection has occurred. In the scripture above, Paul refers to being made alive when God "raised us up" with Christ. Jesus refers to a transformation taking place when one leaves death and becomes alive. According to Paul in the scripture above, Christians are seated in heavenly realms during their physical lifetime. Jesus refers to His followers passing from death into life; this pictures a resurrection:

> *John 5:24 "I tell you the truth, whoever hears my word and believes him who sent me has eternal life and will not be condemned; he has crossed over from death to life."*

While the above verse seems to picture a resurrection, Jesus presents another picture of the new life coming after "being born again."

> *John 3:5-7 "I tell you the truth, no one can enter the kingdom of God unless he is born of water and the Spirit. Flesh gives birth to flesh, but the Spirit gives birth to spirit. You should not be surprised at my saying, 'You must be born again.'"*

Resurrected to new life or being born to new life, one who chooses to follow Jesus can be said to have crossed over from death to life.

If one is in Christ and dies physically before Jesus returns, how does the number 1,000 years relate to all of life? **The Christian's lifespan is eternal!**

A Christian's Life Is Eternal

John 6:50 But here is the bread that comes down from heaven, which a man may eat and not die.

John 6:58 This is the bread that came down from heaven. Your forefathers ate manna and died, but he who feeds on this bread will live forever.

John 8:51 I tell you the truth, if anyone keeps my word, he will never see death.

John 11:25-26 "I am the resurrection and the life. He who believes in me will live, even though he dies; and whoever lives and believes in me will never die. Do you believe this?"

With these thoughts in mind, one can more easily see the meaning of the 1,000 year reign of saints, and the application of the dead who chose to remain dead 1,000 years, their entire lifetime.

Revelation 20:4-6 I saw thrones on which were seated those who had been given authority to judge. And I saw the souls of those who had been beheaded because of their testimony for Jesus and because of the word of God. They had not worshiped the beast or his image and had not received his mark on their foreheads or their hands. They came to life and reigned with Christ a thousand years. (The rest of the dead did not come to life until the thousand years were ended.) This is the first resurrection. Blessed and holy are those who have part in the first resurrection. The second death has no power over them, but they will be priests of God and of Christ and will reign with him for a thousand years.

> **Resurrection Refers to Change from Death to Life.**

This observation was made earlier, and it becomes obvious in the passage above, but the simplicity of the statement has more depth than meets the eye. While being alive physically, those outside of Jesus Christ are spiritually "dead" because of sin. Resurrection is for the dead; a living being has no need of resurrection!

> **Those Who Followed Jesus "Came to Life" (Resurrected) and Reigned with Jesus 1,000 Years.**

When one chooses life and accepts Jesus, he or she dies to a life of sin and is resurrected with Jesus to new life. It is similar to being "born again" *(John 3:1-7)*; new life comes with either explanation.

Revelation 20:4-6	*Romans 6:3-5 ... We were therefore*
They came to life and reigned with Christ a thousand years. ... This is the first resurrection. Blessed and holy are those who **have part in the first resurrection***.*	*buried with him through baptism into death in order that, just as Christ was raised from the dead through the glory of the Father, we too may live a new life. If we have been united with him like this in his death, we will certainly also* **be united with him in his resurrection.**

Further blessings are to come to those who take part in the first resurrection; these promises, just like the "new life," begin during our temporal life on earth. The saints will not only live forever, they will also reign 1,000 years = forever. Both "forever" and "1,000 years" are used to explain the blessings coming to those who make the choice to live.

Revelation 20:6

*... they will be priests of God and of Christ and will **reign with him for a thousand years.***

Revelation 22:5

*... the Lord God will give them light. And **they will reign for ever and ever.***

Along with their eternal reign, they will also be priests of God and of Christ. Peter verifies this truth; those receiving his letter were already priests who were reigning during earth time.

Revelation 20:6

*The second death has no power over them, but they will be **priests** of God and of Christ and will **reign** with him for a thousand years.*

1 Peter 2:9

*... You are a chosen people, a **royal priesthood**, a holy nation, a people belonging to God. ...*

Furthermore, the ones who have had part in the first resurrection will not be harmed by the second death. These blessings cover all of time because of the future tense — "they will be priests" and "will reign with Christ a thousand years." These are blessings received by those who choose to come to spiritual life. What about those who choose to stay dead in sin throughout their lifetimes?

> **The Rest of the Dead Do Not Come to Life Until the End of 1,000 Years.**

Revelation 20:5 (The rest of the dead did not come to life until the thousand years were ended.)

Two resurrections take place; the first brings blessings of life; the second brings the curse of the second death. Observe first that the phrase is in parentheses, separating it from the thoughts presented before and after it. Secondly, be sure to notice there are two resurrections mentioned in *Revelation 20:4-5*, and the resurrection of the dead is the second.

Since the number 1,000 symbolizes all of life for each person, these people had chosen to remain dead in their sins during their entire physical lifespan. This resurrection took place when they "came to life" at the end of 1,000 years (entire lifetime). How interesting that the ones who chose to remain dead in their sins will be resurrected!!! Why would those who made this choice be resurrected at the end of their physical life? They were resurrected to be judged and to join the beast and dragon (Satan) in the lake of fire — the second death. Those choosing life have their names recorded in the "Book of Life." People's names are either in the "Book of Life," or they walk among the dead. Those whose names are not recorded in the "Book of Life" face eternal doom. Observe below the destiny of those who are spiritually dead when they pass from this physical life.

> *Revelation 20:15 If anyone's name was not found written in the Book of Life, he was thrown into the lake of fire.*

Satan Will Be Released at the End of the 1,000 Years

Satan will be unchained to pick up his allies and followers to take them with him to the lake of fire. These are his prisoners of war; he owns the POW's of spiritual warfare. They will come to life to be sent to their death. Christians choose to die to a sinful life and to be resurrected to live eternally. Since the number 1,000 represents all of life, Christians get an extended warranty throughout eternity, while the number 1,000 represents the physical life of those who choose to remain dead in their sins.

> *Revelation 20:7-10 When the thousand years are over, Satan will be released from his prison and will go out to deceive the nations in the four corners of the earth — Gog and Magog — to gather them for battle. In number they are like the sand on the seashore. They marched across the breadth of the earth and surrounded the camp of God's people, the city he loves. But fire came down from heaven and devoured them.*

> *And the devil, who deceived them, was thrown into the lake of burning sulfur, where the beast and the false prophet had been thrown. They will be tormented day and night for ever and ever.*

Satan may pick up his prisoners after each person dies and is resurrected to be sent to the second death, or it could refer to the end of all time, or both. Jesus presented this truth about the fate of those who choose death earlier in scripture.

> *Matthew 25:41 "Then he will say to those on his left, 'Depart from me, you who are cursed, into the eternal fire prepared for the devil and his angels.' ... "*

Comprehending the fate of the spiritual living and spiritual dead helps readers better understand the parable of Lazarus and the rich man in *Luke 16*. The two were not in a condition awaiting judgment; Lazarus was already enjoying heavenly blessings, and the rich man was already in torment. Judgment obviously had already come for the two. Clarity is also given to the following scripture:

> *Hebrews 9:27-28 Just as man is destined to die once, and after that to face judgment, so Christ was sacrificed once to take away the sins of many people; and he will appear a second time, not to bear sin, but to bring salvation to those who are waiting for him.*

It is a no-brainer to say every person faces physical death. The deeper spiritual meaning is that death is a choice; one can choose to die to a sinful life, or one can experience the second death because of the choice to live a sinful lifestyle. As the mechanic said in a television commercial years ago, "You can pay me now, or you can pay me later." Of course, it is after physical death that judgment comes, but the important variable in this situation is not physical death, but which spiritual outcome each person chooses — some choose life, and some choose death! These thoughts will help readers better grasp what happens in judgment as John envisions the throne room and judgment of the dead.

> **John Sees the Throne Room and Judgment of the DEAD!**

This scene presents the clearest picture of what happens to the "spiritual living" and the "spiritual dead" after physical death. When "books" are opened, the DEAD are judged, but there is another book — the BOOK of LIFE. Earlier we learned that those who were resurrected to LIFE would not be harmed by the second death. Now we read that those whose names are not in the BOOK of LIFE are sent to the lake of fire, the second death. In the scripture below, the DEAD have been placed in bold print to help readers see the magnitude of the point. In the middle of the scripture we read about the BOOK of LIFE; the book contained names of those who had chosen ETERNAL LIFE! Be sure to take note of "the BOOK of LIFE"! The DEAD are the ones facing judgment!

> *Revelation 20:11-15 Then I saw a great white throne and him who was seated on it. Earth and sky fled from his presence, and there was no place for them. And I saw the **dead**, great and small, standing before the throne, and books were opened. Another book was opened, which is the Book of Life. The **dead were judged according to what they had done** as recorded in the books. The sea gave up the **dead** that were in it, and **death and Hades** gave up the **dead** that were in them, and each person was judged according to what he had done. Then **death and Hades** were thrown into the lake of fire. The lake of fire is the second death. If anyone's name was not found written in the Book of Life, he was thrown into the lake of fire. (Emphasis is mine.)*

The book of *Revelation* presents many themes concerning what happens to winners and losers of the heavenly war.

WINNERS	LOSERS
Invited to Feast of the Lamb	Eaten by birds of prey
Rejoice over victory	Mourn over loss
Reaped to live eternally	Reaped into winepress
Inherit the city of God	Sent to lake of fire
Live & Reign 1,000 years	Remain dead 1,000 yrs
Names in Book of Life	Suffer the second death

****

How does the preceding information in this chapter fit with all the existing theories of millennialism? For hundreds of years, speculation has taken place about eschatology, the "end times." This is evident in four theories: 1) Dispensational Pre-millennialism, 2) Historic Pre-millennialism, 3) Post-millennialism, and 4) A-millennialism.

The term "pre-millennialism" did not exist before the middle of the 19th century. Primarily it is the belief that Jesus will literally and physically be on the earth for 1,000 years following his second coming; consequently, we are living in that time before his coming and reign. This theory is tied to belief in the "rapture" or transporting of the redeemed into heaven for seven years during a time of tribulation on earth. Adherents believe that the tribulation will be followed by the return of Christ with His saints to the earth for the 1,000 year reign.

Believers in historic pre-millennialism see believers of all ages comprising the redeemed body of Christ. Their concept does not include the "rapture" and the "great tribulation" taking place before the return of Christ to reign with His saints on earth. They see a great apostasy and tribulation taking place along with the reign.

Post-millennialism differs by claiming that Christ will come after the end of a golden age (hence, the word "post") in which Christian principles flourish. Believers look for signs of things changing during earth time to begin the 1,000 year reign before the coming of Christ.

The Latin "a" means "no"; thus, A-millennialism rejects the idea that Jesus will have a literal 1,000 year reign on earth. This theory teaches that Christ's reign is spiritual in nature and is taking place now; at the end of this age, Christ will return in final judgment. The preceding information comes closer to this concept than to any the others.

First, looking at these four concepts, let's consider how the concepts harmonize with scripture. Pre-millennial views take the number 1,000 literally. If this is so, a huge problem exists. Notice that John actually identifies two separate thousand year reigns. In *Revelation 20:4*, John saw saints who "came" to life and "reigned"; these two verbs are past tense, and John saw them 2,000 years ago. To take this literally, their reign came to an end about 1,000 years ago. In *Revelation 20:6*, readers are encouraged to take part in the first resurrection; the ones doing so "will be" priests of God and of Christ and "will reign" for 1,000 years. These verbs are future tense; how can we have two 1,000 year reigns, one in the past and one with blessings for the future? Clue: It can't be literal! This can be harmonized by understanding that the 1,000 years is symbolic, referring to the lifespan of each person — past, present, and future.

Second, three of these concepts downplay the fact that Christ reigns today and that we are priests and reign with Him. Peter said Christians are a "royal" priesthood. Earlier scriptures indicated that Christians "have been lifted up and seated in heavenly realms." In *Romans 5* Paul told his readers that they "reign in life."

Third, these theories cannot harmonize with the symbolic nature of the number 1,000 meaning "all, everything, total," combined with the message of *Revelation 22:5* that saints "will reign forever."

****

The graphic on the following page shows the results of choices we make; the cross is in the center to indicate that Christ died so we might have eternal life. But for humanity to have eternal life, we must choose to die to a sinful lifestyle. The graphic depicts the choices and outcomes one faces when these choices are made.

1,000 Years = ALL of Life for Each Person

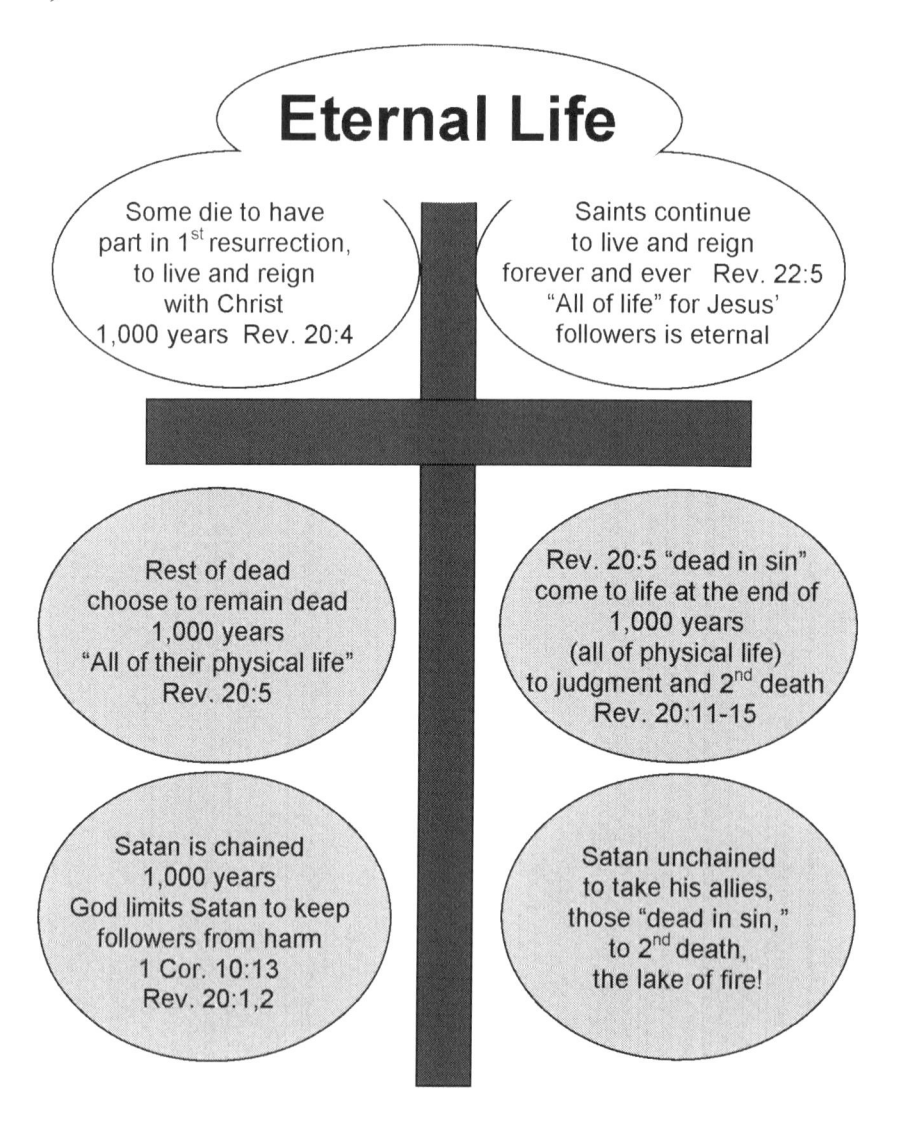

Eternal Life

Some die to have part in 1st resurrection, to live and reign with Christ 1,000 years Rev. 20:4

Saints continue to live and reign forever and ever Rev. 22:5 "All of life" for Jesus' followers is eternal

Rest of dead choose to remain dead 1,000 years "All of their physical life" Rev. 20:5

Rev. 20:5 "dead in sin" come to life at the end of 1,000 years (all of physical life) to judgment and 2nd death Rev. 20:11-15

Satan is chained 1,000 years God limits Satan to keep followers from harm 1 Cor. 10:13 Rev. 20:1,2

Satan unchained to take his allies, those "dead in sin," to 2nd death, the lake of fire!

In the concluding chapter of this volume, we will rejoice with John and those early Christians as they viewed the results of the victory in Jesus Christ. The battle has been won through the blood of the Lamb; everyone must now make the choice to inherit the city of God for all eternity or to suffer the second death in the lake of fire.

Chapter Sixteen

Victory in Jesus

In the final chapters of *Revelation*, John sees scenes of new arrangements God has planned for His followers. The first and second chapters of *Genesis* tell about the beginning of physical life and the fall of mankind. *Revelation*, chapters 21 and 22, detail the great reversal as God restores all by making all things new.

> *Revelation 21:5 He who was seated on the throne said, "I am making everything new!" Then he said, "Write this down, for these words are trustworthy and true."*

> "I am making everything new."

New Heaven and New Earth

Genesis 1:1
In the beginning God created the heavens and the earth.

Revelation 21:1 Then I saw a new heaven and a new earth, for the first heaven and the first earth had passed away, and there was no longer any sea.

Satan and sin tarnished the first home God made for man, but God has a new home prepared for those who overcome. An intriguing statement occurs in verse 1, "... there was no longer any sea." In

Revelation 4:6 the sea separated man from God; in chapter 15 the redeemed were standing near the sea; now **the sea is no more**. Man is finally with God as the Almighty intended; no more barriers exist to continue the separation.

How new will God make things? The following comparison of the way things were after the fall with the new circumstances really emphasizes the gift God has given His followers.

Genesis 3:19 "By the sweat of your brow you will eat your food until you return to the ground, since from it you were taken; for dust you are and to dust you will return."	*Revelation 21:4 "He will wipe every tear from their eyes. There will be no more death or mourning or crying or pain, for the old order of things has passed away."*

The comparison between the beginning of earth time and the entrance of God's followers into eternity helps the reader to follow the theme of victory and "all things being made new" in John's message. That which is necessary for physical life is no longer needed for heavenly life.

Genesis 1:16 God made two great lights — the greater light to govern the day and the lesser light to govern the night. He also made the stars.	*Revelation 21:23 The city does not need the sun or the moon to shine on it, for the glory of God gives it light, and the Lamb is its lamp.*

Adam and Eve lost the tree of life in events surrounding the opening of *Genesis*, but the tree of life (eternal life) is restored for those who believe and trust in God.

Genesis 2:8,9
Now the LORD God had planted a garden in the east, in Eden; and there he put the man he had formed. And the LORD God made all kinds of trees grow out of the ground — trees that were pleasing to the eye and good for food. In the middle of the garden were the tree of life and the tree of the knowledge of good and evil.

Revelation 22:1,2
Then the angel showed me the river of the water of life, as clear as crystal, flowing from the throne of God and of the Lamb down the middle of the great street of the city. On each side of the river stood the tree of life, bearing twelve crops of fruit, yielding its fruit every month. And the leaves of the tree are for the healing of the nations.

From original sin came the curse of separation from God and the curse of pain and death. Sin separated mankind from God, but through Christ, God and humans are once again united. **THE CURSE WAS REMOVED BY THE BLOOD OF JESUS!**

Genesis 3:14
*So the LORD God said to the serpent, "Because you have done this, **Cursed** are you above all the livestock and all the wild animals!*

Revelation 22:3
No longer will there be any curse. *The throne of God and of the Lamb will be in the city, and his servants will serve him.*

Sin was so devastating that Adam and Eve tried to hide from the face of God. But the redeemed will be able to see the face of God. The comparison below graphically displays the change from fall to redemption as all things are made new.

Genesis 3:8
*... **they hid** from the LORD God among the trees of the garden.*

Revelation 22:4
They will see his face, and his name will be on their foreheads.

John said in *John 1:18,* *"No one has ever seen God ..."* *Exodus 33:20* states, *"But," he said, "you cannot see my face, for no one may see me and live."* This reversal appears to go a step beyond the previous ones listed; man cannot see the face of God in this life, but salvation and eternal life make the seeing of God's face reality. The reality may be years away, but the promise is immediate. According to the passage below, the blessings can all be viewed as present while one is living on this planet during earth-time.

> *Ephesians 2:4-6 Because of his great love for us, God, who is rich in mercy, made us alive with Christ even when we were dead in transgressions — it is by grace you have been saved. And God raised us up with Christ and seated us with him in the heavenly realms in Christ Jesus.*

After learning that God is making all things new, what more significant thing to make new than the city of God itself! Jerusalem in Old Testament times was the city of God, but John has a vision of **new Jerusalem**.

Vision of New Jerusalem

> *Revelation 21:2 I saw the Holy City, the new Jerusalem, coming down out of heaven from God, prepared as a bride beautifully dressed for her husband.*

Verses 9 and 10 will later clarify the significance of new Jerusalem as being the bride, the wife of the Lamb. In other words, new Jerusalem is symbolic of the church; the perfection of new Jerusalem contrasts with the imperfections of earthly Jerusalem. New Jerusalem is not a place; it is a collection of God's people! Notice the 10 elements composing Mt. Zion in the following reference:

Hebrews 12:22-24 But you have come

- *to Mount Zion,*
- *to the heavenly Jerusalem, the city of the living God.*
- *You have come to thousands upon thousands of angels in joyful assembly,*
- *the church of the firstborn, whose names are written in heaven.*
- *You have come to God, the judge of all men,*
- *the spirits of righteous men made perfect,*
- *to Jesus the mediator of a new covenant ...*

In the preceding verse "heavenly Jerusalem" is synonymous with "the church of the firstborn" and with those "whose names are written in heaven." Some try to make the description of new Jerusalem the picture of heaven, but this actually describes how God sees the redeemed. Another great clue that new Jerusalem is the church is found in *Ephesians 5:22-33*. Paul draws deep comparisons to show that the relationship of Christ and the church is analogous to the relationship between husband and wife; the church is the bride of Christ.

Vision of the New Tabernacle

Notice that John's visions are moving the redeemed closer to God with every step. First, the new heavens and the new earth; second the new Jerusalem; third a new tabernacle. The new tabernacle is "with men," indicating once more the barriers between God and man have been removed. The NIV uses the word dwelling where other versions use the term tabernacle; tabernacle would be closer to the meaning since this is the place where God at one time dwelled.

Revelation 21:3   And I heard a loud voice from the throne saying, "Now the dwelling of God is with men, and he will live with them. They will be his people, and God himself will be with them and be their God ..."

New Circumstances

In this life man is in a constant state of need and dependence. Man is also plagued by sinfulness which destroys the essence of life. However, in eternity all of these things will be removed for mankind to live in eternal bliss with God.

> *Revelation 21:4-7 "He will wipe every tear from their eyes. There will be no more death or mourning or crying or pain, for the old order of things has passed away." He who was seated on the throne said, "I am making everything new!" Then he said, "Write this down, for these words are trustworthy and true." He said to me: "It is done. I am the Alpha and the Omega, the Beginning and the End. To him who is thirsty I will give to drink without cost from the spring of the water of life. He who overcomes will inherit all this, and I will be his God and he will be my son."*

Sin at one time held reign over the lives of men, and sin brings pain; however, John sees God's turning it all around. God is called the "faithful and true," the "Alpha and the Omega." The Alpha and the Omega are the first and last letters of the Greek alphabet, but the same symbols were also used for the Greek number 1, indicating the Beginning and the number 800, the new Beginning; God is the Creator and is also the Resurrection. In this passage, God is also called "the beginning and the end."

Three characteristics are used, and remember the number 3 is the number of the Trinity. The promises are made to those who are thirsty, reminding one of the beatitude, "Blessed are those who hunger and thirst after righteousness." Rewards are promised to those who overcome, reminiscent of the promises made in chapters 2 and 3 of *Revelation*.

God's followers will definitely receive blessings beyond imagination, but John's message continues by revealing the reverse will be true for those who do not follow God:

Revelation 21:8 *"But the cowardly, the unbelieving, the vile, the murderers, the sexually immoral, those who practice magic arts, the idolaters and all liar —-their place will be in the fiery lake of burning sulfur. This is the second death."*

An Expanded View of New Jerusalem

Beginning with verse 9, the reader is shown the beauty of the redeemed in the eyes of God. An earlier verse compared new Jerusalem to the bride of Christ, and evidence was given that new Jerusalem is a symbolic description of the redeemed. The city of God is now described in all of its beauty; this is another one of those scenes where God's followers are shown to be both from the Old Covenant and from the New Covenant. **The gates represent those who served God before the cross; the foundations are symbolic of those who follow the Lamb.**

An Overview of the City

Revelation 21:9-11 *One of the seven angels who had the seven bowls full of the seven last plagues came and said to me, "Come, I will show you the bride, the wife of the Lamb." And he carried me away in the Spirit to a mountain great and high, and showed me the Holy City, Jerusalem, coming down out of heaven from God. It shone with the glory of God, and its brilliance was like that of a very precious jewel, like a jasper, clear as crystal.*

The above information is vital, for it pictures the redeemed — the bride of the Lamb. In *Revelation 4* the jasper was used in describing the glory of God; now it is used to represent the glory of His people. The walls and gates reveal both beauty and perfection of God's people.

John Tells of the Gates into the Eternal City

Revelation 21:12,13 It had a great, high wall with twelve gates, and with twelve angels at the gates. On the gates were written the names of the twelve tribes of Israel. There were three gates on the east, three on the north, three on the south and three on the west.

Perfection is evident in the number symbols of the vision. The number 12 is comprised by multiplying the world's number 4 by the godhead's number 3; the symbolism indicates God's working with the world. Its having four sides with three gates on each side yields a total of twelve gates; the twelve tribes of Israel set the stage for the arrival of the Messiah. The tribes, therefore, were the gates into the eternal city; furthermore, Judah was the tribe through which Jesus Christ would be born!

John Tells of the Foundations of the Eternal City

Revelation 21:14 The wall of the city had twelve foundations, and on them were the names of the twelve apostles of the Lamb.

The Bible names men other than the original twelve who were called apostles. The word *apostle* means "one sent out"; Barnabas was an apostle of the church in Antioch because he was "sent out" from that sea port on missionary journeys. Twelve were originally chosen as "apostles of Jesus Christ"; after the suicide of Judas, Matthias was chosen as an apostle of Jesus Christ. Saul of Tarsus was chosen to be an apostle of Jesus Christ with a special mission to preach to the Gentiles. Regardless of others who were "sent out" on various missions, the number given is the number 12, God's number for working with the world, and John saw the city founded on twelve apostles.

While reading about the city, one should not forget this is new Jerusalem, the bride, the church, the people of God. It is a perfect city, not because God's people never erred, but because the blood of Jesus perfected those who believe in God.

John Describes the City

Revelation 21:15-18   The angel who talked with me had a measuring rod of gold to measure the city, its gates and its walls. The city was laid out like a square, as long as it was wide. He measured the city with the rod and found it to be 12,000 stadia in length, and as wide and high as it is long. He measured its wall and it was 144 cubits thick, by man's measurement, which the angel was using. The wall was made of jasper, and the city of pure gold, as pure as glass.

Earlier, John was given an instrument to measure the tabernacle, the worshippers, and the worship of God. In *Revelation* 7 the people of God were sealed, and scripture also indicates their names were placed in the Book of Life. It is a major truth — **God knows who belongs to Him!** John reveals the size of the city based on multiples of the number 12 and the cubing of the number 10. The length, breadth and height were equal — 12,000 stadia. Some versions use the word furlongs rather than stadia. If taken literally, this would be 1,500 miles or 250 times the height of Mt. Everest. However, this is a figurative number, the number symbolizing God's working with man — 12, then multiplying this by the cube of the perfect number 10. How large is the city? Large enough! The people of God will have no literal boundaries with protective walls; the redeemed are in a state of perpetual safety.

The wall surrounding the city was tremendously thick — 144 cubits. Since a cubit is approximately 18 inches, this would make a wall 216 feet thick if taken literally. This imagery was used because people during the first century understood the need of thick walls to protect cities. However, there will be nothing to threaten the redeemed; there is no need for this kind of protection. The purpose of the symbol was simply to comfort the readers; there would be no threat to them once they had overcome the tribulations of this life.

An angel did the measuring with a rod of gold; there would be no error with the measurement. The calculations of size were given in earthly terms so humans could understand the message. The thickness was 12 X 12 to equal 144 cubits. The size of the city was 12,000 stadia to the east, 12,000 stadia to the north, 12,000 stadia to the west, and 12,000 stadia to the south. It was 12,000 high, and the thickness was 12 X 12 cubits. There were 12 gates and 12 foundations. Remembering that the number 12 symbolizes God's work with humanity, it should not take the reader long to realize God's purpose is fulfilled in perfecting His followers. The city itself was absolutely beautiful; the walls were made of jasper and the buildings of pure gold. It is thrilling to know the beauty described is the way God views the redeemed.

Description of the Foundations

Revelation 21:19,20 The foundations of the city walls were decorated with every kind of precious stone. The first foundation was jasper, the second sapphire, the third chalcedony, the fourth emerald, the fifth sardonyx, the sixth carnelian, the seventh chrysolite, the eighth beryl, the ninth topaz, the tenth chrysoprase, the eleventh jacinth, and the twelfth amethyst.

Eight of the twelve stones listed were found in the breastplate of the high priest in tabernacle worship of old. Some of the stones are hard to identify with modern stones; however, the overall feeling the reader should experience is excitement over redemption. An earlier verse revealed that the foundations are symbolic of the apostles; this part would represent the redeemed after the time of Christ.

Description of the Gates

Revelation 21:21 The twelve gates were twelve pearls, each gate made of a single pearl. The great street of the city was of pure gold, like transparent glass.

An earlier passage explained the gates symbolized the twelve tribes of Israel. These would depict the redeemed before the time of Christ; however, all salvation was consummated by the death, burial, and resurrection of Jesus.

Hebrews 9:15 For this reason Christ is the mediator of a new covenant, that those who are called may receive the promised eternal inheritance — now that he has died as a ransom to set them free from the sins committed under the first covenant.

The entire scene is one of the beauty of the saved by using metals and gems highly prized on earth. **The very idea of using gold for paving!**

Explanation about the Temple

Revelation 21:22 I did not see a temple in the city, because the Lord God Almighty and the Lamb are its temple.

Earlier material indicated God will not need a physical temple in new Jerusalem, because God perfects His followers, and **they become a temple.** There will be no restrictions to accessing God. The temple of God is not a physical building, but rather, the temple of God is within the redeemed. **God moved from the tabernacle, to the temple, to living within His followers!**

Acts 17:24 The God who made the world and everything in it is the Lord of heaven and earth and does not live in temples built by hands.

I Corinthians 3:16 ... you yourselves are God's temple and that God's Spirit lives in you?

This concept even further strengthens the point that John is not describing a physical place; he is describing how God views those who accept Him through the sacrifice of Jesus Christ.

Further Descriptions of the City

Revelation 21:23 The city does not need the sun or the moon to shine on it, for the glory of God gives it light, and the Lamb is its lamp.

The very first act in the creation of the universe was God's declaration, "Let there be light." There were no sun, moon or stars until the fourth day of creation, but there was light on the first day. In one of his letters, John explained that God is light.

> *1 John 1:5 This is the message we have heard from him and declare to you: God is light; in him there is no darkness at all.*

Jesus came into a world filled with the darkness of sin; He came to bring light. The gospel of John told of the role of John the Baptist and claimed that Jesus was the light God sent to the world.

> *John 1:6-9 There came a man who was sent from God; his name was John. He came as a witness to testify concerning that light, so that through him all men might believe. ... The true light that gives light to every man was coming into the world.*

Very prominent in the teachings of Jesus was His claim to be light sent from God to the world.

> *John 8:12 When Jesus spoke again to the people, he said, "I am the light of the world. Whoever follows me will never walk in darkness, but will have the light of life."*

Continuing with the text in *Revelation*, the reader discovers the followers of God are also a part of the eternal light John envisions.

> *Revelation 21:24-26 The nations will walk by its light, and the kings of the earth will bring their splendor into it. On no day will its gates ever be shut, for there will be no night there. The glory and honor of the nations will be brought into it.*

God is light; Jesus is light, and Jesus said His followers were light.

> *Matthew 5:14 "You are the light of the world. A city on a hill cannot be hidden."*

The light of the Christian is one that must get brighter after death because John says the followers of God will actually be like Him.

> *1 John 3:2 Dear friends, now we are children of God, and what we will be has not yet been made known. But we know that when he appears,* **we shall be like him***, for we shall see him as he is.*

John has already said the redeemed will reign with God in eternity; if Christians are going to reign, what does this make the followers of God? **KINGS!** The phrase "kings of the earth" is a symbolic way of saying "Christians." The redeemed are also referred to in the passage above as "the glory and honor of the nations." The reference to "nations" indicates the redeemed of God will come bringing light from every nation on the face of the earth.

The reason there will be no need for the sun or moon is two-fold. First, because of the sources of light — God is light, the Lamb is light, and the victorious are light. Second, because there will no sources for darkness to exist. **Is it any wonder there will be no night there — IMPOSSIBLE WITH ALL THAT LIGHT!**

> *Revelation 21:27 Nothing impure will ever enter it, nor will anyone who does what is shameful or deceitful, but only those whose names are written in the Lamb's Book of Life.*

With all barriers having been removed, God and man will be bonded forever: 1) artificial light of the sun and moon is no longer needed because God, the Lamb, and the followers are all light. 2) There is no more sea, representing human limitations, to separate man from God. 3) There is no physical temple where God is found because God is located in each of His followers.

As we enter the last chapter of *Revelation,* John sees the tree of life of both sides of the river of life to indicate "life." Mankind, through sin, had lost the right to the Garden of Eden and the tree of life; however, through Christ, the redeemed will regain the beautiful tree of life. The tree in *Revelation* fulfills all the needs; it bears fruit every month, and its leaves have healing power. The tree in *Revelation* is obviously symbolic; since months measure time, months would be absolutely unnecessary in eternity. Also, there will be no need for healing in eternity since there will be no pain, suffering, or sickness. This symbolic message is saying God will take care of the saved. One of the promises to the seven churches of Asia was that those who overcame would be allowed to eat from the tree of life, a **symbol of eternal salvation**. Symbols have been drawn to the Jordan River symbolizing death, and on each side of death the redeemed of God can be found. This is really the negative side of what happens — the river we cross is the river of Life because the redeemed live forever. Jesus promised that if we live in Him and believe in Him we shall never die. John sees the message in the vision below:

> *Revelation 22:1-2   Then the angel showed me the river of the water of life, as clear as crystal, flowing from the throne of God and of the Lamb down the middle of the great street of the city. On each side of the river stood the tree of life, bearing twelve crops of fruit, yielding its fruit every month. And the leaves of the tree are for the healing of the nations.*

After the fall of man in the Garden of Eden, there was a curse placed on the earth and on all participants in the fall. Woman was cursed with pain during childbearing, and she was placed in submission of man. Man was cursed by having to work the ground to survive. All humanity was cursed by having to suffer the pains of death. The serpent was cursed by having to crawl on its belly. The fall brought curses! But forgiveness and salvation through Jesus Christ brought the great reversal

> *Revelation 22:3* **No longer will there be any curse.** *The throne of God and of the Lamb will be in the city, and his servants will serve him.*

When man first sinned, guilt drove Adam and Eve to hide from the face of God. But the redeemed will be able to see the face of God. What a great reversal! This truth was revealed when God spoke to Moses.

> *Exodus 33:20 states, "But," he said, "you cannot see my face, for no one may see me and live."*

Man cannot see the face of God in this life, but salvation and eternal life make the seeing of God's face reality. John himself had written in *John 1:18*, *"No one has ever seen God ..."* But now John sees another great reversal for the redeemed:

> *Revelation 22:4* **They will see his face**, *and his name will be on their foreheads.*

As all things are being made new to reverse the old, the theme is reinforced with the message that there will be no more darkness. Throughout history mankind insisted on worshipping the sun; now the Creator of the sun, the true Light, arranges for eternal light.

> *Revelation 22:5 There will be no more night. They will not need the light of a lamp or the light of the sun, for the Lord God will give them light. ...*

Revelation 20 said the redeemed would live and reign 1,000 years; but as the scripture continues, we see clearly the 1,000 years was a symbol meaning "forever."

> *Revelation 22:5   ... And they will reign for ever and ever.*

THE CONCLUSION OF THE VISIONS

As the book of *Revelation* comes to an end, statements are made to reinforce and to reaffirm earlier points.

> *Revelation 22:6,7 The angel said to me, "These words are trustworthy and true. The Lord, the God of the spirits of the prophets, sent his angel to show his servants the things that must soon take place." "Behold, I am coming soon! Blessed is he who keeps the words of the prophecy in this book."*

Four concepts above were presented in earlier parts of John's message: 1) God is the author of the book. 2) He has sent His angel to tell John these things. 3) The events of John's revelation are going to happen within a short time. 4) The ones who obey the book will be blessed.

For the second time in the book, John falls down before the angel bringing the message.

> *Revelation 22:8,9 I, John, am the one who heard and saw these things. And when I had heard and seen them, I fell down to worship at the feet of the angel who had*

> *been showing them to me. But he said to me, "Do not do it! I am a fellow servant with you and with your brothers the prophets and of all who keep the words of this book. Worship God!"*

John had already been warned about angel worship; the idea is confirmed here. John's visions were so powerful he felt compelled to worship the angel; however, he learned that angels and humans are both on the servant level. God is to be worshipped.

A tremendously important sequence takes place next when John is commanded to keep his book unsealed. **That is the total idea of a revelation! Material is not concealed in a revelation.**

> *Revelation 22:10 Then he told me, "Do not seal up the words of the prophecy of this book, because the time is near."*

The time was to be short from John's visions until fulfillment — unlike Daniel's visions that were sealed because fulfillment was centuries away. The reason for not sealing the prophecy is clearly stated above — "because the time is near." This was true for the Roman Empire when it collapsed in Armageddon, but it has been true of countless other nations that have fallen through their own experience of "Armageddon." It is also true for each person who has ever read the book; the time from birth to death is never that far away.

The condition of souls was to remain constant because the end of these matters was not far away; each had chosen a way of life and a principle to follow. The idea that it was time to reap the results of their actions is found in the passage below:

> *Revelation 22:11 "... Let him who does wrong continue to do wrong; let him who is vile continue to be vile; let him who does right continue to do right; and let him who is holy continue to be holy."*

Jesus speaks next, and many versions recognize this by using red letters. In chapter 21 God calls Himself the Alpha and the Omega, the First and the Last; in chapter 22 Jesus calls Himself the Alpha and the Omega, the First and the Last. This confirms the point that God and Jesus are One. In His message, Jesus indicates that judgment is on the way.

> *Revelation 22:12-16 "Behold, I am coming soon! My reward is with me, and I will give to everyone according to what he has done. I am the Alpha and the Omega, the First and the Last, the Beginning and the End. Blessed are those who wash their robes, that they may have the right to the tree of life and may go through the gates into the city. Outside are the dogs, those who practice magic arts, the sexually immoral, the murderers, the idolaters and everyone who loves and practices falsehood. I, Jesus, have sent my angel to give you this testimony for the churches. I am the Root and the Offspring of David, and the bright Morning Star."*

Once again Jesus claimed to be coming soon; this could be His coming in judgment of Rome, judgment on future nations, judgment of each person who dies physically, or His coming to end earth time. In reality, every fall of a nation gives a glimpse of the end of the world. Those who are faithful and choose to serve Jesus will be given eternal life, and those who seek worldliness will suffer eternal loss. The concepts are true whether it is the "time of the end" of an era, or whether it is the "end of time."

In these concluding comments, Jesus is again revealed as the author of *Revelation*. In the previous citing, Jesus is called the Alpha and the Omega; below, His kingship is mentioned.

> *Revelation 22:16 "I, Jesus, have sent my angel to give you this testimony for the churches. I am the Root and the Offspring of David, and the bright Morning Star."*

Jesus' birth on earth and His throne were to come through Israel, through the tribe of Judah, through the family of David.

> *Romans 1:2-4 ... the gospel he promised beforehand through his prophets in the Holy Scriptures regarding his Son, who as to his human nature was a descendant of David, and who through the Spirit of holiness was declared with power to be the Son of God by his resurrection from the dead: Jesus Christ our Lord.*

An open invitation was given by the Spirit of God and by the church, the bride; this invitation was issued to anyone who was thirsting for spiritual water to follow Jesus. The choice is up to each person whether to accept God through Jesus; the ultimate choice is one between life and death. The fact that the bride says, "Come," indicates the mission of God's family on earth.

> *Revelation 22:17 The Spirit and the bride say, "Come!" And let him who hears say, "Come!" Whoever is thirsty, let him come; and whoever wishes, let him take the free gift of the water of life.*

The last admonition in the book is a warning not to abuse the message the book of *Revelation*.

> *Revelation 22:18,19 I warn everyone who hears the words of the prophecy of this book: if anyone adds anything to them, God will add to him the plagues described in this book. And if anyone takes words away from this book of prophecy, God will take away from him his share in the tree of life and in the holy city, which are described in this book.*

This frightening warning should be heeded carefully by anyone seeking to understand *Revelation*. For this reason, this author has primarily used the Word of God in interpretation rather than the daily newspaper. To understand a revelation, it is absolutely necessary to discover what was sealed or unknown. **The Bible is the best commentary on the Bible!** The final statement ever recorded from the words of Jesus is presented in the closing verses.

> *Revelation 22:20 He who testifies to these things says,* ***"Yes, I am coming soon."*** *Amen. Come, Lord Jesus.*

John's response in saying, "Amen, Come, Lord Jesus," indicates he was ready for the events to unfold and for Jesus to arrive in judgment of the beast and/or to come in final judgment of the world. John gives his final statement in the last verse of *Revelation*.

Revelation 22:21 The grace of the Lord Jesus be with God's people. Amen.

The letter ends as most do with a statement to the intended audience; the church was certainly in need of the grace of Jesus to overcome the persecution about to fall upon them.

God sent His Son to earth during the days of one of the most powerful kingdoms in history. Rome's destiny was determined when the ruling powers crucified Jesus. Some forty years after John penned the letter delivered to him from Christ, Rome reached its peak and began its crumble into oblivion. Although the nation was at one time a tremendous power, the prophecy of Daniel was fulfilled.

The spiritual kingdom of God was created on earth in the hearts of believers and overcame and outlasted all earthly kingdoms. Since the fall of the Roman Empire, many other nations have crumbled because of their godless ways.

Rich lessons are abundant. 1) Only one kingdom was meant to last forever; God's kingdom is all powerful, and one should choose to belong to it above all other kingdoms. 2) All earthly nations are destined to die; our own nation is no exception to this rule. 3) The "time of the end" of any country occurs because of wickedness. 4) One must look for signs of degradation and avoid getting caught up in the sins of the nation. 5) Those who are faithful to Christ will be rewarded, and those who choose worldly pursuits will lose everything in eternity. These messages were important in the first century, and they are important today. *Revelation* is truly a book for all time; the beast named Rome may be dead, but others have existed and more will come to war with God's people. John's warnings have rippled throughout every generation, HE WHO SUPPORTS THE WICKEDNESS OF A NATION, WILL PERISH ALONG WITH IT WHEN THE TIME COMES FOR GOD TO END ITS POWER!

The beauty of *Revelation* cannot be missed; HE WHO IS FAITHFUL TO THE LORD JESUS CHRIST WILL SHARE IN THE VICTORY THAT HAS ALREADY BEEN WON! ***Revelation* is not a book of doom; it is a message of hope for the faithful.**

INDEX

A

Abaddon 195, 196
Abomination of desolation 68, 70-72, 80- 84, 98
Abominations of the earth 247, 250
Abraham 91, 109, 129, 131, 184, 211, 216
Abyss 193, 194, 195, 204, 212, 241, 248, 270
Ahasuerus 46
ak-Hissar 154
Alexander Severus 253
Alexander the Great 47, 49-51, 58, 79, 84, 151
Alpha 123, 140, 226, 290, 300, 301
Alphabet 22, 226, 290
Amethyst 294
Angel 3, 5, 43, 44, 54-57, 76, 81, 104, 112, 114,120, 121, 138, 139, 142, 145, 157, 159, 168-171, 173, 174, 194, 197, 203, 213, 230-233, 247-250, 254, 256, 257, 262, 265, 266, 271, 287, 289, 292, 298-301
Angel (altar of incense) 189, 190, 233
Angel (evil) 212, 213, 223, 280
Angel in the sun 267
Angel of the abyss 193, 194, 197
Angel of Ephesus 145
Angel of Laodicea 161
Angel of Pergamum 151
Angel of Philadelphia 157
Angel of Sardis 157, 274
Angel of Smyrna 148
Angel of Thyatira 154
Angel over fire 113, 233, 240
Angel over waters 239, 240
Angels over winds 129, 182, 240
Angel with chains for dragon 270
Angel with measuring rod 119, 120, 293
Angel with millstone 262
Angel with open scroll 106, 199-201
Angel with seal of God 112, 129, 182, 183
Angel with sickle 233
Angel worship 265, 300
Angels at the Euphrates 197, 242, 274
Angels holding back wind 129, 182, 240
Angels (twelve gates) 120, 242
Angels surrounding throne 185
Angels with seven plagues 235, 237-240, 242, 244, 247, 249, 291

Angels with seven trumpets 189, 190, 191, 193, 197, 207
Anointed 80, 93, 94, 97, 98, 203
Anti-Christ 57, 71, 217, 218, 222, 224, 227, 252
Antioch 61, 292
Antiochus I *Soter* 59
Antiochus II *Theos* 59-61
Antiochus III (The Great) 59, 62, 63, 65, 66
Antiochus IV *Epiphanes* 50, 53-57, 59, 66, 67, 69-72, 75, 76, 81, 83, 89, 211, 215, 217
Antiochus V *Eupator* 59
Antoninus Pius 253
Antipas 151, 152
Apollo 72, 75, 151, 154
Apollyon 195, 196
Apostles 134, 146, 167, 203, 261, 292,294
Archangel 44, 45, 55, 76
Armageddon 1, 7, 27, 212, 243, 247, 255, 256, 258, 260, 265-269, 271, 300
Army 53, 62, 63, 65, 67, 69, 70, 76, 84, 118, 198
Army in heaven 117, 221, 268
Artaxerxes 93
Augustus Caesar 17, 20, 21, 89, 165, 251, 253
Author 3, 6, 15, 19, 27, 34, 53, 61, 87, 103, 104, 114, 117, 142, 144, 151, 154, 157, 162, 163, 164
Authorship (true) 137, 138, 139, 145, 148, 151, 154, 157, 159, 162-164, 299
Aventine hill 23, 251

B

Babylon 7, 12, 15, 16, 17, 22, 25, 26, 31-40, 47, 29, 50, 66, 84, 85, 92, 103, 107, 114, 123, 124, 137, 142, 197, 217, 230, 231, 242, 244, 247, 248, 250, 255, 256, 258, 262, 267
Balaam 152, 164
Barak 243
Bear 12, 16, 25, 34, 35, 40-42, 50, 216, 217, 225
Beast (7 heads) 7, 18
Beast (10 horns) 7, 8, 12, 18, 19, 22, 25, 87, 137, 165
Beast (mark of) 14, 117, 231, 238, 250

Beast (number 666) 22-25, 129, 132, 139, 225, 227, 228
Beasts (comparison of) 8-13
Beasts (wild) 112, 179
Belshazzar 32, 34-37, 39
Belteshazzar 43
Berenice 59-61
Beryl 294
Black (sun turned) 181
Black horse 178
Blood (bulls and goats; sacrifices) 111, 186
Blood (from winepress) 233
Blood (mixed with fire and hail) 190
Blood (moon turned to) 181
Blood of Jesus 95, 96, 107, 140, 167, 174, 272, 180, 182, 186, 214, 230, 271, 281, 283, 292
Blood (of saints) 180, 233, 240, 250, 262, 263
Blood (on door posts) 183
Blood (water turned into) 191, 203, 239
Book of Life 77, 159, 222, 236, 248, 279, 281, 282, 283, 293, 297
Bowl one 238
Bowl two 239
Bowl three 239
Bowl four 240
Bowl five 193, 194, 241, 263
Bowl six 197, 242, 243
Bowl seven 243-245
Bowls 26, 27, 138, 174, 193, 210, 235, 237, 238, 241, 247, 249, 291
Brass (feet of angel/Jesus) 25, 141,142, 154
Brass/Bronze kingdom 17, 32, 40, 42, 47, 49, 85, 87, 89
Bronze 35, 37, 199, 258, 259
Bride of Christ 107, 108, 152, 249, 262-265, 288, 289, 291, 292, 301
Bridegroom 152, 262, 263, 265
Bronze (arms and legs of Jesus) 44, 80, 99
Bronze (burnished) 51, 91, 114, 163, 164, 178
Burnt offering 53, 54, 67

C

Caelian hill 23, 251
Caesar/caesars 8, 17, 22, 23, 89, 143, 163, 178, 179, 219, 243, 249, 251-254
Caesar Augustus 21, 102
Caesars (Year of four) 18, 19
Caesars (deification/worship) 99, 150, 165, 217, 218, 225, 228, 250
Cambyses II 46
Candlestick 118, 146, 147, 164, 168, 204
Caracalla 253

Capitoline 23, 251
Caracalla 125-127
Carnelian 105, 160, 294
Carrion birds of prey 117, 256, 265, 267, 268, 282
Carthaginian 51
Cassander 53, 56
Chaining of Satan 213, 270-272
Chalcedony 294
Cherubim 104, 168, 169, 237
Child (Jesus) 17, 210-214
Children 137, 155, 273, 297
Children of Abraham 109
Chrysolite 44, 80, 99, 294
Chrysoprase 294
Clay (iron and) 32, 85, 87, 92
Claudius 20, 21, 89, 165, 251
Clement of Alexandria 138
Cleopatra 59, 64, 65
Commodus 253
Crown 193, 194, 199, 204, 205, 226, 267, 290, 306
Crown of life 150, 161, 164
Crown of twelve stars 210, 211
Crown (diadem) 167, 168, 176, 266
Crown (evil) 195, 210, 216, 218
Crown (stephanos) 167, 168, 172, 177, 232, 253
Curse 287, 298
Cursed 225, 240, 241, 244, 280, 287, 298
Cyrus I 46
Cyrus II (the Persian aka "The Great") 40, 42, 47

D

Daniel
  (Compared with Ezekiel) 31, 107, 137
  (Dream of four beasts) 25, 40, 86, 87, 217
  (Dream of shaggy goat) 17, 42, 50, 56
  (Explains king's dream) 32, 33, 42
  (Handwriting on wall) 36, 37
Darius the Mede 38, 40, 46, 47
David 118, 126, 131, 160, 177, 229, 301
David (key of) 159, 164
David (Jesus, offspring of) 301
David (Jesus, root of) 173
David (Jesus take throne of) 131
Death
  Death 26, 46, 106, 112, 150, 165, 179, 195, 196, 214, 232, 257, 268, 271, 280, 281, 286, 287, 290, 296, 298, 300
  Death and hades 141, 179, 281
  Death (choose life or death) 273, 275-277, 301

Death (firstborn) 182
Death (Jesus) 91, 96-99, 109, 148, 178, 186, 214, 219, 250, 294
Death (second) 276, 278-283, 291
Death (spiritual) 94, 158, 164, 194, 221, 273, 274
Death (two witnesses 205
Death wound of beast 218, 219
Deborah 243
Deified 89, 99, 165, 217, 220, 252
Demetrius I 59, 69
Devil 5, 150, 213, 270, 280
Domitian 20, 21, 89, 112, 143, 150, 161, 217, 219, 220, 225, 249, 252-254
Dragon 210-216, 218, 219, 223, 228, 242, 243, 270, 281, 279

E

Eagle (face of) 104, 169, 170
Eagle (warnings from) 193
Eagle (woman given wings of) 13, 215
Eagle (Nebuchadnezzar's dream) 34
Eden 55, 116, 287, 297, 298
Elam 117
Elders 167
Elders (of church) 167
Elders (seventy) 107
Elders (twenty-four) 134, 167, 168, 172-175, 209, 210, 229, 236, 264
Emerald 105, 166, 167, 294
End times (time of the end or end of time) 27, 42, 45, 46, 56, 70, 71, 76, 80, 172, 181, 244, 301
Ephesus 59, 60, 144-148
Epistle 4, 6, 143, 219
Esquiline 23, 251
Esther 46
Euphrates 33, 197, 242, 262, 272
Evil (angels) 212, 213, 223, 280
Evil (three evil spirits) 242, 243
Evil-Merodach 35
Eyes (flaming fire) 25, 44, 80, 99, 141, 142, 154, 164
Eyes (Four living creatures) 104, 169, 170, 266
Eyes (seven of the Lamb) 173
Eyes (full of) 118, 195, 196

F

Fasting 42-44
Feast (vultures) 265-268
Feast (wedding) 264, 265, 267, 282
Flavian dynasty 19-21, 89

G

Gabriel 55, 56
Gaius 20, 21, 29, 251
Galba 19, 20, 89
Gardens of Babylon 33
Gaumata 46
Gematria 23, 225
Goat (shaggy with prominent horn) 17, 41, 42, 47, 50, 52, 53, 56
Goats (sacrifices) 111, 129
Goats (separation from sheep) 126
Goats (trade items) 116
Goats Hair (sun turned black as) 181
Gog and Magog 118, 119, 279
Gold
  Gold / Golden (altar) 67, 189, 197, 242
  Gold (belt, sash, girdle) 25, 44, 80, 99, 141, 237
  Gold / Golden (bowls) 174
  Gold (city of God) 293, 294
  Gold (city of wicked glittered) 261
  Gold / Golden (censer) 189
  Gold / Golden (crown) 167, 232
  Gold (crowns of evil locusts) 195
  Gold / Golden (cup in prostitute's hand) 247, 250
  Gold (goblets used by Belshazzar) 35
  Gold (head of) 16, 32-35, 38-40, 85, 92
  Gold / Golden (idols) 35, 37, 73, 74, 129, 198, 199
  Gold / Golden (lampstands) 145, 146, 168
  Gold / Golden (measuring rod) 119, 120, 293
  Gold (prostitute glittered in) 247, 249
  Gold (streets of the city of God) 294, 295
  Gold (talents = 666) 130
  Gold (trade items) 116, 258, 259
Greek alphabet 22, 226, 290

H

Hades 112, 141, 179, 281
Hadrian 253
Hail 190, 210, 217, 244, 245
Hallelujah 263, 264
Hamon Gog 243
Harlot 247-250
Har Mageddon 243
Harran 36
Hebrew alphabet 226
Heliodorus 66
Heliogabulus 253
Herod 71, 97, 99
Herodotus 83

307

I

Iron (breastplates of locusts looked like) 155
Iron and clay (feet of metal man) 32, 85-87, 86, 87, 92
Iron gods 35, 37
Iron scepter 156, 210, 212, 266, 267
Iron teeth (4th beast) 12, 87
Iron (trade items) 116, 258, 259

J

Jabin 243
Jacinth 294
Jasper 105, 166, 291, 293, 294
Jehoiachin 103
Jehovah 55, 131
Jeremiah 16, 31, 33, 37, 191, 264
Jerusalem
  Jerusalem 26, 112, 125, 132, 143, 184, 205, 289
  Jerusalem (Babylonian captivity) 31, 35, 36, 93, 94, 96, 98, 107, 112, 113, 142
  Jerusalem (fall of in 70 AD) 16, 27, 79, 84, 99, 111, 181, 184, 202, 243
  Jerusalem (Persian attacks) 53, 57, 63-70, 83-75, 77, 82, 83
  Jerusalem (new / heavenly / spiritual) 107-111, 119, 120, 161, 166, 202, 216, 229, 233, 288, 289, 291-293
Jesus
  (Judge) 220, 227, 266
  (King of kings) 15-17, 87, 91, 92-95, 97, 113, 118, 176, 209, 252, 254, 266, 267
  (Lamb) 114, 118, 120, 171, 173-179, 181, 182, 185-187, 199, 214, 222, 223, 228-232, 235, 236, 252, 254, 264-267, 272, 282, 283, 285-288, 291, 292, 295, 297, 298
  (Light) 286, 295, 296, 297
  (Lion) 173, 200
  (Mediator) 111, 140, 186, 289, 295
  (Priest) 127
  (Prophet) 127
  (Reaper) 232
  (Son of God) 154, 175, 218, 301
  (son of man) 15, 44, 93, 94, 141, 232,
  (Vine) 113
Jezebel 155, 156, 164
Judge (God is the) 180, 181, 239, 257, 261, 281, 303,
Judgment (results of) 37, 99, 100, 112, 126, 132, 153, 154, 194, 213, 230, 231, 239, 240, 263, 280, 281,
Judgment (of saints) 14, 99, 100, 156, 262
Julio-Claudian dynasty 20, 21, 89

Julius Caesar 18, 165
Justin Martyr 138

K

King of kings 15-17, 87, 91, 92-95, 97, 113, 118, 176, 209, 252, 254, 266, 267
Kingdom of God 15, 26, 32, 86, 87, 90-93, 99, 100, 109, 162, 176, 204, 207, 217, 275, 302,

L

Labash-Marduk 35
Lake of fire 222, 279, 281-283,
Lamb (seven eyes) 173
Lamb (seven horns) 173
Lamb (song of) 235, 236
Lamb (wedding of) 264,
Laodice 59-61
Laodicea 161, 164,
Leopard 12, 25, 42, 47, 50, 53, 216, 217
Lion (Babylon) 12, 16, 25, 33-35, 38, 40, 50, 216, 217
Lion (face of living Creatures) 104, 169, 170,
Lion (heads like that of) 198
Lion of Judah 173, 200
Lion (Satan compared to a) 271, 272
Lion's teeth 195
Little horn 88,
Little scroll 106, 199, 201
Locusts 194-196, 241
Lukewarm 162, 164
Lunisolar 83
Luristan 64
Lydia 154

M

Machaira 178
Magog 118, 119, 279
Marcus Aurelius 253
Maps 10, 11
Mark (of the beast) 14, 117, 231, 238, 250, 268
Mark (seal of God) 112, 129, 183, 194,
Measure (city of God) 119, 120, 134, 293
Measure (temple) 202
Measurements (Babylon's) 33
Measurements (Ezekiel's city) 120
Measuring rod 119, 120, 293
Mediterranean 9, 75, 243
Megiddo 243
Merchants 114, 116, 256, 258-263, 271,
Millennium theories 282, 283
Michael 43-46, 55, 57, 76, 213, 271
Mount Sinai 133

Mount Zion   184, 185, 228, 229, 236, 237, 288, 289
Mountains   71, 132, 181, 244,
Mountains (seven)   23, 26, 27
Mounted troops   197
Mt. Everest   293
Mt. Vesuvius   190

N

Nabonidus   35
Nebuchadnezzar   15, 16, 31-37, 40, 47, 85, 86, 103, 129
Neriglissar   35
Nero   19-21, 89, 150, 152, 219, 251, 254
Nerva   253
Nicolaitans   146, 152, 164
Nineveh   124
Number of beast   22, 25, 129, 130, 225
Number of Jesus   131, 227, 228
Number table (Greek)   226

O

Offspring (Abraham's)   109, 211, 216
Offspring (of David—Jesus)   301
Offspring (of the woman)   210, 211, 215, 216
One Thousand
  1,000 (the number)   124, 134, 183, 184, 196, 206,
  1,000 generations   133
  1,000 (meaning of)   133
  1,000 years   269-271, 273, 276, 277, 278, 282, 299
  1,000 years (meaning of)   275, 279
  1,150 days   55
  1,260 days   203, 210
  1,335 days   83
  1,600 stadia   233
144,000
  (understanding the number)   128, 184
  144,000 sealed   100, 112, 134, 183, 185, 202, 228, 229, 236,
  144,000 on Mount Zion   184, 185, 229, 236, 237

P

Palatine hill   23, 251
Pale horse   179
Palestine   65
Panium   65
Passover   221, 222
Patmos   31, 103, 107, 138, 142, 143
Pentecost   91, 221
Pelusium   67
Pergamum   144, 151, 152, 164, 166,
Philadelphia   144, 159, 164
Philip I   50

Philistines   243
Philo Judaeus   129
Phoenicia   69
Pieria   61
Plagues (ten on Egypt)   133, 182, 191, 192, 204, 237, 239, 241, 243
Plagues (fire, smoke, sulfur)   198
Ptolemy I Lagi *Soter*   59,
Ptolemy II *Philadelphus*   59, 60, 6i
Ptolemy III *Euergetes*   59, 61, 62,
Ptolemy IV *Philopator*   59, 62, 63, 65
Ptolemy V *Epiphanes*   59, 63, 65
Ptolemy VI *Philometor*   59, 66, 69, 70, 75
Purim   221
Pythagoras   123, 124, 225

Q

Quadri-paschal   221
Quirinal hill   23, 251

R

Ram (two horned)   16, 17, 41, 42, 52, 56
Raphia   62, 64
Reaper (of faithful)   232
Reaper (of lost)   233
Red (dragon)   210, 212, 218
Red (horse)   177
Red (stone)   167
Red Sea   206, 215
Reign (sin and death)   290
Reign (of Christ)   15, 94, 207, 209
Reign (of saints)   14, 94, 100, 168, 174, 273, 276-278, 282, 297, 299
Rhomphaia   178, 179
Resurrection   77, 78, 98, 99, 117, 124, 125, 130, 148, 168, 173, 204, 205, 206, 219, 226, 227, 275-279, 290, 294, 301

S

Sacrifice
  Sacrifice (Abraham's five items)   129
  Sacricie (Antiochus stops)   74, 80, 81, 82
  Sacrifice (daily)   54, 55, 68, 70, 72
  Sacrifice (Jesus brings end of)   98, 110, 111, 126
  Sacrifice (Isaac, a picture of Jesus)   131
  Sacrifice (Jesus for world)   109, 110, 111, 126, 173, 176, 178, 179, 186, 280, 295
  Sacrifice (of saints)   147, 178, 179, 180
  Sacrifice (swine)   55, 68, 70
  Sacrifice (to idols/false gods)   72, 154, 155
  Sacrifices for sins   95, 186
Saints
  Saints (judgment of)   14, 99, 100, 156, 262
  Saints (on thrones)   100, 168

Saints (possess the kingdom)   14, 100
Saints (reign of)   14, 94, 100, 168, 174, 273,
  276-278, 282, 297, 299
Saints (righteous acts of)   235, 264, 265
Saints (slain)   14, 152, 178, 180, 182, 189,
  204, 233, 235, 263
Saints (testimony of)   180, 214, 215, 247,
  250, 265, 271, 272, 276,
Sardis   144, 157, 158, 164, 180, 274
Sardius   166
Sapphire stone   294
Sardonyx sstone   294
Scipio Africanus   51, 64, 65
Sea (beasts came from)   9, 42, 87, 216, 217
Sea (Dead)   75
Sea (of glass)   169, 170, 235, 236
Sealed (Daniel's visions)   2, 5, 6, 25, 31, 32,
  79, 80, 300, 302
Sealed (144,000)   100, 134, 182, 183, 184,
  196, 224, 228, 236, 237, 250, 293
Sealed scroll   90, 101, 165, 172, 175, 187,
  199, 200,
Sealed (the abyss)   270,
Seals (Jesus found worthy to open)   172
Seamen   114
Second death   150, 164, 179, 276, 278-283,
  191
Seleucia   61, 62
Seleucus I *Nicator*   59
Seleucus II *Callinicus*   59, 60, 61, 62, 63
Seleucus III *Soter*   62, 63
Seleucus IV *Philopator*   59, 66, 69
Septimius Severus   253
Seven hills of Rome   251
  Aventine
  Caelian
  Capitoline
  Esquiline
  Palatine
  Quirinal
  Viminal
Silence   (about one half hour)   187
Silenced   (Tyre)   114
Silver idols   35, 37, 74, 198, 199
Silver kingdom   16, 17, 34, 35, 39,
Silver part of metal man   32, 40, 85, 92
Silver trade items   116, 258, 259
Smerdis   46
Smyrna   144, 148
Son of man   (Daniel)   5, 56, 79,
Son of man   (Ezekiel)   106, 118
Son of man   (Jesus)   15, 44, 93, 94, 141, 232

Song
  Song (by angels)   170, 174
  Song (by four living creatures)   171
  Song (by four living creatures and elders)
    174, 264
  Song (by elders)   172
  Song (by everything ever created)   175
  Song (multitude shouting "Hallelujah"   263
  Song (new song sung by 144,000)   229
  Song (of Lamb)   235, 236
  Song (of Moses)   235, 236
Stephanos   168, 177, 232
Stone
  Stone (cornerstone)   35
  Stone (hailstones)   244
  Stone (gods of)   198, 199
  Stone (millstone)   262
  Stone (white)   153
  Stones (precious covering angels)   237
  Stones (precious covering prostitute)   247,
    249
  Stones (precious used by Antiochus)   74
  Stones (precious trade items)   116, 258, 259,
    261
  Stones (three in rainbow around God)   166,
    167
  Stones (twelve in breastplate)   294
  Stones (twelve in foundation)   294
Sword
  Sword   19, 68, 71, 112, 117, 179, 223, 224
  Sword (double-edged)   142, 151, 153, 164
  Sword from Jesus' mouth   117, 153, 220,
    266, 267, 268
  Sword (machaira)   178
  Sword (rhomphaia)   178, 179

T

Tabernacle
  Tabernacle (in heaven)   237, 289
  Tabernacle (in Jerusalem)   110, 129, 294,
    295
  Tabernacle (measuring)   293
  Tabernacles (Feast of)   221
Teima   36
Temple
  Temple (body of Christ)   125
  Temple (God and Lamb are the)   120, 295
  Temple (heavenly)   110, 119-121, 161, 164,
    186, 210, 232, 233, 237, 238, 244
  Temple (in Jerusalem)   35, 37, 54, 55, 58,
    67, 70, 80, 82, 83, 237
  Temple (people of God)   200, 201, 202, 295,
    297
Thief   158, 242, 243
Thousand (also see 1,000 under O's)

Thousand (angels—thousands of) 171, 289
Thousand (5,000 baskets) 124
Thousand (generations) 133, 269
Thousand (7,000 killed in earthquake) 206
Thousand (meaning of) 184, 270
Thousand (generations) 153, 309
Thousand (nobles) 35
Thousand (troops—ten thousand X) 198
Thousand years 14, 270-273, 276-278, 289
Throne
  Throne (of a god) 115
  Throne (of beast) 241
  Throne (of David) 118, 131, 301
  Throne (of God) 25, 93, 100, 104, 105, 138, 139, 163, 164, 166-169, 171-175,1 81, 185, 186, 189, 209, 210, 212, 216, 218, 229, 237, 244, 264, 280, 281, 285, 289, 290
  Throne (of God and the Lamb) 121, 287, 298
  Throne (of Greece) 51, 60, 61, 63, 69,
  Throne (of Rome) 7, 19, 20, 25, 89, 137, 143, 251-253,
  Throne (of Satan) 151, 152
  Thrones (of saints) 14, 276
Thytira 144, 154-156, 164
Tiberius 20, 21, 89, 251
Time, Times, and half-a-time 13, 14, 81, 88, 89, 99, 202, 211, 215
Titus 20, 21, 84, 89, 150, 165, 202, 251
Topaz stone 294
Trajan 197, 253, 254
Tribulation 6, 89, 137, 143, 144, 146, 147, 152, 155, 165, 179, 186, 204, 206, 236, 293
Trumpet
  Trumpet (sound of voice) 105, 165, 166
  Trumpet (first) 190, 238
  Trumpet (second) 191, 239
  Trumpet (third) 191, 192, 210, 240
  Trumpet (fourth) 192, 193, 240
  Trumpet (fifth) 192-194, 241, 263, 267, 272
  Trumpet (sixth) 197-199, 206, 242
  Trumpet (seventh) 200, 206, 207, 209, 210, 234
  Trumpets 26, 27, 130, 138, 187, 189, 190, 192, 193, 196, 235
  Trumpeters 262
Twelve
  Twelve (angels) 120, 292
  Twelve (apostles) 167, 292
  Twelve (baskets) 124
  Twelve (crops of fruit) 287, 298
  Twelve (crowns) 243
  Twelve (foundations) 292
  Twelve (gates) 120, 292, 294
  Twelve (pearls on gates) 294
  Twelve (stars on woman's crown) 210, 211
  Twelve (stones) 166, 294
  Twelve (tribes) 120, 134, 167, 211, 292, 294
Tyre 26, 114, 115, 250

U
Ulai 56
Unsealed 6, 32, 80, 300

V
Vespasian 19-21, 89, 111, 142, 143, 150, 165, 190, 251
Vesuvius 190, 241
Viminal hill 23, 251
Vitellius 19, 20, 89

W
War (see Armageddon)
  War 178, 197, 198, 242, 243
  War (beween woman and child) 213
  War (by the beast) 219, 220
  War (Egypt and Syria) 53, 62-67, 69, 74, 76
  War (end of Antiochus) 80, 93
  War (against saints) 12,13, 99, 204, 215, 303
  War (civil war of 69 AD) 18, 89
  War (in heaven) 117, 142, 153, 213, 214, 215, 219-221, 243, 252, 254, 266-268, 271, 30
  War horses 116
Warfare 179, 199, 214, 243
Warfare (Macabees) 55
Woman
  Woman (childbearing) 298
  Woman (Jezebel) 155
  Woman (locusts had hair of) 195
  Woman (Radiant) 13, 210, 211, 213-216
  Woman (Prostitute) 18, 24, 247-251, 255

X
Xerxes 46

Y
Year of the four emperors 18, 19, 21

Z
Zahar 116
Zebulun 120, 183
Zerubbabel 203
Zeus 75, 151
Zeus Olympius 55, 72, 74

Made in the USA
Charleston, SC
31 March 2011